Published by

The Naval & Military Press Ltd
Unit 5 Riverside, Brambleside
Bellbrook Industrial Estate
Uckfield, East Sussex
TN22 1QQ England

Tel: +44 (0)1825 749494

www.naval-military-press.com
www.nmarchive.com

In reprinting in facsimile from the original, any imperfections are inevitably reproduced and the quality may fall short of modern type and cartographic standards.

A HISTORY OF THE NEGRO TROOPS

IN

THE WAR OF THE REBELLION

1861–1865

PRECEDED BY

A REVIEW OF THE MILITARY SERVICES OF NEGROES
IN ANCIENT AND MODERN TIMES

BY

GEORGE W. WILLIAMS, LL.D.

COLONEL AND LATE JUDGE ADVOCATE IN THE GRAND ARMY OF THE REPUBLIC
AUTHOR OF "THE HISTORY OF THE NEGRO RACE IN AMERICA"

The Naval & Military Press Ltd

TO

THE NEGRO SOLDIERS

WHO HEROICALLY SERVED THEIR COUNTRY
IN THE WAR OF THE REBELLION
THIS RECORD OF THEIR VALOR

Is Inscribed

BY THEIR COMRADE IN ARMS

THE AUTHOR

PREFACE.

I HAVE undertaken to write a military history of Negro troops in the War of the Rebellion. I have written only of the military services of Negro troops; and I have used the generic word Negro because, while many mulattoes were in the service, the Negroes preponderated to an overwhelming degree.

In writing of the remote past, the historian has the benefit of the sifting and winnowing to which time subjects historical data; but in writing of events within living memory it requires both fortitude and skill to resist the insidious influence of interested friends and actors, to separate error from truth with an even and steady hand, to master the sources of historical information — to know where the material is, to collect and classify it, although scattered through an almost endless maze of books, newspapers, diaries, pamphlets, etc. — and to avoid partisan feeling and maintain a spirit of judicial candor. How far I have succeeded is left to the considerate judgment of the reader.

Myself a soldier in the volunteer and regular army of the United States, in infantry and cavalry, an officer of artillery in the Republican forces of the Mexican army, and recently an officer of the Sixth Regiment of Massachusetts Volunteer Militia, I may claim some military experience. I participated in many of the battles herein described, including some of the most severe conflicts of Negro troops with the enemy in Virginia. But I have relied very little on personal knowledge, preferring always to follow the official record.

For years an active member of the Grand Army of the Republic, I have heard with deep interest, at camp-fires and encampments, many narratives of the heroic conduct of Negro soldiers, but my enthusiasm has never led me away from the record. I have been intrusted with the journals and orderly-books of officers from the rank of lieutenant to that of major-general, and have been personally acquainted with six major-generals who at one time or another commanded Negro troops.

The data upon which I have relied for the historical trustworthiness of this work are divisible into two classes, *official* and *unofficial*. The *official class* contains the following documents:

"Official Records of the War of the Rebellion," edited by Lieutenant-colonel Robert N. Scott; Confederate Official Records; *Army and Navy Official Gazette; Congressional Record* and *Congressional Globe; Journal of the Confederate Congress;* Executive Documents of the several States; Official Despatches of the War Department; manuscript information furnished me by the Secretary of War, through the courtesy of the Adjutant-general of the army; manuscript information furnished by the Adjutant-generals of the several States; manuscript information furnished by war offices of foreign governments through their ambassadors in Washington; and orderly-books of general officers who commanded Negro troops in the field.

The *unofficial class* contains the following material:

"The Rebellion Record," edited by Frank Moore; the annuals of the "American Encyclopædia" for the period of the War; the principal histories of the War, including the works of Pollard, Stephens, and Davis for the Confederacy; "The Campaigns of the Civil War"—entire series —published by the Messrs. Scribner; "The Army of the Potomac," by John Swinton; the History of the War, by the Comte de Paris; Grant's Military History, by General Adam Badeau; the *Proceedings of the Society of the Army of the Potomac and of the Army of the Cumberland;* the Soldiers' and Sailors' Historical Society publications of Rhode Island; Townshend's War Library; numerous books published by Confederate and Union officers; pamphlets, patriotic speeches, and the files of the *Boston Journal,* the *New York Herald, World, Times,* and *Tribune,* and many other newspapers, both Confederate and Union.

I have availed myself of as much of this material as could advantageously be used in writing a popular history, and have been careful to make due acknowledgment to my authorities.

I am under deep obligations to the Hon. Ainsworth R. Spofford, the librarian of the Library of Congress, for his kindness in placing before me his large manuscript collections, from which I have derived valuable facts. I am happy to return thanks to the Secretary of War and the Adjutant-general of the army for access to sources of information. General Drum is an indefatigable worker, and with his excellent method he will soon place the records of the War Department in a most convenient and accessible shape. I found Colonel Robert N. Scott, who is in charge of the publication of the War records, a most genial and accommodating gentleman. I have enjoyed and appreciated his literary sympathy, and have profited by his wide, varied, and accurate knowledge of the records. I cheerfully acknowledge receipt of personal information from Major-generals B. F. Butler, A. L. Chetlain, James B. Steedman, Thomas J. Morgan, Daniel Ullmann, David Hunter, Majors

William C. Manning and Luis F. Emilio, and many other officers. Of the officers who led the movement to employ Negroes as soldiers or commanded them in battle, the following are still living: Saxton, Terry, Butler, Ullmann, Hinks, Banks, Morgan, Doubleday, Wild, Ferrero, Ames, Thomas, Jackson, Auger, Andrews, and Birney; while Phelps, Weitzel, Ord, Burnside, Hunter, Steedman, D. B. Birney, and Draper are dead. Of these twenty-four, nine were graduates of West Point. And that noble spirit—another Sidney—Adjutant-general Lorenzo Thomas, has entered into his well-earned rest; while Stanton, who was always firm in the conviction that the Negro was capable as a soldier, and the venerable General Casey, who wrote a system of tactics for these troops, are also dead. These names, of the living as well as the dead, with others not mentioned here, will always be held in grateful remembrance by the Negro race.

I judged it proper to give a summary of the military services of Negro soldiers in ancient and modern times, and thus to bring together in one work the necessary facts to understand their military capacity. The chapter on Negro soldiers in ancient times I have prepared with great pains, after carefully weighing all the evidence I could obtain.

In the chapter on Negro soldiers in modern times I have sought, with succinct brevity, to glean the essential facts of the Negro's military services throughout modern Europe, without overshadowing or detracting from his record in the late Rebellion. I personally examined the fields on which Negroes fought in Mexico; and while in England, Germany, and France, I heard from those who had led them in conflicts, and from those who had contended with their valor, but one story of their matchless courage. The Germans have not forgotten the Negro's desperate fighting, and the French will always remember that in their army in 1870 he was "the bravest of the brave."

I have told the story of the Negro's exploits in Hayti from the record, and I have gone for my facts to Frenchmen as well as to Englishmen, to foe as well as to friend. In recording what he did in the war of the Revolution, I have gone to the orderly-books in the State House at Boston, the Department of State, and the Library of Congress at Washington, D. C.; I have examined the descriptive lists of the army under Washington and Ward at Cambridge, Massachusetts. I have found it necessary, in the interest of history and science, to prick some bubbles of alleged history, and to correct the record. Negro soldiers were not in the battle of Red Bank, as many school histories declare; nor were the free Negroes of the colonies enrolled as a part of the established militia. They entered many of the companies in the towns, but not with the approval of either public sentiment or law; it was by tacit consent of local authorities against provincial inhibition.

On the other hand, justice, in many instances, has been denied the Negro soldier of the war of the Revolution, as in the case of the Rhode Island regiment. I have nevertheless kept to the record, hewing to the line, regardless of the direction the flying chips take.

The part enacted by the Negro soldier in the war of the Rebellion is the romance of North American history. It was midnight and noonday without a space between; from the Egyptian darkness of bondage to the lurid glare of civil war; from clanking chains to clashing arms; from passive submission to the cruel curse of slavery to the brilliant aggressiveness of a free soldier; from a chattel to a person; from the shame of degradation to the glory of military exaltation; and from deep obscurity to fame and martial immortality. No one in this era of fraternity and Christian civilization will grudge the Negro soldier these simple annals of his trials and triumphs in a holy struggle for human liberty. Whatever praise is bestowed upon his noble acts will be sincerely appreciated, whether from former foes or comrades in arms. For by withholding just praise they are not enriched, nor by giving are they thereby impoverished.

Nor will the reader find reason for complaint at the spirit of the historian. I have spoken plainly, it is true, but I have not extenuated nor set down aught in malice. My language is not plainer than the truth, my philippic is not more cruel than the crimes exposed, my rhetoric is not more fiery than the trials through which these black troops passed, nor my conclusions without warrant of truth or justification of evidence.

I trust that Congress will adopt my suggestion and name the park in front of Howard University for the brave and beautiful young colonel, Robert Gould Shaw, and there erect a monument to the Negro soldiers who fell in the service of their country. It would be a deserved and fitting tribute to the valor of the Negro soldier, and would have a beneficent influence upon the entire people for all time to come.

I commit this story of the Negro's martial prowess to my countrymen, regardless of section or race, creed or party; entertaining the belief that neither sectional malice nor party rancor can ever obliterate a record that is now, happily in the progress of events, not only the proud and priceless heritage of a race, but the glory of a nation.

GEORGE W. WILLIAMS.

ETONIA, WASHINGTON, D. C.,
July 31, 1886.

CONTENTS.

CHAPTER I.
INTRODUCTORY: NEGRO SOLDIERS IN ANCIENT TIMES 1

CHAPTER II.
NEGRO SOLDIERS IN MODERN TIMES 10

CHAPTER III.
ANTECEDENT FACTS.—FORESHADOWING EVENTS 58

CHAPTER IV.
MILITARY RENDITION OF SLAVES 66

CHAPTER V.
THE NEGRO VOLUNTEER.—MILITARY EMPLOYMENT OF NEGROES . 81

CHAPTER VI.
MILITARY STATUS OF NEGRO TROOPS 145

CHAPTER VII.
NEGRO IDIOSYNCRACIES 167

CHAPTER VIII.
THE OUTLOOK 170

CHAPTER IX.
NEGRO TROOPS IN BATTLE.—DEPARTMENT OF THE SOUTH (1862-1865) 181

CHAPTER X.
IN THE MISSISSIPPI VALLEY (1863) 214

CHAPTER XI.
IN THE ARMY OF THE POTOMAC (1864) 231

CHAPTER XII.
THE FORT PILLOW MASSACRE (1864) 257

CHAPTER XIII.
IN THE ARMY OF THE CUMBERLAND (1864) 273

CHAPTER XIV.
IN THE ARMY OF THE JAMES (1865) 291

CHAPTER XV.
AS PRISONERS OF WAR 304

CHAPTER XVI.
THE CLOUD OF WITNESSES 320

INDEX 343

THE GILLMORE MEDAL.

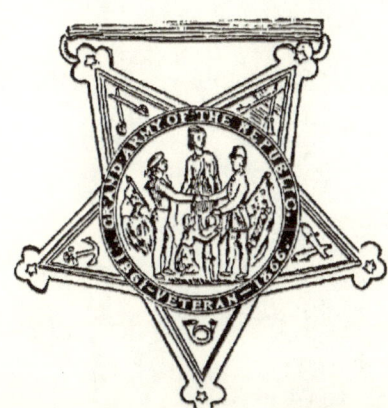 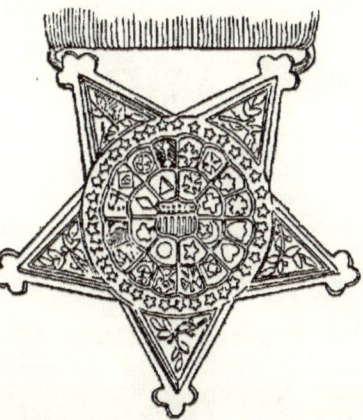

GRAND ARMY BADGE.

THE BUTLER MEDAL.

A HISTORY OF NEGRO TROOPS

IN

THE WAR OF THE REBELLION,

1861-1865.

CHAPTER I.

INTRODUCTORY: NEGRO SOLDIERS IN ANCIENT TIMES.

THE Negro appears in the military history of Egypt for the first time in the Inscriptions of Una, who was crown-bearer, or Secretary of State, under King Pepi during the Sixth Dynasty.[1] Down to this time the Egyptian Empire had enjoyed comparative quiet, but the Sixth Dynasty clearly marks the beginning of the military epoch. A large army had always been in existence in Egypt, but it was seldom called into the field. The military class always ranked high, coming next in order to the priesthood,[2] and was divided into two distinct parts. Herod-

---

[1] The Inscription of Una was found by M. Mariette, and subsequently placed in the Museum of Boulaq, at Cairo. It was translated by the late Vicomte Em de Rougé—"Recherches sur les Monuments: Six Premières Dynasties," 4to, p. 117, and following, pl. 7, 8. Paris, 1866; Brugsch-Bey, "Histoire d'Egypte," 8vo, p. 70, and following. Leipzig, 1875.

[2] The Egyptians were famous for classes; and in order to show the important position of the soldiers the subjoined table is given. The

otus estimates the strength of the Egyptian army at 410,000.[1] On an average of five persons to a family, his figures would bring the military class up to 2,050,000. But Diodorus places the strength of the army at 692,000.[2] The same family average brings these figures up to 3,460,000. This constituted the entire military class. The two great divisions of the army were the Hermotybies and Calasiries. The latter were archers, and inhabited the cantons of Thebes, Bubastis, Aphthis, Tanis, Mendes, Sebennytus, Athribis, Pharbæthus, Thmuis, Onuphis, Anysis, and Myecphoris. With the single exception of Thebes, these districts all lay within the Delta. These Calasiries numbered about 250,000. The Hermotybies were not so numerous, and inhabited only six cantons: Busiris, Saïs, Papremis, Prosopitis, and Natho, also in the region of the Delta, with Chemmis, which was in Upper Egypt. These troops were spearmen and chariot-riders, and numbered about 160,000. The population of Egypt (3000 B.C.) was about 7,500,000. The army, when on war footing, was about one-fourth the population; but after it was recruited, the archers or infantry were disbanded and sent into agricultural districts. But the largest empires of modern Europe, with five times the population of Egypt, find a standing army of 400,000 or 500,000 men an enormous burden. An army of large proportions

---

evidence in favor of the position of the soldiers is absolute. The Negroes must have obtained great favor as soldiers.

Classes of Herodotus.	Classes of Plato.	Classes of Diodorus.
1. Priests.	1. Priests.	1. Priests.
2. Soldiers.	2. Soldiers.	2. Soldiers.
3. Cow-herds.	3. Herdsmen.	3. Herdsmen.
4. Swine-herds.	4. Husbandmen.	4. Husbandmen.
5. Traders.	5. Artificers.	5. Artificers.
6. Boatmen.	6. Hunters.	....
7. Interpreters.	....	....

[1] Herodotus, book ii., pp. 165, 166.   [2] Diodorus, book i., p. 54.

was always necessary under the Egyptian monarchy, and a cheap army became a matter of grave concern.

At a period unknown to history prior to the Sixth Dynasty, the Negro tribes to the south of King Pepi became tributary to the Egyptian Empire. In the second year of Pepi's reign he put his army into the field, and his troops were successful against the Mentu.[1] Elated with this success, he turned his victorious arms against the Amu and Herusha, two peaceable tribes inhabiting the desert to the east of Lower Egypt. The King encountered stout fighting from these children of the desert, and fearing their vengeful spirit, collected and drilled a numerous army. The nucleus of his army was from the native Egyptians in the north; but he soon turned his attention to the Negro tribes to the south, from among which he secured thousands of black levies. "His Majesty made soldiers of numerous ten thousands in the land of the South. . . . The Negroes from Nam, the Negroes from Aman, the Negroes from Uauat, the Negroes from Kau, the Negroes from the land of Takam. His Majesty placed me at head of that army,"[2] says Una.

It was natural that, having honored these Negroes with the Egyptian uniform, King Pepi should place Egyptian officers over them. It does not follow either that the Negroes were degraded, or that there were none of their number capable of a command. The high and important position of the Egyptian army, the severe requirements of its drill and discipline, and the exalted social position of the men who were appointed by his Majesty as officers in this vast Negro army, are creditable to the rank and file. The "nomarchs, the chancellors, the sole friends of

---

[1] Birch's "Ancient Egypt," p. 52.
[2] "Records of the Past," vol. ii., pp. 4, 5.

the palace, the superintendents, the rulers of the nomes of the North and South, the friends, superintendents of gold, the superintendent of the priests of the South and North, the superintendents of the register and at the head officers of the South and the land of the North, and of the cities, [drilled] the Negroes of these lands."[1]

These Negroes evidently had won a reputation for soldierly qualities, else they would not have been recruited for service in the Egyptian army. If this contingent were a "wild and disorderly crew,"[2] as Professor Rawlinson asserts, why were they not enslaved and sent into the Delta to perform agricultural labor? No modern writer on ancient Egypt has a stronger claim upon the confidence and respect of the student of history than Professor Rawlinson, and it is from his own works that this argument is derived. Several things are patent. The eleventh chapter of the first volume of "Ancient Egypt" gives a minute and graphic account of the constitution of the Egyptian army. He deals with its social rank, its divisions, numbers, weapons, and drill. Thus we are led to regard superior physical qualifications and high intelligence as necessary to secure admission to the Egyptian army. The professor will no doubt concede that the captor in Eastern wars had a right in fee-simple to his captive. He could dispose of his labor, sell him, or take his life. Professor Rawlinson says, "In war many cruel and barbarous customs prevailed. Captives were either reduced to slavery or put to death."[3] This is strong and conclusive. These Negroes could not have been captives. Professor Rawlinson must find an explanation, however, for the employment of tens of thousands of Negroes by King Pepi.

---

[1] "Records of the Past," vol. ii., p. 5.
[2] "Ancient Egypt," vol. ii., p. 108.
[3] Ibid., vol. ii., p. 372.

He says, "It is remarkable that we find the negro races of the South already subdued, without any previous notice in any of the Egyptian remains of the time or circumstances of their subjugation. . . . We find the negroes already obedient subjects of Pepi when they are first mentioned as coming into contact with him; and his enlistment of them as soldiers to fight his battles would seem to imply that their subjugation had not been very recent. It is necessary to suppose that some monarch of the Fourth or Fifth Dynasty had made them Egyptian subjects, without leaving behind him any record of the fact, or, at any rate, without leaving any record that has escaped destruction."[1]

But such an inference disregards the custom universal in ancient times of reducing subjugated nations or tribes to slavery.[2] Yet there is no reference to the enslavement of Negroes up to this time, nor are they depicted as captives in the monuments or pictures connected with the military campaigns of the five preceding dynasties. If these Negroes were a "wild and disorderly crew," why should "nomarchs and chancellors, the sole friends of the palace," aspire to commissions as their officers? Evidently because their valor and prowess were well known, and it was esteemed an honor to lead them in battle. And this conclusion is borne out by the deportment of these troops in the campaigns through which they subsequently passed.

When the work of drilling this vast Negro army was completed, it was moved into the enemy's country. The precise location of the country invaded is not certain. Some Egyptologists locate it in Syria, and others think it was in Arabia Petræa. The latest researches indicate the region about Lake Menzaleh. In any case, the country

---

[1] "Ancient Egypt," vol. ii., p. 110.
[2] Hurd's "Laws of Bondage and Freedom."

was distant and the marching difficult. It must have been an inspiring spectacle to behold a large and imposing army of Negroes, officered and drilled by the most accomplished native Egyptians, marching out from the imperial metropolis! These troops went out from the imperial presence to battle for a venerable government whose potency the Orient had long ago felt and acknowledged. The black army must have felt the enthusiasm of the occasion. These black soldiers spoke another language, were from another land, and had felt the influence of another and widely different civilization. No doubt the Nile and the Delta had resounded with the exploits of the veterans that formed the strength of this Negro army, and new perils and new glories awaited them. Five battles were fought during this campaign, in all of which the Negro troops were victorious. Una, the historian of the campaign, furnishes the following account:

"The warriors came and destroyed the land of the Herusha, and returned fortunately home; and they came again, and took possession of the land of the Herusha, and returned fortunately home; and they came and demolished the fortresses of the Herusha, and returned fortunately home; and they cut down the vines and fig-trees, and returned fortunately home; and they set fire to the houses, and returned fortunately home; and they killed the chief men by tens of thousands, and returned fortunately home. And the warriors brought back with them a great number of living captives, which pleased the King more than all the rest. Five times did the King send me out to set things right in the land of the Herusha, and to subdue their revolt by force; each time I acted so that the King was pleased with me."[1]

---

[1] Vicomte de Rougé's "Recherches," p. 125.

It would seem that after so thorough a campaign, in which fields, forts, and houses were destroyed, in addition to the frightful slaughter the Herusha sustained, there would be no necessity for a renewal of hostilities. But another expedition was made by water. Una says, "Safely to Takhisa I sailed again in boats with this force. I subdued this country from the extreme frontier on the North of the land of Herusha."[1] The troops were landed, and the fighting was pushed with vigor and skill. The enemy was defeated and subdued to the extreme border towards the North.

This had not been a constructive period; but now that a successful war had been waged against King Pepi's enemies, the Negro troops were recalled, and arts and architecture revived. What became of this enormous Negro army is not known. It appears suddenly upon the page of Egyptian history, achieves signal success for the ancient empire, and then disappears from view. This may or may not have been the first time Negroes were largely employed as soldiers by the Egyptians. Like many another important event, the record of an earlier employment of troops of this character may have perished.

The military paintings connected with the campaigns of the Egyptians during the Eighteenth Dynasty represent Negro soldiers as numerous. They formed the strength of the army of Shishak, king of Egypt, in 971 B.C., when that intrepid monarch marched against Rehoboam. King Shishak's tomb was opened in 1849, and his depicted army, including an exact representation of the genuine Negro race, in color, physiognomy, and hair. Negroes were also found in large numbers in the armies under Sesostris and Xerxes.

---

[1] "Records of the Past," vol. ii., p. 6.

There is ample and trustworthy evidence of the stable national government and high social organization attained by the Negro tribes in the East before the Christian era.

Mr. Wilkinson, the famous Egyptologist, opened a remarkable Theban tomb, and in 1840 Harris and Gliddon made a very careful examination of it. It abounds in Negro scenes, one of which is described as follows: "A negress, apparently a princess, arrives at Thebes, drawn in a plaustrum by a pair of humped oxen — the driver and groom being red-colored Egyptians, and, one might almost infer, eunuchs. Following her are multitudes of negroes and Nubians, bringing tribute from the upper country, as well as black slaves of both sexes and all ages, among which are some *red* children, whose *fathers* were Egyptians. The cause of her advent seems to have been to make offering in this tomb of a 'royal son of Ke Sh-Amunoph,' who may have been her husband."[1]

It is evident that the Negro government whose representative this princess was maintained a military establishment.

During the reign of Rameses III., a Negro king appears at the head of fourteen captured princes in the sculptures of Medinet-Abou.[2]

From about three thousand years before the Christian era, until the birth and establishment of Christianity, there is an unbroken chain of historical evidence of the military employment of Negroes. Christianity came breathing its spirit of hope and charity into the dead and empty formalisms of the period, and the clash of arms was succeeded by the fierce controversial spirit of the theologians. The dreadful carnage of war did not cease, but the thea-

---

[1] "Types of Mankind," p. 262. 1854.
[2] Brugsch-Bey's "Hist. d'Egypte," vol. i., pp. 150, 151.

tre of strife was transferred from the Orient to the Occident. The Eastern world had fought its way to the front line of martial fame. Its colossal civilization had risen gradually through centuries of painful effort. It had reached the danger-line; and then the effulgent morning of its primal glory was succeeded by the gloaming of its barbarous and costly wars, and yet later by the starless night of its irreparable decay. Christianity turned her radiant face to the West, and all behind her was darkness, silence, and death. For more than sixteen hundred years the Negro's hands were empty of his weapons. Western and north-western Europe were the scene of the struggle for Christian civilization. The Negro was not needed in such a struggle, in such a climate. During all these centuries no facile pen traces the history of the Negro nations in the East. They were left entirely to themselves for sixteen centuries. The problems propounded by Christianity—discovery, empire, letters, and liberty—could well dispense with the remorseless military audacity of the Negro.

CHAPTER II.

NEGRO SOLDIERS IN MODERN TIMES.

It was about fifteen centuries from the time the Negro disappeared from the page of the world's history until his reappearance. The Gospel of Peace had rendered the potent arms of his victorious warfare impotent and obsolete. The spirit of geography and discovery which thrilled the continents in the fifteenth and sixteenth centuries revived interest in the Negro. But it was interest *for* him and not interest *in* him. Spain and Portugal, France and Italy, Germany and England, either by discovery or conquest, had extended their landed domains. The great distances of the new possessions from the seat of these European empires gave rise to problems of vast meaning and difficult of solution. The contiguity of these great States rendered necessary enormous standing armies to watch each other at all times, and this state of affairs made labor dear and laborers scarce. The distant possessions, at a time when steam was unknown, could be reached only by officials or the opulent. Avarice and necessity seized upon Caucasian convicts and Negro slaves to solve the labor problem in North America.

During the three hundred years in which the Latin, Germanic, and English speaking races were engaged in robbing Africa of Negroes for the nefarious traffic in human flesh, the Negro was a non-combatant. He not only did not fight, he scarcely ever offered a protest. To him war was a lost art, and the word *resistance* had no place in his scanty vocabulary. Three centuries of servitude to the dominant races of the world were not without their lessons to the docile Negro. From the dark night of savagehood he moved into the gray dawn of civilization. He occasionally felt the influence of some great impulse towards humanity, and was doubtless conscious, to a certain degree, of the great civilizing forces that were turning the flood-tides in the affairs of the nations he was serving. The tendencies towards republican government in France, and the struggle for independence in America, like a great magnetic current, electrified the Negro's heart, and the old love of valor and liberty went singing through his soul.

In his place upon the cotton, rice, and tobacco plantations of the British colonies in North America, he heard the sullen complaint of Americans against magisterial autocracy and parliamentary encroachments; and from his insular home in the Antilles he heard the low reverberation of the French Revolution, and later, the shock of embattled arms. Here in America he aided the colonies to achieve independent autonomy; there in the Antilles he fought his way to freedom through the veteran ranks of Spanish and French soldiery, and made his way to self-government over the avarice and personal ambition of slave-holding planters.

In the vast system of militia and "minute-men" that guarded the young colonies in America against the savage depredations of the aborigines, the Negro bore an honorable part.[1] In the southern colonies he was assigned to fatigue duty chiefly, although compelled "to train" with his company. In Massachusetts he was found upon the foremost wave of popular indignation at the quartering of

---

[1] Palfrey's "History of New England," vol. ii., p. 30, *note*.

soldiers upon the colonists; and "the shot that was heard around the world" felled the stalwart form of the patriot Negro, Crispus Attucks.¹ When the Revolutionary war began, the Negro was alert. Ministerial and Continental authorities appealed to his courage as a man and his valor as a soldier. He was found under the standards of both armies; but his idiosyncratic instinct led him into sympathy with the American cause. His power of assimilation made him intensely American, and gave him, in his new home, his alphabet of thought. He did not reason about British aggression, he read the cabalistic meaning in stirring events; and his patriotism outran all the reasoning of the colonists, and was early in the breach between liberty and tyranny. He was conspicuous at the first great battle of the Revolutionary War, and by deeds of valor inscribed his name high up upon the scroll of fame.² One of the most decisive events of the battle of Bunker Hill, June 17, 1775, was the death of the British major, Pitcairn, at the hands of private Peter Salem, of Colonel Nixon's regiment of the Continental army.³ No one has ever disputed the claim of the Negro soldier to this deed of valor; and the silvern lips of the most polished orator of Massachusetts have spoken his praise in measured sentences and rounded periods.⁴ Nor was this all. Another Negro soldier distinguished himself; and so great was the impression that he created that fourteen American officers commended his valor to the Congress. The memorial was dated at Cambridge, December 5, 1775, and recited "that, under our own observation, we declare that a negro man called Salem Poor, of Colonel Frye's regiment, Captain

---

¹ Adams's Works, vol. ii., p. 322.
² Bancroft, vol. vii., p. 421. Sixth edition.
³ Washburn's "History of Leicester," p. 267.
⁴ "Orations and Speeches of Everett," vol. iii., p. 529.

Ame's company, in the late battle at Charlestown, behaved like an experienced officer, as well as an excellent soldier. To set forth particulars of his conduct would be tedious. We would only beg leave to say, in the person of this said negro centres a brave and gallant soldier. The reward due to so great and distinguished a character we submit to the Congress."[1]

The random shots at Lexington, in April, 1775, had brought the eastern colonies to their feet. In the grand rally for the protection of their homes and personal rights, the colonists paid little regard to the Negroes who rallied also in great numbers and with patriotic spirit. In the initial battles they had shared the perils of the Continental militia and pastoral minute-men. Most of them were freemen, and naturally felt it their duty to share the perils of freemen, and consequently were scattered throughout the American forces.

But when the smoke of Lexington, Concord, and Bunker Hill had cleared away, and the presence of Negroes was observed in the army, considerable feeling prevailed against them. On the 29th of May, 1775, the "Committee of Safety" for the Province of Massachusetts Bay deemed the question of the employment of Negroes as soldiers of great importance. A resolve[2] was passed reciting that the contest was between Great Britain and the colonies, and concerned the liberties of the latter; and that the admission into the army of any persons as soldiers except freemen would reflect dishonor on the colony; "and that no slaves be admitted into this army upon any consideration whatever." On the 6th of June the committee entertained a resolve for the admission of slaves into the army,

---

[1] "MS. Archives of Massachusetts," vol. clxxx., p. 241.
[2] "Journal of the Provincial Congress of Massachusetts," p. 553.

but it was finally "ordered to lie on the table for further consideration."[1] The majority of the committee opposed the employment of Negroes, and public sentiment did not condemn this action. The army at Cambridge was greatly influenced by the attitude of the people of the province. On the 10th of July, General Gates, in his instructions to recruiting officers, forbade the enlistment of "any stroller, *negro*, or vagabond."[2] But the fact remains that many Negroes *had* secured a place in the army, and honorably kept it until the close of the war. Bancroft records the fact that "the roll of the army at Cambridge had from its first formation borne the names of men of color."[3] He adds, "Free negroes stood in the ranks by the side of white men. In the beginning of the war they entered the Provincial army; the first general order which was issued by Ward had required a return,[4] among other things, of the 'complexion' of the soldiers, and black men like others were retained in the service after the troops were adopted by the continent."[5] In the mean while this question of the military status of the Negro, which had begun as a local matter, had grown to Continental proportions. On the 29th of September the Continental Congress was the scene of an animated debate over a draft of a letter to General Washington, reported by Lynch, Lee, and Adams. Mr. Rutledge, of South Carolina, offered an amendment instructing the commander-in-chief to discharge all free Negroes and slaves in the army. The southern delegates

---

[1] "Journal of the Provincial Congress of Massachusetts," p. 302.
[2] Moore's "Diary of the American Revolution," vol. i., p. 110.
[3] Bancroft, vol. viii., p. 110. 1860.
[4] Ibid., vol. viii., pp. 232, 233. 1860.
[5] I examined the muster-rolls or descriptive lists of the army at Cambridge, and found this statement correct. I have now a large list of Negro soldiers of the army at Cambridge, Massachusetts.—G. W. W.

supported the amendment with spirit; but it was defeated. On the 8th of October a council of war was held at General Washington's headquarters. General Washington presided. There were three Major-generals—Ward, Lee, and Putman—and six Brigadier-generals—Thomas, Spencer, Heath, Sullivan, Greene, and Gates. The arming of Negroes was canvassed with the deepest concern. Two questions were considered; first, whether any Negroes ought to be enlisted "in the new army;" second, whether a distinction should be made "between such as are slaves and those who are free." The record of this "council of war" upon the employment of Negroes as soldiers is explicit. "It was agreed unanimously to reject all slaves, and by a great majority to reject negroes altogether."

When the action of this council of war became known it had a depressing influence upon the Negro population of the eastern colonies. The free Negroes began to discuss the situation, and a spirit of unrest pervaded the slave class. The Negro was seriously discussed as a subject of public interest. Although the Provincial Congress of Massachusetts and the council of war at Cambridge had voted the Negro unworthy of the Continental uniform, there was still a disposition to consider the matter further. On the 18th of October a committee of conference was convened at Cambridge to take into consideration the renovation and reorganization of the army. Benjamin Franklin, Thomas Lynch, and Benjamin Harrison, with the deputy governors of Connecticut and Rhode Island, General Washington, and the Committee of Safety for Massachusetts, constituted the conference. The Negro question entered into their deliberations, and fared as it had on previous occasions—both free and slave Negroes were "rejected altogether."

The adverse action of three distinct bodies, each of them

authoritative in its way, seemed to settle the fate of the Negroes who stood waiting to bear arms in the public defence. It might be imagined that this action was the expression of public sentiment upon the military employment of the Negro, but it was not. The masses had scarcely had time to recover from the shock of an unexpected and unprovoked assault upon their liberties. There had been no adequate expression of public opinion upon the employment of Negroes as soldiers. The most influential journals of the colonies were issued weekly or semi-monthly. Their columns were ablaze with patriotic appeals to the people to stand for the rights guaranteed to them by the British *Magna Charta*. They had not considered the subject of placing arms in the hands of black allies, but the discontent of the Negroes themselves forced the question to popular consideration.

On the other hand, the Royalists were awake to all that occurred within the lines of their enemy. The Earl of Dunmore, who was Governor-general of the colony of Virginia, saw the dangerous policy of the Continental authorities, and grasped the situation. On the 7th of November he issued a proclamation to the slaves of Virginia from on board the ship *William*, off Norfolk. He declared "all indented servants, negroes or others (appertaining to Rebels), free, that are able and willing to bear arms, they joining his Majestie's troops as soon as may be."[1]

This *coup de maître* arrested the opposition to the employment of Negroes as Continental troops, and threw the entire Negro population into violent excitement. No civil or military official could be found now to oppose the enlistment of Negroes in the army at Cambridge. Large bodies of Negroes sought the towns, and agricultural work

---

[1] "American Archives," vol. iii., p. 1385. Fourth Series.

was generally abandoned. Little effort was made to keep the Negro within the narrow limits of the old slave code. He was the most difficult and dangerous problem of the hour. On the 12th of November, before hearing of Lord Dunmore's proclamation, General Washington issued instructions to recruiting officers forbidding the enlistment of Negroes.[1] From the 1st of July to the late autumn of 1775 there had been constant and unremitting opposition in official circles to the enlistment of Negroes beside those who had served at Bunker Hill on the 17th of June. There was even loud complaint against the retention of those already in the army—not, indeed, in the eastern colonies, but from the South. In a letter to John Adams, then in Congress, dated October 24, 1775, General Thomas wrote: "I am sorry to hear that any prejudice should take place in any southern colony with respect to the troops raised in this.... We have some negroes, but I look on them in general equally serviceable with other men for fatigue, and in action many of them have proved themselves brave."

But notwithstanding the feeling in the southern colonies, where the Tory element was strongest, and where slaves were most numerous, the gravity of the situation had greatly tempered public sentiment on this question. In the early autumn, on the evening of the 24th of September, John Adams wrote an account of an interview with Messrs. Bullock and Houston, from Georgia. He thus reports them: "They say that if one thousand regular troops should land in Georgia, and their commander be provided with arms and clothes enough, and proclaim freedom to all the negroes who would join his camp, twenty thousand negroes would join it from the two provinces in

---

[1] Sparks's "Washington," vol. iii., p. 155, *note*.

a fortnight. The Negroes have a wonderful art of communicating intelligence among themselves; it will run several hundreds of miles in a week or fortnight."[1]

Lord Dunmore's proclamation was working most effectually. The Negroes were flocking to the ministerial standards. The planters and Federalists were in consternation. On the 23d of November a Williamsburg (Va.) paper issued a carefully drafted proclamation of "Caution to the Negroes," intended to stop the stampede and win them back to the Federalists. "They" [the negroes], ran the proclamation, "have been flattered with their freedom if they be able to bear arms, and will speedily join Lord Dunmore's troops. To none, then, is freedom promised but to such as are able to do Lord Dunmore service,"[2] etc.

Lord Dunmore had by this time gathered quite a large number of Negroes into his army, and at the battle of Kemp's Landing they behaved like veterans. They met three companies of white troops and delivered battle; when one of the companies broke, the ex-slaves pursued and captured it.[3]

Every day increased the peril of the colonial cause. The Virginia Convention issued an answer to Lord Dunmore's proclamation on the 13th of December, and on the day following published a proclamation "offering pardon to such slaves as shall return to their duty within ten days after the publication thereof."[4]

Only one month had passed since General Washington, on November 12th, had officially forbidden the enlistment

---

[1] Adams's Works, vol. ii., p. 428.
[2] Force's "American Archives," vol. iii., p. 1387. Fourth Series.
[3] Ibid., vol. iv., p. 202. Fourth Series.
[4] Ibid., vol. iv., pp. 84, 85. Fourth Series.

of Negroes. The events of five weeks had changed his mind. On the 15th of December he wrote to Joseph Reed: "If the Virginians are wise, that arch-traitor to the rights of humanity, Lord Dunmore, should be instantly crushed, if it takes the force of the whole army to do it. ... But that which renders the measure indispensably necessary is the negroes, for, if he gets formidable, numbers of them will be tempted to join who will be afraid to do it without."[1]

But the commander-in-chief of the Continental army did not know that numbers of Negroes had already joined Lord Dunmore's forces. All of the disastrous news from Virginia was kept from the army at Cambridge, as far as possible. Two weeks after this letter to Joseph Reed, on the 30th of December, Washington, in General Orders, authorized the enlistment of "free negroes." On the following day he wrote a letter to Congress announcing that he had ordered the enlistment of free Negroes against the decision of that august body, adding, however, that he would "put a stop to it" if objection were made.[2] *Fas est ab hoste doceri!* Congress took no further action; and nearly every one of the colonies secured legislation by which slaves were encouraged to enlist by the offer of emancipation. This new policy met with instant success; and the masters, receiving a handsome sum for the enlistment of their slaves, turned recruiting officers. Considering the numerical strength of the united colonies, one half million slaves were not to be disregarded. At the commencement of the war the slave population in the colonies was estimated as follows:

---

[1] "Life and Correspondence of Joseph Reed," vol. i., p. 135.
[2] Sparks's "Washington," vol. iii., p. 218.

	Negroes.
Massachusetts	3,500
Rhode Island	4,373
Connecticut	5,000
New Hampshire	629
New York	15,000
New Jersey	7,600
Pennsylvania	10,000
Delaware	9,000
Maryland	80,000
Virginia	165,000
North Carolina	75,000
South Carolina	110,000
Georgia	16,000
Total	501,102

besides a considerable population of free Negroes. And, whatever the feeling may have been, and wherever it may have been manifested, the free Negroes who entered the Continental army at the commencement of hostilities remained, and by various ways, and under peculiar circumstances, others enlisted from time to time. Many free Negroes, scattered through New England towns, who had won by upright, industrious lives a secure place in public confidence, joined local companies without remonstrance or remark. When those companies were accepted at the headquarters of the army at Cambridge, the Negro patriots were not excluded. "The negro can take the field," wrote a Hessian officer, October 23, 1777, "instead of his master; and therefore no regiment is to be seen in which there are not negroes in abundance, and among them there are able-bodied, strong, and brave fellows. Here, too, there are many families of free negroes, who live in good houses, have property, and live just like the rest of the inhabitants."[1]

---

[1] Schloezer's "Briefwechsel," vol. iv., p. 365.

The time came when slaves were solicited to don the Continental uniform. Lord Dunmore's influence with the Negroes began to wane. His proclamation had had more influence upon the Continental authorities than upon the slaves. It constrained the former to act in order to counter its influence; and its narrow provisions, giving freedom only to such as would enter his Majesty's service, led the latter to doubt its genuineness, or the motive that inspired it. On the 30th of March, 1776, nearly five months after the issuance of his proclamation, Lord Dunmore reported his failure to raise a black regiment in Virginia to the home government. "A fever crept in amongst them which carried off a great many very fine fellows," he wrote the home secretary. And on the 26th of June he wrote: "Had it not been for this horrid disorder, I am satisfied I should have had two thousand blacks, with whom I should have had no doubt of penetrating into the heart of this colony."[1]

But Dunmore was not the only royalist pursuing a pacific policy towards the Negroes. On the 21st of July, 1776, Brigadier-general Nathaniel Greene, from his camp on Long Island, notified General Washington that his latest advice from the enemy's lines was that he was about organizing a regiment of Negroes "eight hundred" strong.[2] At the siege of Augusta, in 1781, Fort Cornwallis "was garrisoned by four hundred men in addition to two hundred negroes." On the 28th of February, 1781, General Greene wrote General Washington from North Carolina: "The enemy have ordered two regiments of negroes to be immediately embodied."[3] But the great majority of Negro soldiers fought on the side of independence. Negro levies

---

[1] Force's "American Archives," vol. ii., pp. 160, 162. Fifth Series.
[2] Ibid., vol. i., p. 486. Fifth Series.
[3] "Journals of Congress," vol. ii., p. 26.

for the Continental army were sought with intelligent zeal in all the colonies. Congress left the matter of raising troops to fill the quota of each colony with the local authorities. On the 16th of January, 1776, Congress gave permission to the free Negroes of Massachusetts, whose first term of enlistment had expired, to re-enlist in the army at Cambridge.[1] But even before a general policy of emancipation and military employment of Negroes as soldiers had been adopted, a large number had enlisted in the Eastern army. The following official return gives the number of Negroes in the main army under Washington's command two months after the battle of Monmouth:

RETURN OF NEGROES IN THE ARMY, 24TH OF AUGUST, 1778.

Brigades.	Present.	Sick. Absent.	On command.	Total.
North Carolina	42	10	6	58
Woodford	36	3	1	40
Muhlenburg	64	26	8	98
Smallwood	20	3	1	24
Second Maryland	43	15	2	60
Wayne	2	..	..	2
Second Pennsylvania	[33]	[1]	[1]	[35]
Clinton	33	2	4	39
Parsons	117	12	19	148
Huntington	56	2	4	62
Nixon	26	..	1	27
Patterson	64	13	12	89
Late Learned	34	4	8	46
Poor	16	7	4	27
Total	586	98	71	755

ALEX. SCAMMELL, *Adjutant-General.*

The above return does not include the Rhode Island regiment, which had already been organized, nor the troops from Connecticut. Nevertheless, this is a strong

---

[1] Sparks's "Correspondence of the American Revolution," vol. iii., p. 246.

representation of Negro soldiers at so early a period of the war.

On the 29th of March, 1779, Congress enacted a law to enable the colony of South Carolina to raise "three thousand able-bodied negroes," and made provisions for paying the masters of such slaves as might enlist.[1] Shortly after this, Congress commissioned John Laurens, whose father was in Congress from South Carolina, as a lieutenant-colonel, and despatched him to the South to recruit black levies. These are the only two instances in which Congress took any action respecting the military employment of Negroes; and it is the duty of history to record the failure of so noble an enterprise. "But the single voice of reason," wrote Colonel Laurens, May 19, 1782, "was drowned by the howlings of a triple-headed monster, in which prejudice, avarice, and pusillanimity were united."[2]

Moved by the pressing necessities of war, and admonished by the celerity of an insidious enemy, the colonies seized upon the policy of arming their slaves. In the month of May, 1777, the General Assembly of Connecticut passed an act for the enlistment of Negroes; but it was put over one session, and finally defeated by a committee hostile to the project.[3] But, in addition to the free Negroes scattered through the Connecticut regiments, a company of slaves was raised, and assigned to Meigs's, afterwards Butler's, regiment.[4] On the 2d of January, 1778, General J. M. Varnum, of Rhode Island, wrote General Washington concerning a plan he had conceived for the raising of

---

[1] "Secret Journals of Congress," vol. i., pp. 107-110.

[2] Sparks's "Correspondence of the American Revolution," vol. iii., p. 506.

[3] "An Historical Research," pp. 114-116.

[4] "National Portrait Gallery of Distinguished Americans."

troops in Rhode Island. "It is imagined that a battalion of negroes can be raised there;"[1] he wrote. His letter was enclosed by General Washington to Nicholas Cooke, governor of Rhode Island. When the General Assembly convened in February, the correspondence was laid before it, and after some debate an act embodying General Varnum's plan was passed. It provided "that every able-bodied negro, mulatto, or Indian man slave" might enlist, and "that every slave so enlisting . . . be immediately discharged from the service of his master or mistress, and be absolutely FREE." The act provided that the owner of each slave enlisting should be allowed "a price not exceeding £120 for the most valuable slave; and in proportion for a slave of less value."[2] This legislation, so radical and costly, was not secured without violent opposition. There were four reasons for its rejection set forth in a protest signed by six members of the Assembly. They thought that there were not enough Negroes in the Province to justify the scheme of a separate battalion; that slaves ought not to be purchased to fight the battles of freemen; that the expense of such an organization would be much greater than of an organization of white men of the same number; and that both difficulties and dissatisfaction would arise among the masters in reference to the purchase-money.[3] The plan, however, went into operation, and four companies of emancipated slaves were enrolled as soldiers,[4] at a cost of £10,437 7s. 7d. This sum was audited and sworn to at Providence on February 23, 1781.

But the enlistment of slaves in this colony was only

---

[1] "Rhode Island Colonial Records," vol. viii., p. 641. *Vide* General Washington's letter, p. 640, also p. 524.
[2] Ibid., vol. viii., pp. 358–360.
[3] Ibid., vol. viii., p. 361.
[4] "Spirit of '76 in Rhode Island," pp. 186–188.

permitted for four months. In May, 1778, the General Assembly declared in a resolution that the act of February was intended to be temporary only, and "voted and resolved, that no negro, mulatto, or Indian slave be permitted to enlist into said battalion from and after the tenth day of June next, and that the said act then expire and be no longer in force." But the little colony had exhausted all the military material among the Negroes, and the above resolve had little or no effect.

On the 3d of April, 1778, Thomas Kench, a member of an artillery regiment stationed on Castle Island, presented an elaborate plan for raising Negro troops to the Council of the Province of Massachusetts Bay. "We have divers of them," he explained, "in our service, mixed with white men. But I think it would be more proper to raise a body by themselves." He thought that in a separate organization the Negroes would have the *esprit de corps*, and said that no patriot could oppose "this plan, or be against his negroes enlisting into the service to maintain the cause of freedom."[1] But the Council did not feel called upon to amend its record and invite "slaves" to "help fight the battles of freemen." On the other hand the question of the emancipation and enlistment of the slaves had occasioned deep concern and sharp discussion. Several altercations resulting in blows had taken place in the coffee-houses in the lower part of Boston, and the public temper was dangerously excited. Mr. Kench, receiving no reply to his communication, addressed a brief note calling attention to disturbances that had occurred in Boston, adding that he would be brief lest he might give offence. He seems to have realized the temper of the Council.

---

[1] "MS. Archives of Massachusetts," vol. cxcix., p. 80.

"*To the Honorable Council in Boston:*

"The letter I wrote before I heard of the disturbance with Colonel Seares, Mr. Spear, and a number of other gentleman, concerning the freedom of negroes, in Congress Street. It is a pity that riots should be committed on the occasion, as it is justifiable that negroes should have their freedom, and none amongst us be held as slaves, as freedom and liberty is the grand controversy that we are contending for; and I trust, under the smiles of Divine Providence, we shall obtain it, if all our minds can be united; and putting the negroes into the service will prevent much uneasiness, and give more satisfaction to those that are offended at the thoughts of their servants being free.

"I will not enlarge, for fear I should give offence; but subscribe myself

"Your faithful servant,
"THOMAS KENCH.

"CASTLE ISLAND, *April* 7, 1778."[1]

From 1652 to 1656 the free Negroes of Massachusetts were permitted to join the militia by law, but in 1656 a law was passed excluding them. "Henceforth," the law declared, "no negroes or Indians . . . shall be armed or permitted to trayne."[2] And in May, 1680, Governor Bradstreet wrote to the "Committee for Trade," "We account all generally from sixteen to sixty that are healthful and strong bodys, both House-holders and servants, fit to beare Armes, except Negroes and Slaves, whom wee arme not."[3] In the Militia Act of 1775, "*negroes*, Indians, and *mulattoes*" were excepted. And by the act of May, 1776, providing for the reinforcement of the American army, it was declared that "Indians, negroes, and mulattoes shall not be held to take up arms or procure any person to do it in their room." On the 14th of November, 1776, contemplating an improvement of the army, "negroes, Indians, and mulattoes were excluded." And in an order issued dur-

---

[1] "MS. Archives of Massachusetts," vol. cxcix., p. 84.
[2] Moore's "History of Slavery in Massachusetts," App., p. 243.
[3] "Mass. Hist. Soc. Coll.," vol. viii., p. 336. Third Series.

ing this year, to take the census of all males above the age of sixteen, "negroes, Indians, and mulattoes" were excepted. But the gravity of the situation led the General Court to pass a resolve on the 6th of January, 1777, "for the raising of every seventh man to complete our quota," "without any exceptions, save the people called Quakers." As late as the 5th of March, 1778, Benjamin Goddard, representing the selectmen, Committee of Safety, and militia officers of the town of Grafton, protested against the enlistment of the Negroes of that place.

On the 11th of April, 1778, the first letter of Thomas Kench, dated April 3, was read and referred to a joint committee, with instructions "to consider the same, and report." On the 17th of April a copy of the Rhode Island act "for enlisting negroes in the public service" was referred to the same committee; and on the 28th of April an act was passed for the military employment of Negroes, almost in the words of the Rhode Island law of February, 1778. But there is no record of a separate Negro organization in Massachusetts, and, being allowed to enter the service, they enlisted in the white organizations already in the field.

The New England colonies had at length accepted the policy of arming Negroes as inevitable. The Negroes would make powerful allies; their great natural strength, their power of endurance and enthusiasm, made them welcome comrades everywhere. Within three years after the battle of Bunker Hill they were scattered through the eastern army, and their intelligence and valor had been severely tested. But the middle and southern colonies had manifested more conservatism. There were 15,000 slaves in the colony of New York, and most of them in the city of New York. There were 7,600 in New Jersey, 10,000 in Pennsylvania, and 9,000 in Delaware. Sir Henry Clinton was in command of His majesty's forces on the Atlantic seaboard from Nova Scotia to West Florida. He saw that the policy of the Continental authorities in employing Negroes was ruinous to his Majesty's cause, and in order to discourage the military employment of Negroes, Sir Henry issued a proclamation. It was published in *The Royal Gazette*, of New York City, July 3d, 1779.

"PROCLAMATION.

"Whereas the enemy have adopted a practice of enrolling NEGROES among their Troops, I do hereby give notice That all NEGROES taken in arms, or upon any military Duty, shall be purchased for [*the public service at*] a stated Price; the money to be paid to the Captors.

"But I do most strictly forbid any Person to sell or claim Right over any NEGROE, the property of a Rebel, who may take Refuge with any part of this Army: And I do promise to every NEGROE who shall desert the Rebel Standard full security to follow within these Lines any Occupation which he shall think proper.

"Given under my Hand, at Headquarters, PHILLIPSBURGH, the 30th day of June, 1779.   H. CLINTON.

"By his Excellency's command.
     "JOHN SMITH, Secretary."

While Sir Henry's proclamation had little or no effect at the North, many Negroes joined his forces at the South. In the spring of the following year, Colonel Laurens wrote General Washington from Charleston, South Carolina, February 14th: "Private accounts say that General Prevost is left to command at Savannah; that his troops consist of the Hessians and Loyalists that were there before, reinforced by a corps of blacks and a detachment of savages. It is generally reported that Sir Henry Clinton commands the present expedition."[1]

This news seems to have had the effect of convincing the

---

[1] Sparks's "Correspondence of the American Revolution," vol. ii., p. 402.

brave General Lincoln of the importance of raising Negro troops in the South. On the 13th of March, 1780, he wrote Governor Rutledge, of South Carolina:

"Give me leave to add once more, that I think the measure of raising a black corps a necessary one; that I have great reason to believe, if permission be given for it, that many men would soon be obtained. I have repeatedly urged this matter, not only because Congress have recommended it, and because it thereby becomes my duty to attempt to have it executed, but because my own mind suggests the utility and importance of the measure, as the safety of the town [Charleston] makes it necessary." And on the 16th of March, 1779, the Hon. Henry Laurens, of South Carolina, wrote General Washington: "Had we arms for three thousand such black men as I could select in Carolina, I should have no doubt of success in driving the British out of Georgia, and subduing East Florida before the end of July."[1] Free Negroes had enlisted in the Virginia regiments, although there was no law accepting their services. It appears that several slaves deserted their masters, and under the pretence of being free persons, enlisted. And to prevent such enlistments the following law was enacted:

"*Be it enacted*, that it shall not be lawful for any recruiting officer within this commonwealth to enlist any negro or mulatto into the service of this or either of the United States, until such negro or mulatto shall produce a certificate frome some Justice of the Peace for the county wherein he resides that he is a freeman."[2]

There is no record of a separate battalion or regiment of Negroes in the colony of Virginia; but the above act very clearly indicates that there *were* Negroes in the army,

---

[1] Sparks's "Washington," vol. vi., p. 204.
[2] Henig's "Statutes," vol. ix., p. 280.

and that free Negroes *could* enter if they chose. On the 20th of November, 1780, the Hon. James Madison wrote to Joseph Jones, of Virginia: "Would it not be as well to liberate and make soldiers at once of the blacks themselves? . . . And with white officers and a majority of white soldiers, no imaginable danger could be feared from themselves."[1] Virginia did nobly; for in 1783 the General Assembly passed a law entitled "An Act directing the emancipation of certain slaves who have served as soldiers in this State, and for the emancipation of the slave Aberdeen."[2] On the 20th of March, 1781, the General Assembly of New York enacted a law for the embodiment of two regiments of Negro slaves, who, after a term of three years, were to be freemen of the State.[3] And in June, 1781, Maryland was entertaining a project to raise seven hundred and fifty Negro soldiers, to be incorporated with the white troops from that colony.[4]

And so the work went forward, until it was the exception, not the rule, to find no Negro soldiers in any brigade of the army. Everywhere they won the confidence and applause of their white compatriots; and they did their duty so naturally and faithfully that their color was lost sight of. Towards the close of the war their presence was no more a matter of comment than that there were Continental troops from the eastern colonies, or that liberty had votaries among the colonists.

While there were no special engagements in which Negro soldiers bore the brunt, nevertheless they participated

---

[1] "Madison Papers," p. 68.
[2] Henig's "Statutes of Virginia," vol. xi., pp. 308, 309.
[3] "Laws of the State of New York," chap. xxxii. Fourth Session.
[4] Sparks's "Correspondence of the American Revolution," vol. iii., p. 331.

in most of the battles of the Revolution. There were but few separate organizations of Negro troops, and even then their personality was swallowed up in some brigade of white troops. But, side by side with their white compatriots, they fought gallantly for American independence, from Bunker Hill to Brandywine, from Valley Forge to Monmouth, and from Saratoga to Yorktown. They were represented in ten of the fourteen brigades in the main army under General Washington during the first three years of the war; and after the battle of Monmouth (June 28, 1778) they were to be found in eighteen brigades.[1] These gallant black soldiers extended their military exploits from Massachusetts Bay to Lake Ontario; from the battle of Rhode Island to the surrender of Cornwallis. At Bunker Hill they set an example of valor and soldiership admirable to white officers, and which won the applause of the Provincial Congress. In the battle of Rhode Island they shared, with unwavering devotion, the perils of the conflict and the glory of the victory.[2] As early as

---

[1] I have gone over the muster-rolls, as well as the descriptive lists, of the Continental army, and have been rewarded by the discovery that nearly all the regiments from the eastern colonies contained negro soldiers. This I found true, also, of many regiments from the southern colonies.—G. W. W.

[2] One Sidney S. Rider, author of "An Historical Tract" (No. 10) in the Rhode Island series, has striven to ridicule and cast into oblivion the black regiment of Rhode Island during the Revolutionary War. Mr. Rider's tract was published at Providence in 1880. He seeks to disprove the fact that "a regiment" existed; although it is carried on the rolls of the army as a "regiment," and is designated as a regiment by all historians. He seeks to belittle the services of this regiment at the battle of Rhode Island, August 29, 1778, and to show that there was only a handful of insubordinate Negroes in that engagement. Mr. Rider is lacking in judicial temper; and his literary workmanship is very imperfect. He gives a list of the names of the privates—eighty-eight in all—while only nine of these names tally with the roll as it ap-

1776, when the main army from the east was mobilized at New York, there were many Negroes in the regiments. Graydon (p. 147) wrote of Colonel Glover's regiment, from Marblehead, Massachusetts: "But even in this regiment (a fine one) there were a number of Negroes." They

peared on the 1st of May, 1779 (*vide* Saffell's "Revolutionary Records," pp. 153, 154). In Cowell's "Spirit of '76 in Rhode Island" (pp. 186–188), the number of these black soldiers is given (January, 1780) as one hundred and forty-four. All that history claims for this regiment is *just* as well as *true*. The troops fought well; and Major-general Greene wrote the next day after the engagement: "The enemy repeated the attempt three times [tried to carry his position], and were as often repulsed with great bravery." The black regiment was one of three that prevented the enemy from turning the flank of the American army. These black troops were doubtless regarded as the weak point of the line, but they were not.

On the 5th of January, 1781, the Marquis de Chastellux ("Travels," vol. i., p. 454, London, 1789) wrote: "At the passage to the ferry, I met a detachment of the Rhode Island regiment, the same corps we had with us all the last summer, but they have since been recruited and clothed. The greatest part of them are Negroes or mulattoes; but they are strong, robust men, and those I have seen had a very good appearance."

Mr. Rider says (p. 37) that "they were in no engagement after the battle of Rhode Island;" forgetting that he had recorded (p. 29) their engagement at Point Bridge. He says that while here Colonel Greene "was surprised and attacked in the rear by a party of two hundred and sixty of the enemy's light-horse during the night of May 14, 1781. Colonel Greene and Major Flagg were killed, and about forty of the regiment were either killed, wounded, or taken prisoners."

Several facts are clearly admitted here: (1) It was a *surprise* (2) at *night* in the (3) *rear;* and by (4) *two hundred and sixty* (5) *light-horse* upon Mr. Rider's "*eighty-eight Negroes,*" who sustained a loss of about (6) forty men!" Let military students and critics draw their own conclusions, and then read the sneering comments of Mr. Rider (p. 47 *sq.*) in his tract.

As late as 1783 this black regiment was still in the service, and from it General Washington ordered a detail to effect a forced march to, and surprise of, the enemy's post at Oswego (*vide* Sparks's "Washington," vol. viii., p. 385).—G. W. W.

were numerous in the regiments that were despatched to the northward, and so readily adjusted themselves to the profession of arms that no objections were offered to them anywhere. Their splendid feats of valor covered their dark visage as with a halo of glory; and the only way to distinguish them from their white compatriots, so close was the comradeship, is to go over the rolls of the army patiently, name by name. The following partial roll shows that nearly every town in Massachusetts had its Negro representative in the army:

Negro Soldiers.	Age.	Height.	Where from.
Scipio Witt	19	5 ft. 6 in.	Brookfield.
Abner Hibray	31	5 " 6 "	"
Ozias Fletcher	18	5 " 10 "	W. Springfield.
Frederick Way	16	5 " 10 "	"
Peter Lovejoy	17	5 " 7 "	Andover.
Winham Carvey	40	5 " 3 "	Boston.
Isaac Mitchel	36	5 " 5 "	"
Bristol Pratt	35	5 " 10 "	"
Newport Deblois	45	5 " 4 "	"
Boston Foster	32	5 " 8 "	"
Cromwel Barnes	16	5 "	"
Cyrus Kent	30	5 " 4 "	"
Bristol Ballard	25	5 " 6 "	"
Abs'm Northgate	18	5 " 4 "	"
Titus Freeman	37	5 " 2 "	"
James Thomas	22	5 " 8 "	Newburyport.
Cæsar Mills	19	5 " 6 "	Watertown.
Charles Hendrick (Indian)	21	5 " 5 "	Westminster.
Cæsar Sweeten	17	5 " 3 "	Bellingham.
Prince Brewster (mulatto)	17	5 " 6 "	Medway.
Ishmael Coffe (mulatto)	40	5 " 7 "	"
Thomas Gibbs	28	5 " 3 "	Sunderland.
Richard Demmon	59	5 " 7 "	Sutton.
Prince Brown	20	5 " 7 "	Newbury.
Cuff Dowrey	22	5 " 7 "	"
Charlestown Edes	30	5 " 8 "	Groton.
Cambridge Moor	25	5 " 6 "	Bedford.
Cornwallis Negro	18	5 "	Braintree.
Charles Pane	27	5 " 7 "	Franklin.
James Holland (mulatto)	17	5 " 4 "	Braintree.
Jeremiah Crocker	29	5 " 8 "	Medway.
Cammel R. Gould	17	5 " 8 "	Wareham.
Benja Gould	16	5 " 2 "	"
Joseph Warwick (mulatto)	17	5 " 7 "	Marshfield.
Peter Bannister	19	5 " 6 "	Rehoboth.

Negro Soldiers.	Age.	Height.	Where from.
Pompey Wallis	45	5 ft. 6 in.	Stoughton.
Benoni Williams	17	5 " 5 "	Dighton.
Thomas Dean	19	5 " 10 "	"
Peter Winslow	18	5 " 5 "	"
Uriah Tew (mulatto)	17	5 " 7 "	"
John Waben	16	5 " 4 "	Petersham.
Peter Haskall	30	5 " 9 "	Rochester.
Peter Gunn	28	5 " 5 "	Paxton.
Prince Almey	18	5 " 9 "	Dartmouth.
Eben' Prince (Indian)	17	5 " 11 "	"
Solomon Dick (Negro)	17	5 " 4 "	"
Pompey Peckum	28	5 " 8 "	"
London Roger	24	5 " 1 "	Newbury.
Cuff Mitchel	33	5 " 7 "	Bridgewater.
Calvin Jotham	20	5 " 8 "	"
Samuel Mingo	30	5 " 4 "	"
Benj' Oliver	23	5 " 4 "	Salem.
Benj' Thomas (Indian)	22	5 " 8 "	Natick.
Phillip Barrett	19	5 " 9 "	Concord.
Lancaster Bick	20	5 " 9 "	Newbury.
Primus Cobus	16	5 " 4 "	Abington.
Peter Sherron	17	5 " 9 "	Lincoln.
Plato Turner	28	5 " 7 "	Plymouth.
Obadiah Wicket (Indian)	26	5 " 9 "	Sandwich.
Jack Rand	27	5 " 9 "	Woburn.
Cæsar Prescott	47	5 " 6 "	Bedford.
Peter Hazard	22	5 " 9 "	Sandwich.
Fortune Holland	19	5 " 8 "	"
Abraham Demus (Indian)	27	5 " 10 "	"
James Heater (Indian)	16	5 " 6 "	"
Joseph Conant (mulatto)	16	5 " 8 "	"
Peter Warren (mulatto)	39	5 " 6 "	Medfield.
Warwick Green	29	5 " 4 "	"
Newport Green	42	5 " 5 "	"
Paul Cuffee	25	5 " 10 "	Falmouth.
Joshua Robbins (Indian)	20	5 " 5 "	"
Peter Oliver	23	5 " 9 "	Littleton.
Briton Nichols	40	5 " 11 "	Cohasset.
Mark Negro	48	5 " 3 "	Sandwich.
James Crook (Indian)	16	5 " 2 "	Harwich.
Absalom Toby (mulatto)	16	5 " 2 "	"
Robert Pegin (Indian)	36	5 " 9 "	Bridgewater.
Tobe Tarbil (Negro)	45	5 " 6 "	"
Quark Martrick	24	5 " 5 "	"
John Foy	21	5 " 10 "	"
Charles Mingo	18	5 " 9 "	Wrentham.
Peter Buxton	44	6 " 1 "	Danvers.
Zachariah Bray	27	5 " 6 "	"
Jeffery Hemmingway	40	5 " 4 "	Worcester.
Prince Brown	21	5 " 5 "	Falmouth.
James London (mulatto)	19	5 " 2 "	Barnstable.
Asher Freeman	23	5 " 9 "	Scituate.
Nehemiah Sampson (mulatto)	16	5 "	"

Negro Soldiers.	Age.	Height.	Where from.
Toney Rose	18	5 ft. 10 in.	Middleborough.
Jack Negro	16	5 " 2 "	Sandwich.
Adam Tuttle	22	5 " 7 "	Boston.
Cæser Thatcher	32	5 " 5 "	Dorchester.
Ishmael Cutler	36	5 " 6 "	Cambridge.
Prince Cutler	20	5 " 10 "	"
Prince Darby	27	5 " 5 "	Dorchester.
Sharper Freeman	30	5 " 9 "	Stoneham.
Cato Tudor	21	5 " 4 "	Lexington.
Peter Dago	25	5 " 11 "	Natick.
Jacob Spean	26	5 " 8 "	"
Jeremiah Job (mulatto)	20	5 " 11 "	Chesterfield.
Peter Price (mulatto)	26	5 " 4 "	"
Cato Hunt	18	5 " 8 "	Rehoboth.
David Negro	17	4 " 11 "	"
Edward Samms	31	5 " 1 "	Kittery.
Cuff Dole	32	5 " 10 "	Rowley.
Prince Easterbrooks	39	5 " 11 "	Lexington.
Simeon Reed	25	5 " 10 "	Freetown.
Cæsar Elsberry	16	5 " 5 "	"
Cicero Haskell	21	5 " 3 "	Newburyport.
Oxford Task	26	5 " 7 "	"
Uriah Williams	28	5 " 7 "	Berwick.
Samuel Royal	21	5 " 8 "	Salem.
Samuel Craft	18	5 " 9 "	Lexington.

All through this roll of honor we find the word "Negro," or "black." But for this fact, history would have been silent on this important point, which is now, for the first time, established by the record—that Negro soldiers participated in nearly every battle of the Revolutionary War.[1] They witnessed the first flash of war that marked the severance

---

[1] It required two winter seasons to complete an examination of the rolls of the American army of the Revolutionary War. Taking sixty-seven (67) regiments from the entire army, and giving an average of thirty-five (35) Negroes to each of these regiments, the result is two thousand three hundred and forty-five (2345) Negroes. Allowing six hundred and fifty-five (655) for separate organizations, and those in regiments from the Southern States, there were, at the lowest calculation, *three thousand* (3000) *Negro soldiers* in the American army of the Revolutionary War. It is not known how many were among the ministerial troops. Quite a number went to England at the close of the war with General Sir Guy Carleton; some settled in Nova Scotia, and others went to Sierra Leone, West Africa.—G. W. W.

of the colonies from the British Empire, and they beheld Cornwallis's banners go down before the victorious standards of the American army. They were modest, patient, heroic, and efficient from the gray dawn of the struggle until the bright noontide of victory. Their sufferings, sacrifices, and triumphs are now the priceless heritage of a grateful nation.

FRANCE, under the empire and as a republic, never proscribed the Negro in her laws regulating the army. Negroes speaking the French language, and being French subjects, have been admitted to the army at all times. Their presence in the French army has never been commented upon by military writers, because it has always been regarded as natural and normal.

There was no involuntary servitude in France, and the color of the skin was never regarded as a badge of inferiority. In the sea-coast districts and in the large cities of France the Negroes have resided in considerable numbers, and have always contributed their small proportion to the military quota.

The mulattoes soon lose their racial identity, and speaking the French language, and copying French manners, are easily merged in the general population. No one addresses them as Negroes, and a reference to their nationality is always unwelcome. Being few in number, and retaining no Negro characteristics, there is no obstruction to their ambition. A Negro may pass all the grades of the army and reach the rank of a field-marshal if he have military talents.

France has honored herself in recognizing the military services of a brave Negro, Alexander Davy Dumas, who was born at Jérémie, Hayti, March 25, 1762. His father was the Marquis de la Pailléterie, and his mother a Negro girl. He was sent to France to be educated, but, being of a romantic and vivacious temperament, he ran away and joined a French cavalry regiment at the age of fourteen. After two years of service, he reached the rank of a non-commissioned officer. In 1762 the Minister of War, Monsieur De Choiseul, formed a system of promotion for non-commissioned and lower officers. In 1782 the Committee of War manifested a desire to extend a larger opportunity for promotion, but it was not carried into effect until 1790. Nearly all the offices were monopolized by the privileged classes. But three years later this intrepid Negro soldier had won the rank of division commander. Now came a sudden and radical change in his military career. From the monotonous routine of the garrison he was transferred to the active theatre of war. His aptitude for the profession of arms began to be manifest, and by deeds of desperate valor he won the applause of the army and the praise of his commander, Dumouriez. His promotions were rapid, and by September, 1793, he had passed through every grade to the rank of general of division.[1] He served in Italy under Bonaparte, and at the battle of Brixen, single-handed and alone, defended a bridge against the enemy, thus affording the French time to arrive. This feat rendered him quite famous in the French army, and Bonaparte presented him to the Directory as "the Horatius Cocles of the Tyrol." He was ordered to Egypt, where he served with distinction. He died at Villers-Cotterets, France, February 26, 1806. He attained the highest rank and won the greatest distinction as a soldier of any Negro in the world—with the exception of Toussaint l'Ouverture.

The French nation employs an army of Negroes in Al-

---

[1] A general of division is one "who may be charged with the command of armies, corps of the army, active divisions, or special functions" (*vide* Thackeray on the Military of France, vol. i., p. 23).—G. W. W.

giers, but never stations them in France. There are two regiments of these black soldiers, and each regiment is composed of four battalions of one thousand men. When on a war footing, these regiments contain sixteen thousand Negroes. They are commonly called Turcos, on account of their desperate fighting qualities, but are carried upon the muster-rolls of the French army as "*Tirailleurs Algériens.*" They are commanded by French officers, and have attained a high degree of discipline. They are all Mohammedan in religious belief, and rather court death as the beginning of a more desirable life. They are fanatically brave.[1] They served in Mexico in 1865 and 1866, and were justly distinguished by splendid fighting in the war between France and Germany in 1870. They are now winning fresh laurels in the campaign in Tonquin.[2]

THE BRITISH ARMY has employed Negro troops for a century,[3] but on account of dealing with numerous tribes of heathen people, has never commissioned Negroes as officers. This policy has not been directed against the Negro as such, but is general. No foreigner is ever intrusted with a commission in the British army. Several Negroes have, indeed, held commissions as surgeons, but only on the west coast of Africa.

Immediately after the abolition of the slave-trade on

---

[1] During a recent visit to Munich, Germany, the author saw a great military painting in which these troops are represented as conspicuous in the Franco-German war.—G. W. W.

[2] MS. Letter of Commandant De la Chére, of the French Army, to the author.

[3] In reply to a letter of the author, the Secretary of State for War wrote from the Horse Guards, War Office, London, S. W., under date of January 11, 1886: "At the present time there are two regiments of these troops on the Establishment of her Majesty's land-forces, and that negroes have been so employed for the last hundred years."—G. W. W.

the west coast of Africa, in 1807, a local military establishment was constituted. The rank and file of this organization were recruited from recaptures of the British fleet that was policing the coast. As fast as slave-vessels were captured, their living cargo was unloaded at Sierra Leone. Mean as this material may seem, it furnished a splendid corps of soldiers for the British Government. The men were proud of the service, and took the drill and duties of their new employment with intelligent zeal. Seven years after the colony of Sierra Leone had been adopted by the Crown, Mr. Park, the African traveller, wrote: "In the Royal African Corps now [1814] serving at Sierra Leone there are three companies of black men, enlisted from the slaves obtained from numerous slave-trading vessels which have at different times been condemned as prize upon that coast. . . .

"These men, having been trained and disciplined with great care, are become excellent soldiers, and are spoken of by the Governor of Sierra Leone in the highest terms of approbation for their obedience, steadiness, and general good conduct. They are, of course, inured to the climate, are accustomed to hardships and fatigues, and capable of the greatest exertions. They are, at the same time, courageous and high-spirited, feeling a pride and elevation from the advantages which they enjoy, and the comparative *rank* to which they have attained; and they are warmly attached to the British Government."[1]

"Her Majesty's Government do now actually employ colored regiments in the British West Indies, known as the West Indian regiments, composed of West African Negroes;"[2] and they are reputed to be excellent soldiers.

---

[1] Park's "Travels," vol. ii., pp. 142, 143. London edition, 1816.

[2] MS. Letter of the British Minister at Washington to the author. See also Major A. B. Ellis's "History of the First West Indian Regiment."

And while their services are local, these troops have attained a remarkable proficiency in the manual of arms and field manœuvres. And here the Negro is included in a general policy, as it has been noted he was excluded from being an officer by a general policy. It is a general policy of the British Government to use native troops in the colonies, and the Negro is thus included in this policy on the west coast of Africa and in the British West Indies.

In modern as well as in ancient NUBIA Negro troops are employed in large numbers. "The Sultan of Wara, or *fasher*, as he is likewise called (*fasher* being the term applied to the open place where he gives audience), has among his troops many Negroes."[1] At Mocha Negroes were "highly esteemed as soldiers, and as such were kept in numbers by some of the more powerful chiefs of southern Arabia."[2] In BRAZIL many Negroes are employed in the police and military, while a few have obtained rank and distinction. And in PERU dead Negro priests have not only been canonized, but among the military Negroes may be found, "together with a much larger proportion of persons of mixed origin, zamboes and mulattoes."[3]

But the scene of modern Negro soldiership is HAYTI. Here, during the last century, an army of Negroes, with officers from their own class, met in the field and successively and successfully fought the Spanish, French, and English; and by their own unaided efforts established a Negro republic. Several black generals came to the front in this memorable struggle, but the most commanding character was Toussaint l'Ouverture. He was born May 20,

---

[1] Burckhardt's "Travels in Nubia," p. 441. Second Edition. London, 1822.

[2] Pickering's "Races of Men," vol. ix., p. 186.

[3] Ibid., vol. ix., p. 184 *sq.*

1743, on the Island of Santo Domingo, and died April 27, 1803, in the damp, dark, and earless dungeon of Joux, on the Jura Mountains, in France.

When the French throne was rocking amid the angry waves of the Revolution of 1789, the mulattoes of the Island of Santo Domingo — a considerable element in the population — intelligent and wealthy, took advantage of the movement for justice and humanity, and asked for manhood suffrage. They despatched a deputation to Paris, headed by Lieutenant-colonel Vincent Ogé, to lay at the foot of the French throne six million francs to help liquidate the national debt. The deputation pledged the mulatto population to the payment of an annual sum towards the reduction of the French debt, and asked in return that they might not be taxed without representation.

The French Assembly enacted a law making all free men, regardless of complexion, eligible to office. On October 17, 1790, Colonel Ogé landed at Cape Haytien, and marched at the head of two hundred men to La Grande Revière, where he went into camp. He wrote a letter to the Assembly of the Island, requesting them to put into execution the French act making free men of color eligible to office. His letter was read and laid upon the table. A planter seized it and tore it into atoms, and then threw it upon the floor. The excitement was so great that the Assembly broke up in uncontrolled confusion, the members exclaiming, "We will every one die before we will consent to share our political rights with a bastard and degenerate race!"

Ogé was attacked and defeated, and subsequently captured. His trial was most memorable in the annals of the island. It continued three months, when he and his lieutenant, Shevanne, were sentenced to be broken alive upon the wheel. The four quarters of the palpitating body were hung up at the four principal cities of the island. This was intended to menace the mulattoes, and suppress any desire for the enforcement of their newly acquired rights. But its effect was to arouse their indignation. On the night of August 21, 1791, the mulattoes aroused the plantation Negroes, and within thirty hours reduced the island, by torch and sword, to a smouldering heap of ruin. Every city of the island was now in ruins, and property and human life were little prized and in great peril. The slaves left the plantations in large groups, and were everywhere insolent and threatening.

Although the war began in the interest of the mulattoes, and is known to history as the "Mulatto War," it was now transferred to the hands of the hardy Negroes. They organized an army, and placed Jean François, Biassou, and Jeannot, three black brigadier-generals, in command. Toussaint made his appearance in the army as brigade-surgeon on the staff of General François. Being a man of understanding and some education, he proved himself an apt student in this practical school of war. He attracted wide-spread attention, and his talents gave promise of large usefulness.

The planters rallied under the British flag, and the Assembly formally requested the aid of his Majesty's troops stationed at Kingston, British West Indies. The Negroes espoused the cause of Spain, and King Charles IV. conferred upon Toussaint the commission of a brigadier-general. He gathered these black brigands with a firm hand, and organized them for victory. On May 27, 1795, he fought and won his first battle, taking Marmelade after eight hours of stubborn resistance. While his troops were flushed, he marched upon Dondon, and caused the place to capitulate. He fortified these commanding positions, assumed the defensive, and subjected his troops to the severest discipline and drill. As soon as his forces yielded to military law, and began to desire the honor of the military profession, he made a forced march to the mountains, and fell upon Ennery like a bolt of thunder. The garrison yielded to his summons, and another point of commanding importance was now under his control. Surely, if slowly, he was moulding his Negro army with a master-hand. He was a student during times of inaction, and his military books were Claison's "History of Alexander and Cæsar," Marshal Saxe's "Military Reveries," Guischardt's "Military Memoirs of the Greeks and Romans," Lloyd's "Military and Political Memoirs," Cæsar's "Commentaries," etc. He always kept a Bible at headquarters—for he could pray as well as fight.

When he was ready he set his army in motion, and began to attack the enemy in his intrenched positions. He was possessed with wonderful military intuition. He could sweep a line of battle with a glance, and detect a weak point. He could steady a wavering column by his presence, and by his peerless example could inspire his troops to the most desperate fighting against the greatest odds. He drove the British troops at the point of the bayonet, and those who were fortunate enough to escape the fury of the Negro army hastened back to Jamaica.

The French troops in the island had revolted against their commander, General Laveaux, and had caused him to be cast into prison. Toussaint defeated the French in a pitched battle, took Laveaux out of prison, and installed him at the head of the French troops. In his admiration of this brilliant performance, a French officer exclaimed, "*Cet homme fait ouverture partout!*" From this incident he received the affix to his name, L'Ouverture (the opening).

General Toussaint l'Ouverture had administrative ability as well as the talents of a fighter. He was capable of broad plans and successful execution, and knew that skilful planning is one-half of military success. He won the sympathy of Europe by issuing a military proclamation declaring all slaves within range of his bayonets forever free, and thereby secured to himself an enthusiastic support equal to an army corps. The diplomacy of his military orders was not less effective than his manœuvres in the field. While wearing the uniform of a brigadier-general in the service of his Majesty the King of Spain, he learned that his royal master was friendly to the slave-trade. The English had rendered aid and comfort to the planters, and the mulattoes had formed an unnatural alliance with the men who had not only disputed their rights but had murdered their leaders. The French Assembly had not only enfranchised the mulattoes, but had, on February 4, 1794, declared the island free. The black general knew that the Revolution in France had done much for liberty, and that the government of the French nation would not be likely to go backward. He had the island in his control, and finally, with great deliberation, gave it to France. This bold, strategic stroke of policy was as hurtful to Spain as it was helpful to France. The news of the *coup de grace* kindled Paris into a blaze of enthusiasm. The name of the Negro general was pronounced with honor in the rounded periods of orators, while in military circles he was hailed as *Le noir Napoleon*. In Santo Domingo the English feared him, the Spanish hated him, the planters respected him, and the populace trusted him.

As a reward for his distinguished services, the French Government appointed him commander-in-chief of the army of Santo Domingo. By order of the governor he was inaugurated by a magnificent civic and military display, and before the army made the following speech:

"CITIZEN COMMISSIONERS: I accept the eminent rank to which you have just raised me, only in the hope of more surely succeeding in entirely extirpating the enemies of Saint Domingo, of contributing to its speedy restoration to prosperity, and of securing the happiness of its inhabitants. If to fulfil the difficult task which it imposes, it sufficed to wish the good of the island, and to effect it, is all that depends upon me, I hope that, with the aid of the Divine Being, I shall succeed. The tyrants are cast down upon the earth; they will no more defile the places where the standard of liberty and equality ought to float alone, and where the sacred rights of men ought to be recognized. Officers and soldiers, if there is a compensation in the severe labors which I am about to enter on, I shall find it in the satisfaction of commanding brave soldiers. Let the sacred fire of liberty animate us, and let us never take repose until we have prostrated our foes!"

Although a soldier, he felt that the true mission of the sword is to conquer peace; and in time of peace he recognized that true prosperity reposes upon the industry of all the people. Consequently he issued a general amnesty, and encouraged the blacks to cultivate the fields. Agriculture and commerce were of great moment, and business prosperity came as the sequence of a general confidence in Toussaint. His proclamation of amnesty was published at Cayes, August 1, 1800, and from their hiding-places Frenchmen and Englishmen, Spaniards and mulattoes, hurried back home to enjoy the security of a Negro's protection. Prejudices and grudges, distinctions and differences, disappeared amid the general prosperity that healed the wounds of the past. The great Negro soldier called about him able advisers of both races, and made a constitution and built a republic.

Restrained by his powerful hand, the Negro regiments left in garrison did little harm; and the distinctive elements of French administrative policy diffused a feeling of security throughout the entire island. By his striking individuality and marvellous executive ability he had organized an army out of a mob; and with his splendid talents he saw that the ends of victory were freedom and republicanism. In building a republic he adhered to certain fundamental principles. Santo Domingo had been monopolized by a few planters who had enjoyed enormous gains from the unrequited toil of slave labor. The island had had little or no communication with the outside world. Now that slavery and the slave-trade were gone, Toussaint saw the necessity of building up trade with the outside world. With no industries to compete with the manufactured goods of other countries, his constitution declared in favor of "*free-trade.*" Citizenship was broad as the island; and the passport to political station was the possession of character and competency. History records him a Catholic; and some have held this to be a synonyme for bigotry and intolerance. And yet this "intolerant bigot" makes his critics look small in placing these noble sentiments in his constitution: "I would not jeopardize the sacred rights of conscience, so dear to every man, but grant all the privilege of worshipping God according to the dictates of their conscience."

The nineteenth century opened auspiciously for the great Negro soldier and the cause he represented. Under his military administration new roads had been constructed, streams had been bridged, carriages had been introduced for the first time, and increasing confidence and growing trade had led to large expenditures in magnificent private residences and commodious public buildings. The transition from bondage to freedom was effected without arrogance, pomp, or social convulsion. With gratitude restrained by humility, the ex-slave turned to his new relations, duties, and responsibilities. Everything was changed for the better. Treason and rebellion had been buried in the bloody and inhospitable trenches of an internecine war. The after-thought of the planters made them the advocates of free labor, the friends of freedom, and the supporters of republican government. Well-mounted forts policed the bay, and slave-vessels found no market here for their human chattels. France, England, Spain, and Holland found a ready market for their manufactured goods; while the raw products of the island were eagerly sought. Peace and prosperity prevailed throughout the Spanish and French portions of the island, and an era of gladness and good feeling had dawned upon all the people.

But the greatest soldier of modern times was upon the French throne. Bonaparte was a soldier by nature, art, and practice. However, he was a stranger to the impulses of humanity, the dictates of reason, and the principles of justice. The fame of the Negro general of Santo Domingo excited his jealousy, and from his throne he plotted for his destruction. On the 20th of May, 1801, Napoleon issued a decree abrogating all the laws of Santo Domingo conferring freedom upon the slaves and extending manhood suffrage to the island. Rightly measuring the strength of the Negro commander-in-chief, an expedition was ordered to reduce the island to submission. An army of thirty-five thousand men was sent forward in sixty of the best vessels of the world. Spain and Holland hired their ships to the arch-enemy of human liberty. The troops were the flower of the French army. The snowy Alps of northern Europe, the arid sands of southern Egypt, the Rhine and the Nile, had witnessed their exploits and resounded with their triumphs. These famous veterans now left homes and government and lands that boasted of high civilization to bear chains to another people in their little insular home. The ocean was covered with a magnificent armament to punish a contumacious slave, and to put back the hands upon the clock of civilization because, forsooth, a Negro soldier had set them forward by his sword. General Leclerc, a fine soldier, and brother-in-law to Bonaparte, commanded this extraordinary expedition.

In due time the French troops reached the scene of a most remarkable struggle to turn a revolution backward. Toussaint was absent in the Spanish portion of the island when Leclerc sent word ashore that he intended to land. His message came to the hands of a brave black brigadier-general named Christophe, who was in command at the Cape. "Tell General Leclerc," responded the Negro general, "that I cannot permit him to land without orders from the commander-in-chief."

"But the French are about to land," rejoined the officer from the expedition.

"In that case tell General Leclerc that if he attempts to land his troops on this island I will fight him on the ashes of a burning city!" exclaimed the black Spartan.

The French army began to land towards the end of the day. General Christophe took a torch, and with his own hands first fired his beautiful residence recently completed by Parisian decorative artists. He ordered his troops to fire the city, and fought falling back towards the hill-country. The scenes that followed defy description.

In every house in Santo Domingo there were peace and plenty — the sweet angels of domestic charity. Fathers were just home from toil that was lightened and sweetened by the love that waited and watched for them at the door or gate; mothers were lifting high their babes to the plodding churl in the mountains; whose wife and children were his rulers, and his home their throne. Little lights were beginning to blink along the streets of the Cape, and over many an evening meal there were healthy laughter and good cheer. The whole scene was admirable. No news of invasion or conquest had reached these simple islanders; no treaty negotiations had been inaugurated; no insult had been offered to France by her insular subjects. No principal of law, no sentiment of justice, no interest of humanity had been violated. And, without warning or knowledge, the remorseless mailed hand of military power was at the throat of human liberty.

The roar of cannon, the rattle of musketry, the rushing, devouring flame of fire, was the prelude to this monstrous military tragedy. General Leclerc sent forward his troops in four columns of echelon; but these columns were penetrated and thrown into confusion by the boundless fury and matchless bravery of Christophe's black soldiers. The men who but a few hours before were as gentle as lambs in the imagined security of their homes, were now like wild beasts stirred for the life of their young. The pets of the Imperial household never encountered fiercer fighting. The old, infirm, and helpless children were hurried to the mountains, and women turned Amazons and fought with perfect abandon. The wounded refused to yield their place in battle, and most of them fought while strength endured. The dying scornfully declined to be succored by the invader, and died pronouncing curses and imprecations upon the French. Negro soldiership wrote its certificate for valor in the prodigal blood that dyed the streets of the city of the Cape on that eventful night. When the battle was at its height, Toussaint l'Ouverture appeared upon the scene. He gazed a moment at the carnage and destruction, and then, rising in his stirrups, reined in his horse, and, above the tumult of battle, cried, "Burn the city, children! poison the wells! fly to the mountains! and make this island the hell the white man comes to!" He had taken in the situation at a glance, and his heroic order at first checked the pulse of battle; but in a moment the magnetic shock of his presence and words flew like lightning to the heart of every Negro soldier. The fainting, wavering, tugging columns of his brave troops that were staggering heroically against the veterans of the French army took courage. New life flowed through the Negro columns like a gift from the gods. Toussaint's voice was as new wine to their fainting hearts, and his inspiring presence was now their glorious ensign of battle.

The Negro army fell back gradually from the charred and burning city, but rallied on the plains under the mountains. They threw themselves with desperation upon the wavering columns of Leclerc, and hung upon his flanks. The whole scene had deeply affected the French troops, and their fighting was little more than self-defence. The hollow square was ordered to save the veterans from being routed, but the Negro troops formed and struck the squares on three sides with dauntless valor and crushing effect. Back went the Negro column to form again. This time the black troops charged, singing "La Marseillaise:"

> "Allons, enfants de la Patrie:
> Le jour de gloire est arrivé!
> Contre nous de la tyrannie
> L'étendard sanglant est levé!" etc.

And as they reached the trembling squares of the invaders, they sang aloud:

> "Aux armes! Citoyens; formez vos bataillons;
> Marchez! marchez! qu'un sang impur abreuve nos sillons!"

Doubtless French soldiers could fight ex-slaves, but they could not fight their national hymn. Many French soldiers cheered, others wept, and the entire command, exhausted and shattered, staggered back to the coast. The Negro troops retired to the mountains, fortified every defile, and subsequently defended them like the Spartans at Thermopylæ.

Nature seemed to abhor the invasion, for she became the ally of the Negro forces. A destructive fever attacked the French troops. The Negroes were fed by nature from spontaneous vegetation, and was as good a commissariat as these hardy soldiers could wish for. Thirty thousand French soldiers fell in battle, and died of wounds and fever. The French contingent was recruited again and again, but could not conquer the Negro troops and a tropical fever.

Leclerc sent proposals of peace to Toussaint, but he spurned any peace that denied his compatriots the boon of liberty. At the council, where he appeared in the uniform of a French general, Leclerc asked him, in rather a factious spirit, "What would you have done for arms if I had continued the war?" "I would have taken yours," was Toussaint's sharp reply.[1]

An honorable peace was concluded, and the black army melted back among the populace, and began to repair the prodigal waste of war. No plotter or hireling of the French Empire could influence Toussaint's serenity. He declined the offer of the governorship of the island that came to him from Paris with high-sounding phrases of adulation. He preferred to retire to private life after having accomplished the object of his public endeav-

---

[1] It is estimated that the losses in this war reached 30,000 men, 1,500 officers of all grades, among whom were 14 generals, and 700 physicians and surgeons.—G. W. W.

ors — the freedom of his race and the pacification of the island.

In Paris, where Bonaparte was either hated or feared, there was much feeling respecting this costly expedition that came to grief by falling into the hands of an accomplished Negro soldier. But everywhere, among all classes of the people, there were respect, admiration, and sympathy for Toussaint. The soldiers of the great Napoleon had scratched the Negro only to find the Frenchman there. The Negro army spoke French, and was characteristically French in its enthusiasm and fighting. These facts were more formidable than bullets, and the end of the campaign was hailed by the French people and their army with tumultuous acclamations of joy.

Pauline Bonaparte, sister to the First Consul and wife of General Leclerc, a lady of surpassing beauty, engaging manners, and rare accomplishments, had perished of fever in Santo Domingo. Thus had Bonaparte recklessly laid the most costly treasures upon the altar of his cruel ambition.

The expedition against the Negro soldier of Santo Domingo increased the French debt several million francs, but added no territory or revenue to the empire. The Negro government was not built of untempered mortar. It was not erected upon the shifting sands of political ambition. It was built upon the impregnable foundations of Justice, Equality, and Liberty. The guns of Bonaparte could not destroy such a government.

Reflections upon his failure to destroy the Negro republic and to reduce its citizens to involuntary servitude excited the wrath of Bonaparte. He determined to secure Toussaint by fair or foul means, and a dinner-party was the trap in which the Negro general was caught. Unwarned and unattended, he was seized by French officers, and hurried from the festivities held in his honor to a vessel awaiting his arrival. As it sailed out of the harbor, he said, as he gazed upon the theatre of his active life, "They have only felled the tree of the freedom of the blacks; branches will sprout, for the roots are numerous and deep."

He was landed at Brest, August 13, 1802, and hurried across the empire to the Jura Mountains, on the line between France and Switzerland. He was incarcerated in the dungeon at Joux. Bonaparte made no explanation of this kidnapping, and Toussaint was never arraigned upon any charge. Letter after letter was sent from this living tomb to the cruel monster on the French throne, but no sentiment of justice, mercy, or humanity could be found in the heart of Bonaparte. The distinguished Negro prisoner courted an early, impartial, and searching investigation into every act of his official life. If he had been guilty of even a technical violation of the law, he was willing to suffer the penalty. But no word of compassion reached his dungeon, no ray of hope penetrated its gloom, and no recognition of his consummate services to France, or his rank in her service, was made. He was the victim of studied neglect and a murderous plot. His dungeon was always damp, and had ice on the floor and walls for at least five months of the year. The eternal snows looked down upon his prison, and the piercing gales from the north swept it with relentless fury. He was kept in close confinement, and even the coarse food allotted him was reduced in quantity. It was tossed to him as if he were a dog; and the inhuman keeper was not slow in discovering that the way to the royal favor was over the dead body of his prisoner. With the key to Toussaint's dungeon, it was only necessary for this keeper to absent himself in Switzerland for four days. Upon his return, he found that his work had been well done. The great Negro soldier had succumbed to hunger and cold, and his solitary but vicious companions, the rats, had gnawed his body. He expired on the 27th of April, 1803, after nearly a twelve-month of hunger, cold, and neglect. This tragedy was commemorated in song and story, and civilized Europe thrilled with passionate grief at the news of Toussaint's death. And the wail that swept from the Antilles told the world how the great Negro soldier had attached himself to the cause of humanity.

The Nemesis of retribution is the divine ingredient in history. The Negro general was kidnapped at the instance of the First Consul, and was transported from the warm climate of the south to the cold climate of the north. He was then left to perish from cold, hunger, and neglect. Time swept apace; the mutations of political fortune at length made Bonaparte a national prisoner. The man from the north was then transported to the south; and amid the heat and thunder and lightning of St. Helena, Toussaint's imperial murderer died far from kindred and friends.

Let the muse of history behold the damp dungeon floor of Joux, where the virtuous Negro soldier died in loneliness and want; next gaze at the magnificent tomb of Napoleon Bonaparte at Paris, and then look upon the exquisite tomb of the Prince Napoleon at Windsor Castle. There is no monumental marble or brass to commemorate the noble acts of the Negro soldier; but in his island home the little republic he built still stands a monument to his valor as a soldier and sagacity as a statesman; while his deeds, like stars, illumine the page of history, and his Christian character and shining example have an immortal place in the literature of the world. Magnificent as is the tomb of the First Consul, nothing that he accomplished while alive remains. Not only did the idea he entertained of universal empire fail, but the monarchy for which he fought so many famous battles has long since been supplanted by a republic; and the tendency of the State he strove to coerce is now strongly republican. The Prince Napoleon was killed by Zulus in Africa, and thus the last representative of the French military empire was cut off by the very race from which Toussaint's grandfather sprang—for the blood of kings flowed in the veins of Toussaint!

"Though the mills of God grind slowly, yet they grind exceeding small;
Though with patience He stands waiting, with exactness grinds He all."

Mexico never discriminated against or proscribed any of its citizens on account of race or complexion. Negroes have carried the musket and worn shoulder-straps in the Mexican army; and in the war for the independence of that country many Negroes distinguished themselves upon the battle-field.[1]

In the War of 1812 in the United States of America free Negroes participated in the land and naval forces. On the 21st of September, 1814, Major-general Andrew Jackson, commanding the seventh military district, with headquarters at Mobile, Alabama, issued an appeal to the free Negroes of Louisiana to join his army. He confessed that "a mistaken policy" had hitherto excluded them from the army, but declared that it should be so "no longer." Every free Negro volunteering to serve during the "contest with Great Britain" was to "be paid the same bounty in money and lands" that were given to "white soldiers of the United States;" and this consisted of one hundred and

---

[1] Manuscript letter of the Mexican Minister to the author.

twenty-four dollars "and one hundred and sixty acres of land." The General reserved the right to appoint their officers, but the non-commissioned officers were to be taken from among the troops. These Negro soldiers were to be formed into a separate regiment, and "pursuing the path of glory," were to "receive the applause and gratitude" of their countrymen.[1]

The enlistment of the free Negroes of Louisiana was begun towards the end of September, 1814, under the supervision of the Governor of the State. The recruits came forward in large numbers and with patriotic enthusiasm. The great majority of them were educated freeholders, capable of speedy discipline. Within sixty days they were organized and drilled, and ready for the field. On Sunday, December 18, 1814, General Jackson reviewed the American army in front of New Orleans. The British forces were pushing their way up the Mississippi River from the Gulf of Mexico. A battle was impending, and New Orleans was in a state of feverish excitement. General Jackson had written an address to the army, and a portion of it was addressed to the Negro troops. Adjutant-general Edward Livingston rode to the head of the troops, and read, in rich, sonorous tones, an address to the Negro soldiers. They were praised for the possession of all physical qualities necessary to the profession of arms, and assured that they had surpassed the General's hopes. "I have found in you," continued the General, "united to these qualities, that noble enthusiasm which impels to great deeds."[2]

On the battle-field these troops justified the expectations of the Government and fulfilled the hopes of General Jack-

---

[1] Niles's "Register," vol. vii., p. 205.
[2] Ibid., vol. vii., pp. 345, 346.

son. They were found to be brave and steady, performing with cheerfulness and celerity every order that was given them.

On the 24th of October, 1814, one month after the call for Negro volunteers in Louisiana, the Legislature of New York enacted a law for the incorporation of two regiments of free Negroes. The men were to receive the same pay and bounty as white soldiers, and were to be placed upon a regular army footing. They were to be stationed within and for the defence of the State; but if the United States would furnish pay and subsistence they might be transferred from state to national service. Even slaves, obtaining written permission from their master or mistress, could enlist in either of these two regiments. But at the end of three years' faithful service, or upon honorable discharge, such slaves as had enlisted were emancipated. If such manumitted persons became infirm after being in the service, they were to be maintained by the town where they were registered.[1]

By an order promulgated by the War Department, Captain William Bezeau, Twenty-sixth United States Infantry, was ordered to take charge of the recruiting station at Philadelphia, Pennsylvania. He served in this capacity from July, 1814, till the spring of 1815. From the 30th of August, 1814, till the 15th of February, 1815, he recruited and mustered into the United States Army two hundred and forty-seven Negroes.

During this war the recruiting officers of the United States Army accepted Negro recruits, and by July, 1815, over three hundred had been mustered into the service.

---

[1] "Laws of the State of New York," chap. xviii. Thirty-eighth Session.

CHAPTER III.

ANTECEDENT FACTS.—FORESHADOWING EVENTS.

The two years immediately preceding the Rebellion were teeming with unprecedented events. Almost every question of public interest was directly or indirectly connected with one phase or another of the slavery problem. Thirty years of vigorous anti-slavery agitation had forced men into or out of parties; had made them declare for the restriction or extension of slavery—its nationalization or extinction. Slavery was like a dangerous coast with hidden reefs, where wild gales and stormy breakers blow and dash. It overshadowed every other question of national importance, and against its hidden reefs and treacherous currents the fierce gales of public events seemed driving the Ship of State. Two great political parties were confronting each other on the vital question—Freedom national and slavery sectional. The Democratic party had administered the Government for a longer period of time than any other party in modern times in the Western world. It had degenerated in leadership, was poverty-stricken for issues, and was now unworthy of its founders. Having been long kept together by the cohesiveness of public plunder, it was in a state of senility.

The Republican party was young, but had recruited its ranks from a dozen different detachments, which, although fighting on their own responsibility, were nevertheless seeking the preservation of the union of the States against the menaces of the slave power. This new political organization, with the ardor of youth and the zeal of truth, was united upon the question of the restriction of the slave power. The opposing party was divided upon a number of vital questions. On the 11th of May, 1859, a Southern convention at Vicksburg, Mississippi, representing eight States, passed resolutions favoring the reopening of the African slave-trade. This had a bewildering effect upon many Northern Democrats, and threw anti-slavery men and Republicans into violent unrest. On the 8th of June the slave-holders of Maryland met in convention at Baltimore, with county representation, and at the same time there was a wide-spread feeling in favor of making slave property more secure throughout the Southern States. But the concern respecting slavery was not all on one side. Already the mild Quaker views of Lundy were giving away to the stalwart opinions of the aggressive party under the leadership of Captain John Brown. The South had startled the North by insolence and brutality in the National Congress, and by its offensive assertions of its right to carry slave property into any State, and of its intention to leave the family of States. But Captain John Brown gave the South the most tremendous fright it had ever had, until the embattled guns of a victorious army put the Confederacy and the slave-power in the dust of defeat. On Sunday night, October 16, 1859, Captain John Brown, at the head of twenty-one men, took possession of the United States arsenal at Harper's Ferry, Virginia, and held it against the military forces of Virginia and Maryland until the morning of the 18th, when it was stormed by the United States Marines. A mail-train was detained six hours; Colonel Lewis Washington, a descendant of George Washington, was arrested, and the quiet town of Harper's Ferry thrown into intense excitement. The news of this remarkable occurrence struck terror to the heart of the South, and was the event of absorbing interest for months. On the 19th of November the village of Charlestown, Virginia, was excited by the rumor of an attempt to rescue John Brown; and on the 30th of the same month a resolution was offered in the South Carolina Legislature declaring in favor of secession with other slave-holding States. On the 2d of December John Brown was hanged; and on the 20th the medical students from the South, in Philadelphia, resolved to secede and join Southern colleges.

The year 1860 opened amid the greatest excitement. The John Brown tragedy had dragged its ghastly length into the new year, and on the 16th of March Hazlitt and Stevens, compatriots of John Brown, were publicly executed at Charlestown, Virginia. The National House of Representatives was in great excitement over the slavery question. Messrs. Potter and Pryor made a scene on the floor of the House on the 5th of April, and the Southern press was impatient, insolent, and impulsive. On the 23d of April the National Democratic party met at Charleston, South Carolina. There were delegates from thirty States in the Union, numbering three hundred and three (303). This venerable organization, that had moved steadily to battle in other days like a Roman phalanx, was now rent by schism and weakened by conflicting interests. The question of slavery in the Territories, the Dred Scott decision, the validity of slave property under the Constitution, the Douglas theory of popular sovereignty, and other lesser questions were pressing for solution. After many ballots, boisterous sessions, and much fruitless labor, the convention adjourned on the 4th of May—having sat for ten days—to convene again at Baltimore on the 18th of June.

Meanwhile a Constitutional Union Convention met at

Baltimore on the 9th of May, representing twenty States, and nominated for President John Bell, for Vice-President Edward Everett. On the 16th of May the National Republican Convention convened at Chicago, and on the 18th nominated for President Abraham Lincoln, of Illinois, for Vice-President Hannibal Hamlin, of Maine. The proceedings were harmonious; the platform report was received without debate, and on the third ballot Mr. Lincoln received 354 votes out of 446. On the 1st of June the Maryland House of Delegates prohibited the manumission of slaves in that State; and on the 23d of June the National Democratic party nominated Stephen A. Douglas, of Illinois, for President, by a vote of $173\frac{1}{2}$, and for Vice-President Senator Benjamin Fitzpatrick, of Alabama, by acclamation. On the same day and in the same city the seceding delegates from the Charleston convention met and nominated for President John C. Breckinridge, of Kentucky, for Vice-President General Joseph Lane.

The canvass that followed these conventions was the most remarkable in the annals of political parties. The meetings were numerous and largely attended, and the speeches of the orators rang with fiery earnestness from one end of the country to the other. The Republican party was making its second contest—and it was the Republican party against the field. It proved itself worthy of admiration and support. It had the courage to assert its convictions and principles upon the political arena. It boldly opposed the extension of slavery into the Territories, and maintained that slavery could exist only by local positive law. Slavery was regarded as an evil threatening the national life, and it was urged that its ultimate extinction should be contemplated by the Government. The Southern wing of the Democratic party, under the lead of Breckinridge, boldly asserted the moral and legal right to buy, sell, own, and transport slaves into the Territories, and maintained that there could be no judicial interference with slavery outside of the States, except by prescription of the Constitution. The Douglas wing of the Democratic party adhered to the doctrine of State sovereignty, and evaded all other issues. The American party, led by Mr. Bell, kept before the people its ideas of emigration and naturalization, but would not commit itself upon the slavery question.

On the 6th of November, 1860, Lincoln and Hamlin were elected by a popular vote of 1,866,452, securing 180 electoral votes. Mr. Douglas secured 1,375,157 ballots from the people, but only 12 votes in the Electoral College. Mr. Breckinridge obtained 847,953 votes at the polls, and secured 76 electoral votes. Mr. Bell's vote reached 570,631, securing for him 39 electors.

Unfortunately, the South regarded the election of Mr. Lincoln as a *casus belli*. The wildest confusion and disgust prevailed at the South, while the North hailed the result as friendly to the country. On the 22d of November the banks of Philadelphia, Baltimore, and Washington suspended specie payment, and the business of the country was almost paralyzed. And as if to shock business confidence all over the country, the United States Treasury suspended specie payment on the 5th of December.

The Republic seemed trembling on the verge of some impending catastrophe. A committee of thirty-three members of the National House of Representatives was appointed and charged to take into consideration measures for the preservation of the Government on the 6th of December; and on the 11th Howell Cobb, Secretary of the Treasury, resigned. On the day following, General Winfield Scott arrived in Washington and conferred with the President. The country was excited and anxious, but no one could tell what a day would bring forth. On the 14th of December Lewis Cass, Secretary of State, resigned, and the next day President Buchanan appointed January 4th as a day of fasting and prayer. A Secession Convention at Charleston, South Carolina, passed an ordinance to withdraw that State from the Union on the 20th, and thenceforward there was little doubt in the public mind that the South would attempt to dissolve the Union. On the 24th an effort to remove the ordnance from the Pittsburg, Pennsylvania, arsenal was successfully resisted by patriotic citizens. Two days later Major Robert Anderson was compelled to evacuate Fort Moultrie and retire to Fort Sumter. John B. Floyd, Secretary of War, resigned his portfolio on the 29th, and the next day the citizens of Charleston seized the Government arsenal at that place. And so the year ended in excitement, and amid efforts to dissolve the Union.

On the 4th day of January, 1861, Fort Morgan, in Mobile harbor, was seized by Alabama troops, and four days later two more forts, Johnson and Caswell, in North Carolina, were seized by State troops. On the same day Jacob Thompson, Secretary of the Interior, resigned. Mississippi voted herself out of the Union on the 9th, and the first guns of the Rebellion were fired from the forts on Morris Island, South Carolina, upon the *Star of the West*, and she was driven to sea. Florida seceded on the 10th, and Alabama on the 11th; and on the 12th the revenue-cutter, *Lewis Cass*, was captured by State authorities at New Orleans; the Pensacola, Florida, navy-yard was seized on the same day. The United States Senators from Mississippi resigned their seats on the 14th, and on the 21st the Alabama delegation in Congress withdrew. Congress was in a state bordering on panic, and the press of the North was impotent to restore public confidence. On the 26th Louisiana seceded, and the news created deeper concern for the safety of the Union. The month of February was ushered in by an organized attempt on the part of the people of Charleston to besiege Fort Sumter, and Texas voted herself out of the Union. On the 2d of February the gold in the United States mint at New Orleans was seized by the State authorities. This action swept the country with a wave of indignant excitement, and the Senators from Louisiana—Slidell and Benjamin—withdrew from the Senate four days later. But at last an incredulous North was forced to believe that the nation was on the eve of a great civil struggle. On the 9th of February, 1861, Jefferson Davis, of Mississippi, was elected President, and Alexander H. Stephens, of Georgia, Vice-President, of the Southern Confederacy, by a convention representing the seceding States, at Montgomery, Alabama. On the 13th the Electoral College formally declared the result of the national election, viz., that Abraham Lincoln and Hannibal Hamlin had been duly elected President and Vice-President of the United States. Five days later Messrs. Davis and Stephens were inaugurated at Montgomery, Alabama. Thus perished the last hope of averting a rupture of the Union.

A feeling of melancholy pervaded the minds of Northern leaders as they saw the Southern States place themselves outside the sisterhood of States. But when, on the 22d, the birthday of George Washington, a plot to assassinate President-elect Lincoln was discovered in Baltimore, a feeling of horror and anger stirred the heart of the entire North. Men who had felt like exhausting every measure of pacification and concession were now eager for war. The patience of peace-men was subject to the most provoking strains almost daily. On the 4th of March, 1861, Abraham Lincoln was duly inaugurated President of the United States for four years; and thus the National Republican party accepted from the American people a government rent by a sectional feud, and soon to be drenched in fraternal blood.

On the 11th of April General G. T. Beauregard demanded the surrender of Fort Sumter; and the demand not having been complied with, he began a bombardment on the next day. This lasted during the night of the 12th, and on the morning of the 13th Major Robert Anderson surrendered. On the 14th he marched his garrison out with arms, field-music, and flying colors, receiving a salute with the honors of war. The war of the Rebellion was thus formally opened by the South; and on the 15th of April, 1861, the President of the United States issued a call for 75,000 troops. On the 29th the President issued another call for an additional volunteer force, making 158,000 in all, and raising the force of the regular army to 85,000 officers and enlisted men.

The curtain was rung up, and the civilized world beheld the first act of the bloody tragedy of war. Neither the South nor the North admitted the Negro into the army. Negro slavery was the evil genius that was rending the Republic. From the forum of political debate and the courts of law this question of Negro slavery was appealed to the Court of Civil War; and the argument begun at Sumter was to be concluded at Appomattox, with a decision in favor of UNION, LIBERTY, EQUALITY, AND FRATERNITY.

CHAPTER IV.

MILITARY RENDITION OF SLAVES.

At first the faintest intimation that Negroes should be employed as soldiers in the Union Army was met with derision. By many it was regarded as a joke. The idea of arming the ex-slaves seemed ridiculous to most civil and military officers. From the period of the introduction of this people into the British colonies in North America down to the breaking out of the Rebellion in the South, they had been subjected to a most rigorous system of bondage to the white race. Transported from his wild African home, the barbarian, without language, tradition, memorials, or monuments, was kept in a lowly condition of servitude. Every lesson of obedience was enforced and illustrated by the lash. He was fenced in by the laws—met by force at every point. His whole existence was a struggle with force in nature and in man. Eventually the wild, free, and impetuous spirit of the African became pliable, docile, and submissive.

The first generation of Africans in America were more tractable than their fathers. Having been reduced to chattels by a code of laws enacted by the white race, which claimed that it was Christian charity to enslave the African under the influence of civilization rather than leave him to barbarism, he was to be kept in this state. The slave code presupposed the natural and native spirit, the aptitude and intelligence of the slave. It was not enough that he was bound with chains, because he was less to be feared physically than mentally. In his abject ignorance his enslavers thought they should find security. That portion of the slave code which denied the Negro slave facilities and privileges of learning was a compliment to his natural ability to acquire knowledge.

The Negro slave was excluded by law from printing-offices, libraries, drug-stores, and from all places and employments where a knowledge of letters and figures was required.[1] He was sedulously kept in ignorance from the first, until ignorance had almost become a second nature to him. He was reduced to a machine. Calm and apparent contentment followed resistance and unrest. The affections, once so instinct with life, scarcely quivered with emotion at the sound of the auctioneer's voice or the crack of the whip. Only the sharp cry of the slave mother, whose famishing child was torn from her withered bosom, or the deep sobs of the wife separated from her husband, indicated that a nerve of sensation or sentiment of affection was yet alive. They were callosed and hardened by cruel blows and barbarous treatment. But they were not dead; they needed only the salve of human sympathy and kindness to call them into action.

Most observing and thoughtful people concluded that centuries of servitude had rendered the Negro slave incapable of any civil or military service. When the Civil War commenced, the Negro was not regarded as a help in preserving the American Union, although the unknown quantity in the problem of war. His flight from Southern bondage was often arrested under the Union flag, and his way back to the hell of slavery lighted by the gleam of Federal bayonets. Every attempt to gain his freedom

---

[1] Many slaves were taught the trades of machinists and carpenters for economic reasons, but their skill was utilized on the plantation where they belonged.—G. W. W.

by reaching the Union lines was met by levelled muskets in the hands of the defenders of a free republic!

The war found the United States Government without a settled policy respecting the slavery question. There were, however, two well-defined views before the civil and military leaders. The President had announced to the army that the real object of its service was "to *restore* the seceding States" to their constitutional relation to the Union. It was thought that the truant States would come back into the Union within three months at the point of the bayonet. Another period was fixed upon, and nine months was thought to be ample time in which to "*restore*" the rebel States. The slavery question had no place in the early military policy of the Union Army. *Slave property* was regarded as *recognized* and *sustained* by the *Constitution*. It was necessary, therefore, to prescribe a more definite object for the army.

The Southern States were guilty of treason, and the moment they levied war against the United States their slaves were *ipso facto* free. But a conservative, vacillating, hand-to-mouth policy held sway for nearly two years, with but one exception. Major-general B. F. Butler, commanding the Union forces at Fortress Monroe, inaugurated a new policy. It was operative in his department, received the approval of the Secretary of War, but was rendered inoperative within less than a month. In the month of April 1861, Flag-officer G. J. Pendergrast, in command of the frigate *Cumberland*, at that time on blockading service in the Roads, captured and restored to their masters, at Norfolk, several fugitive slaves. A few days after this occurrence, the flag-officer, General Butler, Captain Grier Tallmadge, and the correspondent of the *New York Times* chanced to meet on the ramparts of Fortress Monroe. Captain Tallmadge referred to the action of the flag-officer, and disapproved his course in returning the slaves. Turning to General Butler, Captain Tallmadge continued: "General, it is a question you will have to decide, and that, too, very soon; for in less than twenty-four hours deserting slaves will commence swarming to your lines. The rebels are employing their slaves in thousands in constructing batteries all around us. And, in my judgment, in view of this fact, not only slaves who take refuge within our lines are contraband, but I hold it as much our duty to seize and capture those employed, or intended to be employed, in constructing batteries, as it is to destroy the arsenals or any other war-making element of the rebels, or to capture and destroy the batteries themselves." It is interesting in this connection to know that General Butler himself, on the 23d of April, 1861, had written to Governor Thomas H. Hicks, of Maryland, as follows: "I have understood within the last hour that some apprehensions are entertained of an insurrection of the Negro population of this neighborhood. I am anxious to convince all classes of persons that the forces under my command are not here in any way to interfere with, or countenance an interference with, the laws of the State. I am therefore ready to co-operate with your Excellency in suppressing most promptly and effectually any insurrection to the laws of the State of Maryland." The patriotic governor of Massachusetts, John A. Andrew, wrote General Butler as follows: "If I rightly understand the telegraphic despatch, I think that your action in tendering to Governor Hicks the assistance of our Massachusetts troops to suppress a threatened servile insurrection among the hostile people of Maryland was unnecessary."

This declaration was made in the early part of the month of May, and within two days General Butler put the views of Captain Tallmadge into practical operation.

Three slaves, the property of one Colonel Mallory, of the Confederate forces in front of the Union lines at Fortress Monroe, came in. They told the officer of the picket-line that their master was about to send them to the North Carolina seaboard to work on rebel fortifications, and that the fortifications were intended to bar that coast against the advance of the Union forces. General Butler, having heard the statement of the fugitives, said, "These men are *contraband* of war; set them at work."

On the 27th of May, 1861, General Butler wrote to Lieutenant-general Scott that the question of slave property was becoming more embarrassing; that the enemy was using large numbers of Negroes in the work of constructing batteries on his front; and that the women and children of these laborers were to be sent South by the rebel authorities. However, many slaves were escaping within his lines, and women and children in large numbers were coming in also. General Butler employed the effective at fair wages, caused rations to be issued to them, and charged the support of the non-laborers against the wages of the laborers. The General maintained that by this action he was depriving the enemy of the services of these slaves, delaying the construction of his fortifications, and securing valuable aid to the Union forces. He submitted the entire matter to his chief, and forwarded a duplicate despatch to the Secretary of War.[1]

The Secretary of War responded: "Your action in respect to the Negroes who came within your lines from the service of the rebels is approved." But the Secretary, after some explanations, hastened to qualify: "While, therefore, you will permit no interference, by persons under your command, with the relations of persons held to

---

[1] Greeley's "American Conflict," vol. ii., p. 238.

service under the laws of any State, you will, on the other hand, so long as any State within which your military operations are conducted remains under the control of such armed combinations, refrain from surrendering to alleged masters any persons who come within your lines."

The War Department was careful to employ the exact language of the Constitution—"*any person;*" and the words slave and slavery were avoided. Not only the Department of War, but the entire Administration, was scrupulously following that portion of the Constitution that recognized property in man; that gave legal sanction to the cruel curse of human slavery—but always couched in cowardly phraseology—it calls no names!

There was considerable comment in the press, in the pulpit, and in political as well as in military circles, respecting General Butler's order making fugitive slaves contraband of war. Most Union leaders approved his action; but the Government kept to its slow-coach ideas. There was no doubt of the novelty of General Butler's view and action; and in truth it was startling and revolutionary. The doctrine of property in man had long since been expurgated from the jurisprudence of Western Europe, and the brave and patriotic men on this continent who had espoused the cause of stolen Africans forcibly held to bondage maintained that there could be no property in man. All branches of the anti-slavery party maintained that the slaves were illegally held, and that in view of the enlightened sentiment of Europe our laws on the subject were barbarous and without moral support. To have acknowledged the right and fact of property in man would have changed the history of the anti-slavery movement; would have made a holy band of philanthropists a mob of law-breakers. Slavery was wrong both morally and legally, and upon this ground the New England anti-slavery movement stood.

General Butler was born and educated in New England; and with a commission from Massachusetts, in the second month of the Rebellion, reversed "the New England idea" by recognizing property in man! He rated Negroes with mules, wagons, muskets, and stands of colors. He decided that Negroes were property, and that he could, under the rules of modern warfare, appropriate any property of the enemy he could secure. But while this false idea was adopted by the Secretary of War, it died almost before the country was certain it ever had official countenance.

The Army kept at its work of returning fugitive slaves to their rebel masters. Even free Negroes were often arrested on suspicion of being slaves. Two free Negroes from Frederick, Maryland, boarded the train that conveyed Colonel A. E. Burnside's regiment from Baltimore to Washington. When they reached Washington, Colonel Burnside, supposing them to be runaway slaves, returned them in charge of a detail, and had them cast into prison at Baltimore.[1] On the 4th of July, 1861, a day hallowed by Revolutionary memories, Colonel Tyler, of the Seventh Ohio Regiment, made a speech to an audience of West Virginia rebels, to assure the slave-holders of the security of their property. "As our enemies have belied our mission," said Colonel Tyler, "and represented us as a band of Abolitionists, I desire to assure you that the relation of master and servant as recognized in your State shall be respected. Your authority over that species of property shall not in the least be interfered with. To this end I assure you those under my command have

---

[1] *Baltimore American*, June 22, 1861.

peremptory orders to take up and hold any Negroes found running about the camp without passes from their masters."

The monotony of the military slave-hunt was relieved by a bold move on the part of General John C. Fremont, commanding the "Western Department." On the 6th of August, 1861, Congress passed a law entitled "*An Act to Confiscate Property Used for Insurrectionary Purposes.*" An examination of its text, as well as the fiery debate through which it passed, prove that it was not intended to apply to slave property; nor was it intended to supplement General Butler's action. On the 31st of August General Fremont, taking advantage of the new law, issued a military proclamation from his headquarters in St. Louis declaring Missouri under martial law. All persons found with arms in their hands were to be tried by court-martial, and if found guilty were to be shot.

"The property," recited the proclamation, "real and personal, of all persons in the State of Missouri who shall take up arms against the United States, or shall be directly proven to have taken active part with their enemies in the field, is declared to be confiscated to the public use; and their slaves, if any they have, are hereby declared free men."[1]

It was gratifying that General Fremont's proclamation did not deal with Negroes as contraband; they were not mixed with personal or real property, but were "*declared free men.*" This was one of the most effective measures of the war. It was the heroic treatment demanded by the condition of affairs at the time. It wrought great good within twenty-four hours; was exerting excellent and moral influence throughout the South. But the Presi-

---

[1] Greeley's "American Conflict," vol i., p. 585.

dent was not pleased with that portion of the proclamation that emancipated the slaves of the men who were endeavoring to destroy the Government. He requested General Fremont to modify that portion of the proclamation liberating the slaves. This the General declined to do, and wisely left the President to take the responsibility in an Executive proclamation. Accordingly, on the 11th of September, the President, in an open letter, cut out the heart of the Fremont proclamation, and General Fremont was subsequently removed, and the good work of subduing rebels and freeing Negroes was suspended.

In the month of October, 1861, General Thomas W. Sherman, occupying the defences of Port Royal, issued a proclamation to the people of South Carolina. He announced that he had landed a small force on their shores; that his mission was one of good-will and peace; that he recalled many pleasant days spent among them, and assured them that their "local institution" would not be disturbed.[1] Fugitive slaves found no refuge in his camps, and the Rebellion received no serious check at his hands.

On the 13th of November, 1861, General John A. Dix, upon entering the counties of Accomac and Northampton, Virginia, issued a proclamation declaring to the people the nature of his advent. He assured the people that he came as their friend, and consequently would "invade no right of person or property." The laws and institutions of the people were to be respected, and special orders were issued to the troops "not to interfere with the condition of any person held to domestic servitude." All fugitive slaves were to be excluded from the Union lines.[2] General Halleck's famous "Order No. 3," November 20, 1861,[3]

---

[1] Greeley's "American Conflict," vol. ii., p. 240.
[2] "Rebellion Record," vol. iii., Doc., p. 376.
[3] "Official Record of the War of the Rebellion," vol. viii., p. 370.

excluded fugitive slaves from his lines in Missouri; and on the 23d of February, 1862, he issued "Order No. 13," directing among other things that "fugitive slaves" should not "be admitted" within his "lines or camps, except when specially ordered by the General commanding." A few days before this (18th of February), an order was issued by General A. E. Burnside, declaring (in a proclamation) that the Government simply required recognition of "its authority," and that all laws, usages, and local institutions would be respected. This action was not the exception, but the rule, among Department commanders.

General Grant early set an example which ought to have been emulated by other commanders. His action was not only in accord with the highest military wisdom and law, but was consonant with the dictates of humanity. The order given below was the first of its kind issued during the war, and, therefore, entitles General Grant to high consideration in connection with this phase of the war.

"Headquarters District of West Tennessee,
"Fort Donelson, *February* 26, 1862.

"*General Orders* No. 14.

"I. General Order No. 3, series 1861, from headquarters Department of Missouri, is still in force and must be observed. The necessity of its strict enforcement is made apparent by the numerous applications from citizens for permission to pass through the camps to look for fugitive slaves. In no case whatever will permission be granted to citizens for this purpose.

"II. All slaves at Fort Donelson at the time of its capture, and all slaves within the line of military occupation that have been used by the enemy in building fortifications, or in any manner hostile to the Government, will be employed by the quartermaster's department for the benefit of the Government, and will under no circumstances be permitted to return to their masters.

"III. It is made the duty of all officers of this command to see that all slaves above indicated are promptly delivered to the chief quartermaster of the district.

"By order of Brigadier-general U. S. Grant.

"JNO. A. RAWLINS, A. A. G."

General D. C. Buell, commanding the Department of the Ohio, with headquarters at Nashville, Tennessee, wrote, on the 6th of March, 1862, to Mr. J. R. Underwood, of Frankfort, Kentucky, that fugitive slaves did "sometimes make their way improperly into" his lines. He said that "in every instance . . . the master has recovered his servant and taken him away." He characterized the men who harbored fugitive slaves in his camps as "lawless and mischievous," and declared that it was not the policy of his troops to invade the rights of slaveholders.

On the 26th of March, 1862, General Joseph Hooker, while in command of the "Upper Potomac," issued the following order:

"*To Brigade and Regimental Commanders of this Division:*

"Messrs. Nally, Gray, Dunnington, Dent, Adams, Speake, Price, Posey, and Coby, citizens of Maryland, have Negroes supposed to be with some of the regiments of this division. The Brigadier-general commanding directs that they be permitted to visit all the camps of his command in search of their property; and if found, that they be allowed to take possession of the same, without any interference whatever."

On the 23d of June, 1862, one Benjamin Bronson, a rebel of New Orleans, was walking in the street, when he saw, in the uniform of a United States soldier, "something which appeared to be dressed like a man," but which was simply a chattel in men's clothes, whereupon he wrote the following letter:

"New Orleans, *June* 23, 1862.
"*Colonel F. S. Nickerson, Fourteenth Maine Regiment, U. S. A., Lafayette Square:*

"DEAR SIR,—My slave Calvin, a light mulatto, absconded last Friday, 16th inst. On Saturday, as I was passing by Lafayette Square, I found the said slave, with a United States uniform on, standing guard just above the Brooks House on Camp Street, enlisted as a United States soldier, assuming to be a white man; and I have the documents to prove him a slave. I lay these facts before you, trusting you will give me every assistance to recover my lawful property.

"Very respectfully,
(Signed) "B. Bronson,
"Per E. W. Herrick,
"Carriage Repository, 74 Carondelet Street.

"The above slave being a very light color, it would be difficult matter for a stranger to recognize him as a colored man.
(Signed) "B. Bronson,
"Per E. W. Herrick."

Having examined the case, General Butler issued the subjoined order:

"Headquarters Department of the Gulf,
"New Orleans, *July* 7, 1862.
"*Colonel Nickerson, Fourteenth Maine Regiment:*

"Sir,—It having been represented to the General Commanding that you have enlisted a slave (nearly white) by the name of Calvin, the property of B. Bronson, Esq., who will be recognized and pointed out by Mr. E. W. Herrick, you will forthwith discharge him. This by order of the General Commanding. By order of
(Signed) "Major-General B. F. Butler.
"G. Weitzel,
"Lieut. U. S. Eng. and Asst. Military Commander."

The rebel slave-holders, armed with General Hooker's order, went under the American flag, and dragged their human chattels from before the guns of the Union army! But the truckling subserviency of the army to slave-holders had not yet come to an end. Major-general George B. McClellan issued a proclamation from "Headquarters Army of the Potomac, July 7, 1862," in which he declared that the "Rebellion has assumed the character of a war." He concluded by announcing: "Neither confiscation of property, political executions of persons, territorial organization of States, nor forcible abolition of slavery, should be contemplated for a moment."

General McClellan was in command of the Union army at this time, and this declaration respecting slavery did great harm to the humane and patriotic sentiment of the troops. But the most remarkable fact about General McClellan's utterances on the slavery question is, that on the 4th of December, 1861, William H. Seward, Secretary of State, called his attention, by direction of the President, to the fact of the arrest of fugitive slaves in the city of Washington, part of his military district. "Persons," wrote the Secretary, "claimed to be held to service or labor under the laws of the State of Virginia, and actually employed in hostile service against the Government of the United States, frequently escape from the lines of the enemy's forces, and are received within the lines of the Army of the Potomac. This Department understands that such persons, afterwards coming into the city of Washington, are liable to be arrested by the city police, upon presumption, arising from color, that they are fugitives from service or labor."

Mr. Seward then goes on to cite the "Act to Confiscate Property used for Insurrectionary Purposes," approved August 6, 1861. Continuing, he said: "Persons thus employed and escaping are received into the military protection of the United States, and their arrest as fugitives from service or labor should be immediately followed by the military arrest of the parties making the seizure."

Notwithstanding this order, General McClellan, nearly a year later, was still opposed to freeing fugitive slaves. All that General Fremont had done was consonant with the Act of August 6, 1861, alluded to before. He had confiscated the property of persons who were engaged in insurrection, and the slaves of such persons "were declared free men."

Major-general David Hunter assumed command of the "Department of the South" on the 31st of March, 1862. His military district comprised the States of Georgia,

Florida, and South Carolina. On the 25th of April he declared those States under martial law; and on the 9th of May, in "General Order No. 11," declared that "Slavery and martial law in a free country are altogether incompatible." He therefore proclaimed that the slaves of those States were "forever free."[1]

But on the 19th of May, 1862, the President abrogated the order of General Hunter in a long proclamation. In sixty days from this time public sentiment had undergone a change for the better. The Army had caught many slaves who had sought its protection; had fought a few battles, and sustained defeat. On the 19th of August, 1862, Horace Greeley, editor of the *New York Tribune*, published an editorial entitled "The Prayer of Twenty Millions." It was addressed to the President; but while it did not seem to move that dignitary, it thrilled the popular heart, and went through the army like a battle order. The first sentence, like a Damascus blade, struck at the dangerous and suicidal policy of using the army to catch slaves. Mr. Greeley wrote: "On the face of this wide earth, Mr. President, there is not one disinterested, determined, intelligent champion of the Union cause who does not feel that all attempts to put down the Rebellion, and at the same time uphold its inciting cause, are preposterous and futile; that the Rebellion, if crushed out to-morrow, would be renewed within a year if slavery were left in full vigor; that army officers who remain to this day devoted to slavery can at best be but half-way loyal to the Union; and that every hour of deference to slavery is an hour of added and deepened peril to the Union."

Even the "Confiscation Act" had remained a dead let-

---

[1] Greeley's "American Conflict," vol. ii., p. 246.

ter to most general officers in the army; and Mr. Greeley urged its enforcement. "What an immense majority," continued Mr. Greeley, "of the loyal millions of your countrymen require of you is a frank, declared, unqualified, ungrudging execution of the laws of the land, more especially the Confiscation Act. That Act gives freedom to the slaves of rebels coming within our lines, or whom those lines may at any time enclose; we ask you to render it due obedience by publicly requiring all your subordinates to recognize and obey it."

This "prayer of twenty millions" was worth millions of dollars to the Government, and fired the heart of many good and honest men who had been halting between two opinions. It set in motion a strong current of public sentiment friendly to the slave, and in favor of a vigorous prosecution of the war. This current of sentiment gathered strength every day, and the President and his Cabinet were borne along in the right course. Many officers who had entertained strong opinions in favor of non-interference with slavery began to see that, from behind this dark institution, the rebels were aiming at the life of the republic. Changes of opinion were numerous and sudden.

CHAPTER V.

THE NEGRO VOLUNTEER.—MILITARY EMPLOYMENT OF NEGROES.

The South took the initiative in employing Negroes as soldiers; but they were free Negroes, and many of them owned large interests in Louisiana and South Carolina. During the latter part of April, 1861, a Negro company at Nashville, Tennessee, offered its services to the Confederate Government.[1] A recruiting-office was opened for free Negroes at Memphis, and the following notice was issued:

"ATTENTION, VOLUNTEERS!

"*Resolved by the Committee of Safety*, That C. Deloach, D. R. Cook, and William B. Greenlaw, be authorized to organize a volunteer company, composed of our patriotic free men of color, of the city of Memphis, for the service of our common defence. All who have not enrolled their names will call at the office of W. B. Greenlaw & Co.

"F. W. Forsythe, Secretary.   F. Titus, President."

Louisiana had the largest population of free Negroes in the South; many of them were men of large means, and some of them actually owned slaves.

The first law enacted by any State, whether in or out of the Union, and before the United States Congress or the Confederate Congress had entertained any proposition contemplating the military employment of Negroes, con-

---

[1] *Charleston Mercury*, April 30, 1861.
[2] *Memphis Avalanche* and *Memphis Appeal*, May 9, 10, and 11, 1861.

ferring upon the black man military privileges and duties, was the following:

"*An Act for the Relief of Volunteers.*

"SECTION 1. *Be it enacted by the General Assembly of the State of Tennessee,* That from and after the passage of this act, the Governor shall be, and he is hereby authorized, at his discretion, to receive into the military service of the State all male free persons of color between the ages of fifteen (15) and fifty (50) years—or such number as may be necessary, who may be sound in his mind and body, and capable of actual service.

"SEC. 2. *Be it further enacted,* That all such free persons of color shall be required to do all such menial service for the relief of the volunteers as is incident to camp life, and necessary to the efficiency of the service, and of which they are capable of performing.

"SEC. 3. *Be it further enacted,* That such free persons of color shall receive, each, eight dollars per month as pay, for such person shall be entitled to draw, each, one ration per day, and shall be entitled to a yearly allowance, each, of clothing.

"SEC. 4. *Be it further enacted,* That in order to carry out the provisions of this act, it shall be the duty of the Sheriffs of the several counties in this State to collect accurate information as to the number and condition, with the names of free persons of color subject to the provisions of this act, being and situated within the limits of their respective counties, and shall, as soon as practicable, report the same in writing to the Governor.

"SEC. 5. *Be it further enacted,* That a failure or refusal of the Sheriffs, or any one or more of them, to perform the duties required by the fourth section of this act, shall be deemed an offence, and on conviction thereof shall be punished for misdemeanor, at the discretion of the Judge of the Circuit or Criminal courts having cognizance of the same.

"SEC. 6. *Be it further enacted,* That it shall be the duty of officers in command to see that the class of persons who may enter the service under the provisions of this act do not suffer from neglect or maltreatment.

"SEC. 7. *Be it further enacted,* That in the event of a sufficient number of free persons of color to meet the wants of the State shall not tender their services, then the Governor is empowered, through the Sheriffs of the different counties, to impress such persons until the required number is obtained; in doing so, he will have regard to the population of such persons in the several counties, and shall direct the Sheriffs to determine by lot those that are required to serve.

"Sec. 8. *Be it further enacted*, That the expenses incurred in this branch of the service shall be regarded as a part of the army expenses, and provided for accordingly.

"Sec. 9. *Be it further enacted*, That when any mess of volunteers shall keep a servant to wait on the members of the mess, each servant shall be allowed to draw one ration.

"Sec. 10. *Be it further enacted*, That the Adjutants of Regiments may be selected from the private soldiers in the line of the service, as well as from the officers in the service.

"Sec. 11. *Be it further enacted*, That this act take effect from and after its passage.

"W. C. WHITTHORNE,
"Speaker of the House of Representatives.
"B. L. STOVALL,
"Speaker of the Senate.
"Passed June 28, 1861." [1]

While this law did not provide for the incorporation of Negroes in regiments, the first section brings them into the military service.

On the 23d of November, 1861, there was a grand review of the Confederate troops stationed at New Orleans. An associated press despatch announced that the line was seven miles long. The feature of the review, however, was "one regiment" of "fourteen hundred free colored men." Another grand review followed the next spring, and on the appearance of rebel Negroes a local paper made the following comment: "We must also pay a deserved compliment to the companies of free colored men, all very well drilled and comfortably uniformed. Most of these companies, quite unaided by the administration, have supplied themselves with arms without regard to cost or trouble." [2] On the same day one of these Negro companies was pre-

---

[1] "Public Acts of Tennessee," 1861, pp. 49, 50.
[2] The *New Orleans Picayune*, February 9, 1862.

sented with a flag, and every evidence of public approbation was manifested. It was intended to use troops of this character for garrison, but the first victories of the Confederate troops quite turned the head of the rebel government. Negro troops were soon dispensed with, although a few were retained for a brief period. On the 4th of February, 1862, the *Baltimore Traveller* announced that several regiments of Negroes were forming at Richmond for the defence of the Confederate capital. On the 24th of May, 1862, *The Nashville Union* printed the following editorial note from *The Intelligencer and Confederacy*, published in Georgia: "We must 'fight the devil with fire' by arming our negroes to fight the Yankees. There is no doubt that in Georgia alone we could pick up ten thousand negroes that would rejoice in meeting fifteen thousand Yankees in deadly conflict. We would be willing almost to risk the fate of the South upon such an encounter in an open field."[1]

But while Negroes were not used by the Confederate States to any great extent, the following Act shows that they had learned the value of the Negro in time of war as well as in time of peace.

"Adjutant and Inspector General's Office,
"Richmond, Virginia, *March* 11, 1864.
"*General Orders No.* 32.

"I. The Act of Congress relative to the employment of Free Negroes and slaves in certain capacities, and the Instructions of the War Department relative to its Execution, are published for the information of those concerned.

"*An Act to increase the Efficiency of the Army by the Employment of Free Negroes and Slaves in certain Capacities.*

"*Whereas*, the efficiency of the army is greatly diminished by the withdrawal from the ranks of able-bodied soldiers to act as teamsters,

---

[1] "Rebellion Record," vol. v., p. 22.

and in various other capacities in which free Negroes and slaves might be advantageously employed;

"*Therefore*, the Congress of the Confederate States of America do enact, that all male free Negroes, and other free persons of color, not including those who are free under the treaty of Paris, 1803, or under the treaty of Spain of 1819, resident in the Confederate States, between the ages of eighteen and fifty years, shall be held liable to perform such duties with the army, or in connection with the military defenses of the country, in the way of work upon fortifications, or in government works for the production or preparation of materials of war, or in military hospitals, as the Secretary of War or the commanding General of the Trans-Mississippi Department may, from time to time, prescribe; and while engaged in such duties shall receive rations and clothing, and compensation at the rate of eleven dollars a month, under such rules and regulations as the said Secretary may establish:

"*Provided*, that the Secretary of War or commanding General of the Trans-Mississippi Department, with the approval of the President, may exempt from the operations of this act such free Negroes as the interest of the country may require should be exempted, or such as he may think proper to exempt, on grounds of justice, equity, or necessity. . . .

   (Signed)   "THOMAS S. BABCOCK,
                     "Speaker House of Representatives.
              "R. M. T. HUNTER,
                   "President pro tem. of the Senate.
"Approved February 17, 1864.
              (Signed)   "JEFFERSON DAVIS."

The order of the Inspector-general following this act directed in detail the carrying out of its provisions. A regularly established Bureau for Conscriptions was charged with seizing such number of slaves as was required by the exigencies of the public service, making compensation therefor. If such slaves were killed or died in the public service their owners were paid the market value of their chattels.

Fortunately for the future of the republic, the people were far in advance of the generals in the field and the statesmen at Washington. If the Administration of

President Lincoln had a policy—beyond upholding the rebels by preventing their slaves from entering the Union lines—it was the result of evolution; it was forced upon it by the potent voice of public sentiment. There were here and there patriotic and humane men who saw, from the opening of civil war, that the quickest way to win victory and conquer peace was to employ in the military service *all* loyal men. During the national campaign in the summer of 1860, General J. Watts De Peyster, anticipating a war between the Government and Southern States, wrote a letter to a journal of Hudson, New York, advocating the arming of Negroes. In a speech made at Worcester, Massachusetts, in the early days of the war, Charles Sumner said, "I do not say carry the war into Africa; but carry Africa into the war." His colleague in the United States Senate, Henry Wilson, urged similar views upon the country.

Governor Yates, of Illinois, had written, on the 11th of July, 1863, an eloquent letter urging the President to accept *all* loyal men, regardless of color, to aid in suppressing the Rebellion. Once in a while an influential and courageous clergyman would urge the military employment of Negroes. Excellent work was done for the Negro in sections of the country friendly to his emancipation and enlistment in the Union army. Congress was in advance of the President. That body had passed laws sufficient to enable the President to employ as many persons of African descent as he saw fit in any capacity for which they should be found qualified. The Confiscation Act, approved August 6, 1861, empowered the President to receive into the service of the United States as many persons of African descent as he might deem proper for the suppression of the Rebellion. And the Secretary of War, in his letter of instructions to General Thomas W.

Sherman, who assumed command of the Union forces at Port Royal, South Carolina, in October, 1861, gave permission "to employ all loyal persons offering their services for the defense of the Union." General Sherman did not avail himself of this order to secure fugitive slaves, but General Hunter, who relieved him on the 31st of March, 1862, did employ Negroes in the capacity of soldiers.

The indiscriminate return of fugitive slaves to their rebel masters aroused a public sentiment that almost amounted to indignation. On the 10th of March, 1862, the House of Representatives enacted a law providing a new "Article of War," prohibiting army officers to return fugitive slaves. It passed the Senate without amendment, by a vote of 29 to 9. On the 17th of July, 1862, an act passed Congress emancipating the slaves of rebels, and public feeling towards the Negro was greatly mollified.

Although the Confiscation Act of August 6, 1861, and the order of the War Department to the commanding general at Port Royal, warranted and justified the employment of fugitive slaves in a military capacity, no direct legislation had been secured to enroll the Negro as a soldier. Only the fugitive slaves of persons in actual rebellion against the United States had been contemplated thus far. No attention was paid to the free Negro population of the Northern States, that could have supplied twenty-five thousand able-bodied, patriotic Negro soldiers. In nearly every Northern city meetings were held by the Negro citizens; patriotic speeches were made; resolutions pledging themselves to support the Government, and tendering the services of their military organizations, were passed. But their offers were unnoticed or contemptuously declined. In fact, many peace-democrats looked upon the Negro as the cause of the war, and quiet Negro populations were threatened with mob violence.

The first direct legislation that sought the Negroes' military assistance was merely an enabling act. On the 16th of July, 1862, Henry Wilson, of Massachusetts, introduced a bill in the United States Senate, amending the Act of 1795, prescribing the manner of calling out the militia to suppress insurrections. It empowered the President to accept "persons of African descent, for the purpose of constructing intrenchments or performing camp service, or *any* war service for which they may be found competent." This was a half-hearted measure. General Wilson found that his bill could not be passed without many obnoxious amendments, so he accepted it in an emasculated form. It was hurried over to the House, where Thaddeus Stevens, of Pennsylvania, took charge of it. He skilfully parried every attempt to strike it down with deadly amendments, and under call of "the previous question" passed it. On the day following, the 17th of July, 1862, the President signed it, and thus it became a law. But the President was still opposed to the employment of Negroes as soldiers. No one could put the new law in operation but the President.

On the 4th of August, 1862, the *New York Herald* published an editorial on an "Important Decision of the President." "The efforts," said the *Herald*, "of those who love the Negro more than the Union to induce the President to swerve from his established policy are unavailing. He will neither be persuaded by promises nor intimidated by threats. To-day he was called upon by two United States Senators, and rather peremptorily requested to accept the services of two Negro regiments. They were flatly and unequivocally rejected. The President did not appreciate the necessity of employing the Negroes to fight the battles of the country, and take the positions which white men of the nation, the voters, and sons of patriotic sires, should be proud to occupy; there were employments in which the Negroes of rebel masters might well be engaged, but he was not willing to place them upon an equality with our volunteers, who had left home and family and lucrative occupations to defend the Union and the Constitution, while there were volunteers or militia enough in the loyal States to maintain the Government without resort to this expedient."

The President was not only explicit in his views in opposition to the military employment of Negroes, but the editorial continues to inform the country that the President was willing to resign, and one of the Senators told him that "he wished to God he would resign!"

A strong feeling was now manifested all over the country in favor of a vigorous war policy, and in many quarters the arming of the Negroes was regarded with favor. In the largely populated cities of the North the clergy took a deep interest in the affairs of the Union. A large and enthusiastic meeting of the evangelical denominations of Chicago sent two delegates to present a strong and patriotic address to the President. The Rev. William W. Patton, D.D., and his colleague, the Rev. Dr. John Dempster, on the 13th of September, 1862, urged upon the President the emancipation of the slaves and the arming of the Negroes. "If we were to arm them," said the President, "I fear that in a few weeks the arms would be in the hands of the rebels."[1]

No people grow so rapidly in the right direction as Americans. The reverses that the Union arms had suf-

---

[1] Greeley's "American Conflict," vol. ii., pp. 251, 252.

fered, the peril that threatened the republic, had a salutary effect upon the public mind. Army officers in active service, who were more loyal to the Union than to the idea of the inviolability of slave property, could see the necessity and utility of employing Negroes as soldiers. In the extreme South the mortality among the Union troops was very great. The high temperature, the malaria, local fevers, and ague crowded the hospitals with hapless victims. The Government had reluctantly accepted the services of the fugitive slaves of its enemy to construct fortifications and to furnish the muscle for the army. Why not put a musket in the same potent hands? asked several general officers.

In May,[1] 1862, General David Hunter, in command of the Department of the South, issued orders from Port Royal, South Carolina, for the recruitment of a regiment of Negroes. A detail of patriotic and competent white officers was made from the regiments of Union soldiers in the Department, to take charge of and drill the black levies. The Negroes were eager to enter the armed service, and they responded to General Hunter's proclamation with spirit and alacrity. Within a few months the "First South Carolina Volunteer Regiment" was full, armed and uniformed. This was the first regiment of Negroes organized during the Civil War. It was a bold move; and while it was approved by many officers in the army and patriots in Congress, it was denounced by many of the enemies of the Negro in official station. Some officers talked of resigning if Negroes were to be called upon to fight the battles of a free republic. The privates in regiments from large cities and border States were bitter and

---

[1] Sergeant C. T. Trowbridge was detailed to recruit Negroes May 7, 1862, in S. O. 84.—G. W. W.

demonstrative in their opposition. The Negro volunteers themselves were subjected to indignities from rebel civilians within the Union lines, and obtained no protection from the white troops.

A large portion of the Press of the North condemned General Hunter's action, and general apprehension was felt in Congress. On the 9th of June, 1862, Hon. C. A. Wickliffe, a member of the House from Kentucky, introduced a resolution calling upon the Secretary of War for information respecting General Hunter's Negro regiment. Mr. Wickliffe desired to know, first, whether General Hunter had raised "a regiment of South Carolina volunteers for the defense of the Union composed of black men (fugitive slaves), and appointed the Colonel and officers to command them;" second, Mr. Wickliffe was anxious to know whether the War Department had authorized General Hunter "to organize and muster into the army of the United States, as soldiers, the fugitive or captive slaves;" third, whether he had "been furnished with clothing, uniform, etc., for such force;" fourth, whether he had "been furnished, by order of the Department of War, with arms to be placed in the hands of the slaves;" and, in the fifth instance, Mr. Wickliffe desired the correspondence between General Hunter and the War Department.

The Secretary of War promptly, on the 14th of June, replied to Mr. Wickliffe's resolution. He informed Mr. Wickliffe that the War Department was not aware that any regiment of Negroes had been constituted by General Hunter; that the commanding officer of the "Department of the South" had not been instructed to "muster into the army of the United States the fugitive or captive slave;" that General Hunter had "been furnished with clothing and arms for the force under his command, without instructions as to how they should be used;" and that General Hunter had "not been furnished by order of the Department of War with arms to be placed within the hands of 'those slaves.'". The correspondence between General Hunter and the Department of War was denied Mr. Wickliffe, because the President believed it would "be incompatible with the public welfare."

The Hon. Edwin M. Stanton, Secretary of War, had forwarded Mr. Wickliffe's resolution to General Hunter, and requested a categorical reply to the questions of the resolve. On the 23d of June General Hunter received the Secretary's letter with its enclosure. It was late Saturday when the communication reached the General's headquarters, but he hastened forward his reply so that it went by Monday's steamer for New York. This letter has no parallel in the military correspondence of the war. It was terse, piquant, and brilliant. In the first place, General Hunter informed the Secretary of War that no regiment of "fugitive slaves" had been organized in his Department. He said that there was, "however, a fine regiment of persons whose late masters are 'fugitive rebels'—men who everywhere fly before the appearance of the national flag, leaving their servants behind them to shift as best they can for themselves. So far, indeed, are the loyal persons composing this regiment from seeking to avoid the presence of their late owners, that they are now, one and all, working with remarkable industry to place themselves in a position to go in full and effective pursuit of their fugacious and traitorous proprietors." General Hunter then explained that the instructions issued by the Hon. Simon Cameron, late Secretary of War, to Brigadier-general Thomas W. Sherman, were turned over to him for his instruction and guidance; that the instructions authorized him "to employ all loyal persons offering their services in defense of the Union and the suppression of this Rebellion." There was "no restriction as to the character or color of the persons to be employed," continued General Hunter, "or the nature of the employment, whether civil or military, in which their services should be used." He thought the instructions warranted his enlistment of Negroes as well as whites, so that they were loyal; and that he was equally empowered "to enlist 'fugitive slaves' as soldiers, could any such be found" in the Department of the South. "No such characters, however," he continued, "have yet appeared within view of our most advanced pickets, the loyal slaves everywhere remaining on their plantations to welcome us, aid us, and supply us with food, labor, and information. It is the masters who have in every instance been the 'fugitives,' running away from loyal slaves as well as loyal soldiers, and whom we have only partially been able to see—chiefly their heads over ramparts, or, rifle in hand, dodging behind trees—in the extreme distance. In the absence of any 'fugitive-master law,' the deserted slaves would be wholly without remedy, had not the crime of treason given them the right to pursue, capture, and bring back those persons of whose protection they have been thus suddenly bereft." The closing paragraph of General Hunter's admirable letter was the most concise statement on the question of making the Negro a soldier uttered during the war. It is splendid:

"I must say, in vindication of my own conduct, that had it not been for the many other diversified and imperative claims on my time and attention, a much more satisfactory result might have been hoped for; and that in place of only one, as at present, at least five or six well-drilled, brave, and thoroughly acclimated regiments should by this time have been added to the loyal forces of the Union. The experiment of arming the blacks, so far as I have made it, has been a complete and even marvellous success. They are sober, docile, attentive, and enthusiastic; displaying great natural capacities for acquiring the duties of the soldier. They are eager, beyond all things, to take the field and be led into action; and it is the unanimous opinion of the officers who have had charge of them, that, in the peculiarities of this climate and country, they will prove invaluable auxiliaries—fully equal to the similar regiments so long and successfully used by the British authorities in the West India islands."[1]

General Hunter's communication was sent to the Hon. G. A. Grow, Speaker of the House, and by that officer ordered to be read. It created the wildest merriment and entire satisfaction among the members who earnestly desired the suppression of the Rebellion; but it was a severe blow to those members who thought to catch General Hunter violating the law. Mr. Wickliffe was morally prostrated by the reply of the General; but his colleague, Mr. Dunlap, introduced a resolution, the day following, declaring that General Hunter's letter was "clothed in discourteous language;" that he had insulted the Congress and people of America and the "brave soldiers in arms," and thought the General deserved to be censured. But the resolution was never acted upon. General Hunter deserves well of history. He inaugurated a bold policy, and conducted it with consummate skill. He won the confidence of the slaves in his Department, and excited the fear of the enemies of his country. His work was conducted with a masterly hand. Every

---

[1] Executive Document, 37th Congress, 2d Session, No. 143.

slave who enlisted was given his freedom papers. This policy put new life and zeal into the hearts of his Negro soldiers, and made them feel that they were fighting for something. The following is a copy of a "free paper."

"Headquarters Department of the South,
"Port Royal, South Carolina, *August* 1, 1862.

"The bearer, Prince Rivers, a sergeant in First Regiment South Carolina Volunteers, lately claimed as a slave, having been employed in hostility to the United States, is hereby, agreeably to the law of the 6th August, 1861, declared *free forever*. His wife and children are also free. D. HUNTER,
"Major-general Commanding."

The entire work that General Hunter had done in his Department was in accord with law, common-sense, and patriotism. Moreover, there could have been no more effective measure adopted than to deplete the vast Negro population of his Department that were bread-winners for a hostile army. He not only offered the Negro the American uniform and the protection of the Union flag, but each soldier was to have the pay and rations of a United States soldier, and his wife and children were to be free.

But this policy was not in accord with the ideas of Mr. Lincoln, and General Hunter was not supported by the Administration in his noble effort to place arms in the hands of the blacks.[1] He asked to be relieved rather than remain inactive. A correspondent of the *New York Times*, in a letter to that journal dated September 4, 1862, said, "There is little doubt that the next mail from the North will bring an order from the War Department

---

[1] From the 7th of May until the first week in August this "Hunter's Regiment," as it was called, was kept at drill. It was disbanded, however, all but one company. This company was sent to garrison St. Simon's Island, August 5, 1862, under Sergeant Trowbridge, as acting captain. This company was the first, and was in continuous service longer than any other company of Negro soldiers.—G. W. W.

recalling Major-general Hunter to a field of greater activity. The Government had not lent him a hearty support in carrying out his policy of arming the blacks, by which alone he could make himself useful in this Department to the national cause; and, therefore, more than two months since he applied to be relieved, rather than to sit supinely with folded hands when his military abilities might be found of service elsewhere." The regiment was reorganized and the first company mustered November 7, 1862.

While to General Hunter belongs the honor of placing muskets in the hands of Negroes, there were, nevertheless, other officers who shared his views with earnestness and zeal. General J. W. Phelps, of Vermont, a graduate of West Point and a practical man, was in command of the Union forces occupying Carrollton, Louisiana. General B. F. Butler was in command of the forces in the State, and had issued orders forbidding too many fugitives to crowd his camps, as they consumed rations that he needed for his effective force. General Phelps saw that he could utilize the Negroes who flocked to his lines seeking freedom and labor. On the 16th of June, 1862, General Phelps communicated the following views to General Butler, who had established his headquarters at New Orleans: "The enfranchisement of the people of Europe has been, and is still going on, through the instrumentality of military service; and by this means our slaves might be raised in the scale of civilization and prepared for freedom. Fifty regiments might be raised among them at once, which could be employed in this climate to preserve order, and thus prevent the necessity of retrenching our liberties, as we should do by a large army exclusively of whites; for it is evident that a considerable army of whites would give stringency to our Government; while an army partly of blacks would naturally operate in favor of freedom and against those influences which at present must endanger our liberties." [1]

General Butler made no reply, and after waiting a while General Phelps wrote his chief, July 30, 1862, another letter upon the subject of arming Negroes to help subdue the Rebellion: "I think that, with the proper facilities, I could raise the three regiments proposed in a short time. Without holding out any inducements, or offering any reward, I have now upward of 300 Africans organized into five companies, who are willing and ready to show their devotion to our cause in any way that it may be put to the test. They are willing to submit to anything rather than to slavery. . . . If we reject his services, any petty military chieftain, by offering him freedom, can have them for the purpose of robbery and plunder. It is for the interests of the South, as well as for the North, that the African should be permitted to offer his block for the temple of freedom. Sentiments unworthy of the man of the present day—worthy only of another Cain—could prevent such an offer from being accepted." [2]

General Phelps suggested that the cadets from West Point graduating that month (June) should be sent into South Carolina and Louisiana to drill Negro recruits, and that non-commissioned officers and privates already in the service should be appointed as line officers in such organizations. He concluded by giving it as his opinion that, if the policy of arming Negroes was adopted, "an early restoration of peace and unity" [3] would be secured.

At length General Butler replied to General Phelps;

---

[1] "Official Records of the War of the Rebellion," vol. xv., p. 489.
[2] Ibid., vol. xv., p. 535.
[3] Greeley's "American Conflict," vol. ii., pp. 517, 518.

and while he was willing to acknowledge the Negro as contraband of war, he was unwilling to accept his services as a soldier. Therefore, he instructed General Phelps to use the Negro as a laborer, but not as a soldier.

Thwarted and discouraged, General Phelps felt it his duty to resign; and on the 31st of July, 1862, wrote General Butler: "I am not willing to become the mere slave-driver you propose, having no qualifications that way."[1] He tendered his resignation and went back to Vermont, that had given him convictions of duty and right as firm as the mountains of his native State.

But the Northern people in sympathy with freedom welcomed the clarion notes of Generals Hunter and Phelps. Time was needed to turn the strong tide of public opinion that had set against the military employment of the Negro. It was slowly but surely turning; and there was an occasional plea made for the policy which General Hunter had inaugurated and General Phelps had urged.

On the 4th of August, 1862, Governor Sprague, of Rhode Island, officially appealed to the Negro citizens of the State to enlist as soldiers. This was the first call for Negro troops at the North.[2] General Butler saw, from his headquarters in New Orleans, that there was evident feeling at the North on account of his rejection of General Phelps's plan to organize Negro troops. He saw that it was but a question that would, sooner or later, be settled by receiving Negroes into the service. Accordingly, in less than three weeks after General Phelps had left the Department, General Butler, on the 22d of August, 1862, issued an appeal[3] to the free Negroes of New Or-

---

[1] "Official Records of the War of the Rebellion," vol. xv., p. 535.

[2] "Rebellion Record," vol. v., D., p. 53.

[3] "Official Records of the War of the Rebellion," vol. xv., pp. 556, 557.

leans to volunteer their services in a military capacity in defence of the union of the United States. Under the treaty of 1803, between France and the United States, the rights and immunities of citizenship had been guaranteed to "free colored Creoles." There was a large number of this class in the city of New Orleans. Many of them were descendants of the Negroes who fought under General Jackson in 1815. By their uniform good behavior the free Negro population of New Orleans had won public favor. In April, 1861, they had formed a part of the State militia; and when General Butler occupied the city these organizations still had a nominal existence. The free Negroes read General Butler's appeal with pleasure, and by the 27th of September, 1862, a full regiment of free Negroes was mustered into the service of the United States Government. It was constituted as the "First Regiment Louisiana Native Guards," but its designation was changed to the "First Regiment Infantry Corps d'Afrique," June 6, 1863. Another regiment of Negroes was accepted on the 12th of October, 1862, under the designation of the "Second Regiment Louisiana Native Guards;" changed, however, to the "Second Regiment Infantry Corps d'Afrique," June 6, 1863. On the 29th of November, 1862, a Negro regiment of heavy artillery was mustered into the service. It was designated as the "First Regiment Louisiana Heavy Artillery." On the 19th of November, 1863, it was changed to the "First Regiment Heavy Artillery Corps d'Afrique." On the 24th of November, 1862, the fourth regiment of Negroes was mustered into the service of the Government as the "Third Regiment Louisiana Native Guards;" but on the 6th of June, 1863, with the other regiments, it was designated as the "Third Regiment Infantry Corps d'Afrique."

From the date of General Butler's appeal to the free Negroes of New Orleans, August 22d, till the date of the muster in of the fourth regiment, November 24th, was three months. During this brief period three regiments of infantry and one of heavy artillery, all composed of Negroes, had volunteered and been organized and accepted by the United States. The enthusiasm of the men and the short time in which they prepared themselves for service was unprecedented. The news of this work in the city of New Orleans revived the hopes of those who had advocated the policy of arming the Negroes. It is a remarkable fact that on the very day that General Butler's call for Negro troops appeared—the 25th (it was dated the 22d) of August, 1862—the Secretary of War sent General Rufus Saxton, who had relieved General Hunter at Port Royal, South Carolina, the following order:[1]

"3. In view of the small force under your command, and the inability of the Government at the present time to increase it in order to guard the plantations and settlements occupied by the United States from invasion, and protect the inhabitants thereof from captivity and murder by the enemy, you are also authorized to arm, uniform, equip, and receive into the service of the United States such number of Volunteers of African descent as you may deem expedient, not exceeding five thousand; and may detail officers to instruct them in military drill, discipline, and duty, and to command them. The persons so received into service, and their officers, to be entitled to and receive the same pay and rations as are allowed by law to Volunteers in the service.

"4. You will reoccupy, if possible, all the islands and plantations heretofore occupied by the Government, and secure and harvest the crops, and cultivate and improve plantations.

"5. The population of African descent that cultivate the lands and perform the labor of the rebels, constitute a large share of their military strength, and enable the white masters to fill the rebel armies and wage a cruel and murderous war against the people of the North-

---

[1] Captain Robert Smalls, of the steamer *Planter*, carried the order from Washington to South Carolina.—G. W. W.

ern States. By reducing the laboring strength of the rebels their military power will be reduced. You are therefore authorized by every means in your power to withdraw from the enemy their laboring force and population, and to spare no effort consistent with civilized warfare to weaken, harass, and annoy them, and to establish the authority of the Government of the United States within your Department."[1]

Notwithstanding the official and stubborn opposition to the military employment of Negroes, before the closing days of 1862 the army of the United States Government bore upon its rolls four regiments of Negroes. Much hatred of the Negro, and opposition to a policy seeking his aid as a soldier, expired with the old year, and the opposing armies in winter-quarters gave the country that repose so necessary to reflection.

The question of the military employment of Negroes came before the country early in January, 1863, as if it were unfinished business pressing for attention. Kansas, the child of many prayers and tears, the youngest in the sisterhood of States, consecrated by the blood of freemen to the cause of freedom—she had not yet accomplished her days of mourning for the martyrdom of John Brown —took the initiative of raising troops in the North. "The First Regiment Kansas Colored Volunteers" was recruited from July to October, 1862, and was organized on the 4th of January, 1863, at Fort Scott, Kansas, by the indefatigable Colonel James M. Williams. On the 2d of May, 1863, its organization was completed, and it was ready to take the field.[2] And to the State of Kansas belongs the honor of organizing the first regiment of Northern Negro troops during the Civil War.

[1] "Official Records of the War of the Rebellion," vol. xiv., pp. 377, 378.
[2] The first recruits were obtained on the 6th of August, 1862, but the organization was not completed until January, 1863.—G. W. W.

In October, 1862, Brigadier-general Daniel Ullmann, upon being released from Libby prison, called upon President Lincoln and urged the military employment of Negroes. His views were not at once accepted, but doubtless made an indelible impression upon the President's mind. As soon as the Emancipation Proclamation had been issued, on January 1, 1863, the President instructed the Secretary of War to authorize General Ullmann to organize regiments of Negro troops. Authority was issued to him by Secretary Stanton on the 13th of January. General Ullmann was instructed to raise four regiments of infantry and a battalion of six companies of mounted scouts. He was to officer these troops; and from the entire army he was to make the selection of men who had distinguished themselves as soldiers. He established his headquarters in New York City, and at his suggestion several of the loyal governors furnished him with a roll of honor—"the bravest of the brave"—containing the names of privates and officers of white regiments who had already proved themselves heroic in battle and deserving of promotion. He secured a large number of officers with exceptional records who were willing to engage in the difficult and perilous service of commanding Negro soldiers in the field. It was a brave and brilliant company of gentlemen. General Ullmann says of them:

"I transferred the *Cadre* of my command to the designated field of duty in the Department of the Gulf. I had with me more than two hundred officers, a large majority from the Army of the Potomac, who had seen nearly two years' service in the field, and many of whom bore the scars of honorable wounds; some were officers of the Regular Army; one was a son of the Vice-President; one an European prince; several nephews of Kossuth; others officers who had served with distinction in the armies of Europe; and all, with few exceptions, educated gentlemen."

General Ullmann established his headquarters at New Orleans, and entered upon the discharge of his peculiar duties with intelligence, zeal, and patriotism. On the 10th of June, 1863, in General Orders No. 7, he pointed out to his officers the nature of their delicate duties, and made a touching appeal to the Negroes to rally under the Union standards.

Governor Andrew secured permission for the employment of Negro troops by the Commonwealth of Massachusetts. The following order was issued by the Secretary of War:

"War Department, Washington City,
"*January* 26, 1863.

"Ordered, that Governor Andrew, of Massachusetts, is authorized, until further orders, to raise such number of volunteer companies of artillery for duty in the forts of Massachusetts and elsewhere, and such corps of infantry for the volunteer military service as he may find convenient. Such volunteers to be enlisted for three years, unless sooner discharged, and may include persons of African descent, organized into separate corps. He will make the usual needful requisitions on the appropriate Staff Bureaus, and officers for proper transportation, organization, supplies, subsistence, arms, and equipments of such volunteers.

(Signed) "EDWIN M. STANTON,
"Secretary of War."

The Commonwealth of Massachusetts was now the theatre of a new and, some thought, difficult experiment. But Governor Andrew, and the people who had clothed his official action with the majesty of "executive authority," had an unfaltering faith in the Negro. Massachusetts had been the storm-line of the anti-slavery agitation movement for thirty years, and the people were well-informed upon the questions that had excited the fratricidal conflict. If any State could solve the problem of raising black levies, Massachusetts could. Governor Andrew hastened home from Washington, and threw all the energies of his great personality into the work of arming Negro volunteers in Massachusetts. The following is the first order for their recruitment:

"Commonwealth of Massachusetts,
"Headquarters Boston, *February* 9, 1863.
"*Ex-Special Order* No. 68.

"Mr. Philip Backus, of Lenox, is hereby authorized to enlist a company of colored men in Massachusetts for service of the United States in the regiments of the Massachusetts volunteers.

"A premium of two dollars for each recruit obtained is offered by the United States. This may be expended by the person authorized from these headquarters to recruit, in the employment of agents.

"By order of his Excellency,
"JOHN A. ANDREW,
"Governor and Commander-in-chief.
(Signed) "WILLIAM SCHOULAR,
"Adjutant-general."

The Governor authorized John W. M. Appleton to superintend the recruiting of a regiment to be designated as the "Fifty-fourth Massachusetts Volunteer Infantry," composed of "persons of African descent." A rendezvous was established at "Camp Meigs," Readville, Massachusetts, February 21, 1863. It began with a squad of twenty-seven, and afterwards the recruits arrived almost daily. The greatest enthusiasm prevailed among the Negro citizens, and many patriotic meetings were held in their churches or places of public convenience. On the 12th of April following the Fifty-fourth Regiment was full to overflowing. Two other regiments were constituted of "persons of African descent," the Fifty-fifth Infantry and the Fifth Cavalry. The small Negro population of Massachusetts was soon depleted, and Governor Andrew despatched his recruiting agents to other States to secure levies to complete the new organizations. The work was carried forward with patriotic enthusiasm, and the results were grateful to the hearts of the courageous few who had stood for the Negro in other and less enlightened days.

The year 1862 was a period of great peril to the Republic. The Administration was endeavoring to secure the return of the seceding States with as little effusion of blood as possible. It was endeavoring to please the Democratic party at the North, and to conciliate the rebels at the South, by employing the army to return fugitive slaves. This service was not applauded at the North nor appreciated at the South. This policy had failed. In the autumn of 1862 there was to be an election of Congressmen. The Administration had to look for its supporters from the New England, Middle, and Western States. What policy could it appeal to the people to sustain? Certainly not a slave-catching policy, for the men in the North who would be most likely to approve such a policy were uncompromisingly opposed to the Administration. Nothing that the Administration might do or forbear to do would mollify the malice of its enemies and traducers. So, on the 22d of September, 1862, the President took a bold step. He issued an emancipation proclamation. It was an extreme change on the eve of the election, and to many it seemed a bid for political support, and not the result of an expanding and generous sentiment. Even the men who had urged a policy of emancipation were in doubt how to regard the proclamation, while anti-Administration men cried, it is "the Negro and not the Union that Lincoln is endeavoring to save." It was too near the autumn elections to have a fair expression of opinion on the proclamation, and thus the Administration was loser in the contest. There were now seventy-eight Republicans to thirty-seven Democrats, but the election resulted in giving the opposition a majority of ten in the new Congress. There were many evidences of a bitter feeling towards the Administration on the part of the people and their journals. But progressing public sentiment soon broke the opposition in Congress, and the Administration secured the support of the majority for an earnest and radical policy.

On the 1st of January, 1863, the President signalized "New-year's-day" by another proclamation declaring the slaves *forever free;* and thus 1863 was inaugurated by a vigorous and humane policy. It is apparent, therefore, that the policy of arming Negroes was both logical and inevitable. While Kansas and Massachusetts were recruiting Negro soldiers, the Administration decided not only to receive fugitives within its military lines, but to seize them—men, women, and children—and *bring* them in. The object was to deplete the labor force of the enemy and to put the American uniform upon the Negro.

General Halleck, who was at the head of the army, in the following letter to Grant clearly outlined the policy of the Government in receiving and arming all Negroes capable of military service who came within the Union lines.

"Headquarters of the Army, Washington,
"March 31, 1863.

"*Maj.-gen'l U. S. Grant,*
"*Comd'g Dept. of the Tenn. near Vicksburg.*

"GEN'L—It is the policy of the Government to withdraw from the enemy as much productive labor as possible. So long as the rebels retain and employ their slaves in producing grains, etc., they can employ all the whites in the field. Every slave withdrawn from the enemy is equivalent to a white put *hors de combat.*

"Again: it is the policy of the Government to use the Negroes of the South, as far as practicable, as a military force for the defense of forts, depots, etc. If the experience of General Banks near New Orleans should be satisfactory, a much larger force will be organized during the coming summer; and if they can be used to hold points on the Mississippi during the sickly season, it will afford much relief to our armies.

"They certainly can be used with advantage as laborers, teamsters, cooks, etc. And it is the opinion of many who have examined the question without passion or prejudice, that they can also be used as a military force. It certainly is good policy to use them to the very best advantage we can. Like almost anything else, they may be made instruments of good or evil ; in the hands of the enemy they are used with much effect against us, in our hands we must try to use them with the best possible effect against the rebels.

"It has been reported to the Secretary of War that many of the officers of your command not only discourage the Negroes from coming under our protection, but by ill-treatment force them to return to their masters; this is not only bad policy in itself, but is directly opposed to the policy adopted by the Government. Whatever may be the individual opinion of an officer in regard to the wisdom of measures adopted and announced by the Government, it is the duty of every one to cheerfully and honestly endeavor to carry out the measures so adopted.

"Their good or bad policy is a matter of opinion before they are tried; their real character can only be determined by a fair trial, when adopted by the Government it is the duty of every officer to give them such a trial, and to do everything in his power to carry the orders of his Government into execution.

"It is expected that you will use your official and personal influence to remove prejudices on this subject, and to fully and thoroughly carry out the policy now adopted and ordered by the Government. That policy is, to withdraw from the use of the enemy all the slaves you can, and to employ those so withdrawn to the best possible advantage against the enemy.

"The character of the war has very much changed within the last year. There is now no possible hope of reconciliation with the rebels. The Union party in the South is virtually destroyed. There can be no peace but that which is forced by the sword. We must conquer the rebels or be conquered by them. The North must conquer the Slave Oligarchy or become slaves themselves, the manufacturers mere hewers of wood and drawers of water to Southern aristocrats.

"This is the phase which the rebellion has now assumed. We must take things as they are. The Government, looking at the subject in all its aspects, has adopted a policy, and we must cheerfully and faithfully carry out that policy.

"I write you this unofficial letter simply as a personal friend, and as a matter of friendly advice. From my position here, where I can survey the entire field, perhaps I may be better able to understand the tone of public opinion, and the intentions of the Government, than you can from merely consulting the officers of your own army.

"Very respectfully, your ob't serv't,
"H. W. HALLECK."

On the 19th of April, 1863, General Grant wrote to General Halleck from Milliken's Bend, Louisiana, and, among other things, refers to the policy of the military employment of Negroes as follows:

".At least three of my Army Corps commanders take hold of the new policy of arming the Negroes, and using them against the enemy with a will. They, at least, are so much of soldiers as to feel themselves under obligations to carry out a policy (which they would not inaugurate) in the same good faith and with the same zeal as if it was of their own choosing. You may rely on me carrying out any policy ordered by proper authority, to the best of my ability."

His promise to Halleck was no mere lip service, and a few days later he issued the following order to facilitate the organization of colored troops in his department:

"Headquarters Department of the Tennessee,
"Milliken's Bend, Louisiana, *April* 22, 1863.
"*General Orders, No.* 25 [Extract].

"I. Corps, division, and post commanders will afford all facilities for the completion of the negro regiments now organizing in this department. Commissaries will issue supplies and quartermasters will furnish stores on the same requisitions and returns as are required from other troops.

"It is expected that all commanders will especially exert themselves in carrying out the policy of the administration, not only in organizing colored regiments and rendering them efficient, but also in removing prejudice against them. * * *

"By order of Major-general U. S. Grant.

"JNO. A. RAWLINS, A. A. G."

In order to put this policy into immediate and effective operation, General Lorenzo Thomas, Adjutant-general of the United States Army, was despatched to the Mississippi Valley. He was clothed with plenary powers to enforce the new policy of the Administration. He was ordered to dismiss and to commission officers according as they were against or for the new policy without referring their cases to Washington. On the 8th of April, 1863, at Lake Providence, Louisiana, he addressed the United States Army, and expounded the policy of the Administration. "You know full well," said General Thomas, " for you have been over this country, that the rebels have sent into the field all their available fighting men—every man capable of bearing arms—and you know they have kept at home all their slaves for the raising of subsistence for their armies in the field. In this way they can bring to bear against us all the strength of their so-called Confederate States, while we at the North can only send a portion of our fighting force, being compelled to have behind another portion to cultivate our fields and supply the wants of an immense army. The Administration has determined to take from the rebels this source of supply—to take their Negroes, and compel them to send back a portion of their whites to cultivate their deserted plantations; and very poor persons they would be to fill the place of the dark-hued laborer. They must do this or their armies will starve."

This was the first clear official announcement of the new policy of the Administration. The old enterprise of turning the fugitive away—compelling him at the point of the bayonet to go back to the "service and labor" from which he had flown—was abandoned at last. Instead of being turned out of the Union lines he was to be taken in; and the black arms of iron and fingers of steel that had lifted the burdens and held the hoe for the Confederacy were to be converted to the service of the United States Government. "On the first day of January last the President issued his Proclamation," continued General Thomas, "declaring that from that day forward all the slaves in the States then in rebellion should be free. You know that vast numbers of these slaves are within your borders, inside of the lines of this army. They came into your camps, and you cannot but receive them. The authorities in Washington are very much pained to hear, and I fear with truth in many cases, that some of these poor unfortunates have, on different occasions, been turned away from us, and their applications for admission within our lines have been refused by our officers and soldiers. This is not the way to use freedmen." Speaking of the practical operation of the new policy, he said, "All of you will some day be on picket duty, and I charge you all if any of this unfortunate race come within your lines that you do not turn them away, but receive them kindly and cordially. They are to be encouraged to come to us. They are to be received with open arms; they are to be fed and clothed; they are to be armed.

"This is the policy that has been fully determined upon. I am here to say that I am authorized to raise as many regiments of Blacks as I can. I am authorized to give commissions, from the highest to the lowest, and I desire those persons who are in earnest in this work to take hold of it. I desire only those whose hearts are in it, and to them alone will I give commissions. I don't care who they are or what their present rank may be. I do not hesitate to say that all proper persons will receive commissions.

"While I am authorized thus, in the name of the Secretary of War, I have the fullest authority to dismiss from the army any man, be his rank what it may, whom I find maltreating the freedmen. This part of my duty I will most assuredly perform if any case comes before me. I would rather do that than give commissions, because such men are unworthy the name of soldiers."

In recapitulating the policy of the Administration, General Thomas concluded:

"I would like to raise on this river twenty regiments at least before I go back. I shall take all the women and children, and all the men unfit for our military organizations, and place them on these plantations; then take these regiments and put them in the rear. They will guard the rear effectually. Knowing the country well, and familiar with all the roads and swamps, they will be able to track out the accursed guerilla and run them from the land. When I get regiments raised you may sweep out into the interior with impunity.

"Recollect, for every regiment of Blacks I raise, I raise a regiment of whites to face the foe in the field. This, fellow-soldiers, is the determined policy of the Administration. You all know full well when the President of the United States, though said to be slow in coming to a determination—when he once puts his foot down, it is there, and he is not going to take it up. He has put his foot down; I am here to assure you that my official influence shall be given that he shall not raise it."

The entire speech of the Adjutant-general of the Army of the United States was telegraphed to the North, and the enthusiasm over this new business-like policy made many friends for the Administration. It was scarcely less a surprise to the North than it was to the South to learn that a change so sweeping had taken place in the policy of the Government. The magnificent sentiment of the speech of Adjutant-general Thomas touched the heart of the Christian world, and the horrors of civil war were mitigated by the noble idea of practical emancipation. The question of property was definitely settled so far as the slaves of persons and States in actual rebellion against the authority of the United States Government were concerned. The Negroes of such States were absolutely free, and their services were sought by the Government. The grand policy of emancipation and the military employment of the American slave having been officially proclaimed, it swept forward with the force and majesty of its importance. General Thomas was unremitting in his labors in this behalf, and visited Memphis, Helena, and Vicksburg. The prejudice of white troops was melting away every day, and the experiment was winning favor everywhere.

General Thomas reported to the Secretary of War from Lake Providence in the following despatch:

"Lake Providence, Louisiana, *April* 9,
"*Via* Cairo, Illinois, *April* 15, 1863.

"*Hon. E. M. Stanton:*

"I arrived at this place early yesterday morning, and made arrangements for addressing Generals McArthur's and Logan's divisions of General McPherson's army corps. I announced to the former division in the morning, four thousand being present, the policy of the Government respecting the black race, and in the afternoon to General Logan's division, some seven thousand. The troops received it with great enthusiasm, and many speeches were made by officers of different rank, fully indorsing the policy. I must refer to the eloquent remarks of General Logan, who not only fully indorsed my own remarks, but went far beyond them, stating most emphatically that he would never return to his home, from which his wife and child had been driven by an unnatural father, until this wicked rebellion shall be utterly crushed. I asked from each of these divisions officers to raise two Negro regiments, but the difficulty will be to restrict them to that number, for at least ten regiments can be obtained. My first arrangements are for ten regiments, and after these shall have been raised further arrangements will be made for others. Ten thousand pairs of Negro shoes of large size should at once be forwarded to Memphis. Also, arms for that number, including those that may be in the depot at that place. I shall write to Captain Eddy to make requisition for clothing for ten thousand men. I have overtaxed my strength, and am far from well, but hope a day or two rest may recruit my energies.

"L. THOMAS, Adjt.-gen."

General N. P. Banks was now in command at New Orleans. Upon his assumption of the command of the "Department of the Gulf," he found the Negro regiments that had been organized by General Butler. He was so much pleased with their appearance and drill that he issued an order (No. 40) for "the organization of a Corps d'Armée of colored troops, to be designated as the Corps d'Afrique."[1] The order was issued on the 1st of May, 1863, and contemplated "eighteen regiments, representing all arms — infantry, artillery, cavalry — making three brigades of two regiments each, and three divisions of three brigades each, with appropriate corps of engineers, and flying hospitals for each division." The general went on to remark in his order that the efficiency of troops depended largely upon the character of the officers; that small regiments of troops of this character were more easily disciplined; and that details of officers of the highest standing would be made to instruct the black levies. General Banks brought rare patriotism, high intelligence, and splendid tact to the work of organization; while the freedmen responded to his call and complied with his terms with enthusiasm.

The enterprise of recruiting and organizing Negro troops grew to such proportions that competent and appropriate machinery had to be constituted at Washington. In General Orders No. 143, dated Washington, May 22, 1863, a bureau was established for the conduct of all matters referring to the organization of Negro troops. A detail of clerks was made, and a competent officer placed at the head of the new bureau. Three or four field-officers were detailed to inspect the work of recruiting at different points where stations were to be maintained by

---

[1] "Official Records of the War of the Rebellion," vol. xv., pp. 716, 717.

order of the War Department. Boards were to be convened, at such points as the War Department might designate, to examine applicants for commissions in Negro regiments, the applicants first receiving permission from the Adjutant-general to appear before such boards. Persons who desired to recruit Negroes for the army were required to pass an examination before a board, and the maximum of such service was one regiment to each person specially authorized by the War Department. Each candidate was given rank according to the character of his examination. An applicant for a colonelcy might only get a captaincy. Negro troops were to be accepted by companies, the regiments formed from time to time taking their number according to the date of muster. All matters respecting "United States Colored Troops" were to be referred to the Adjutant-general in care of the War Department.

With efficient methods and a matchless head like Adjutant-general Thomas, the work of employing Negroes as soldiers was soon systematized, and worked out the best results both for the Negro and the Government. The former was proud of the generous invitation to aid in destroying slavery and in preserving the Union, and the latter was pleased with the efforts of its new policy upon the country and the progress of the war. In August, 1863, the Administration despatched Adjutant-general Thomas to the South-west, still further to enlarge the scope of the enlistment of Negroes. He was empowered to continue the work of "organization into the military service of the United States of all able-bodied male persons of African descent who may come within our lines, or who may be brought in by our troops, or who may have already placed themselves under the protection of the Federal Government."

The Administration was so earnestly committed to the work of the organization of Negro troops that the Secretary of War sent the following telegram to the commanding officer at Memphis, requiring the removal of Colonel Martin, who had opposed the policy of the Government:

"War Department, *September* 25, 1863.
"*Major-general Hurlburt, Commd'g at Memphis:*
"This Department is satisfied that the good of the service requires the removal of Colonel Martin from command at Paducha, and the assignment of some officer there who will not permit the surrender of slaves to rebel masters, nor oppose the policy of the Government in organizing Colored troops. If Paducha is within your command, you will please relieve Colonel Martin and assign some officer of active loyalty, who may be intrusted with the duty of organizing a Colored regiment for the service. EDWIN M. STANTON,
"Secretary of War."

Thus far the Negro recruits had been taken from States where the slave-holders were engaged in armed rebellion. The Administration now began to look about for new fields in which to recruit Negroes. The border slave States and portions of the seceded States were exempted from the provisions of the Emancipation Proclamation; and the slaves could not be taken without compensation to loyal masters. On the 13th of October, 1863, in General Orders No. 329, the War Department established recruiting stations in Maryland, Tennessee, and Missouri; Delaware was included October 26th, and the methods were carefully prescribed. "All able-bodied free Negroes, slaves of disloyal persons, and slaves of loyal persons, with the consent of their owners," were declared to be eligible for military employment. The county and State furnishing Negro recruits were to be credited with them, and loyal masters consenting to the enlistment of their slaves were to receive three hundred dollars for each one, after filing proof of ownership and furnishing a deed of manumission. It was required, however, that a sufficient number of recruits should be obtained within thirty days from the date of opening the recruiting station, otherwise the slaves could be taken without obtaining the consent of the loyal owners. They were to be compensated, nevertheless, as in the former case. Special boards were created in these States to determine the claims of owners and to facilitate the work of obtaining black levies.

The feeling in New York State, and especially in the city, was not friendly to the Negro. The State Government was Democratic, and the foreign element in the large cities was restless and threatening. But there were many patriotic men in New York who were in hearty accord with the Administration in placing arms in the hands of the Negroes. The Union League Club, of New York City, finding that the State authorities would not entertain the proposition to employ Negroes as soldiers, on the 12th of November, 1863, appointed a committee to devise means for raising Negro troops. Colonel George Bliss, Jr., was chosen chairman, and the committee entered at once upon the discharge of its duties. The War Department preferred to have the concurrence of the State Government when it extended its authority to individuals to raise Negro troops. On the 23d of November, 1863, the committee addressed a letter to the Governor of New York—Horatio Seymour—stating that as he could not grant the committee authority to enlist Negroes as soldiers, and in view of the desire of the War Department to have the committee's work indorsed by the State, they would be greatly obliged if his excellency would grant the committee his official approval.

The Secretary of War addressed the following telegram to General Strong, of New York City:

"War Department, *November* 24, 1863.
"*General William K. Strong, New York:*
"On application by suitable persons special authority will be granted to raise Colored troops in New York, according to the rules and regulations relative to organizing and raising Colored troops. The troops so raised will be credited to the State. Until Congress shall authorize it no bounty can be paid, and the pay is limited by the act of Congress to ten dollars a month. The Department will recommend that in this respect the act be amended so as to make the pay the same as other soldiers. They will be enrolled as United States Volunteers, and the officers be appointed and commissioned by the President.

"EDWIN M. STANTON,
"Secretary of War."

On the 27th of November the Governor wrote the committee that he was entirely without authority to grant them permission to employ Negroes as soldiers, and that they must apply to the authorities at Washington. The committee knew all of this before, but were now thoroughly convinced that they would look in vain for sympathy in this quarter. On the 3d of December, 1863, the War Department granted the committee—George Bliss, Jr., and his associates—authority to recruit and organize the "Twenty-fifth Regiment United States Colored Troops." Having been armed with proper authority to recruit a regiment of Negroes, the committee indulged the hope that the Governor would be disposed to countenance and aid the committee in their patriotic labors. The committee accordingly wrote to Governor Seymour: "We express the hope that, so far as in your power, you will give the movement your aid and countenance." The Governor never answered this most reasonable request, but the committee went forward in its noble work. Its zeal was equalled only by the enthusiasm of the Negro volunteers, who responded to their country's call for defenders.

On the 4th of January, 1864, Colonel George Bliss, Jr., wrote a letter to Secretary Stanton from the headquarters of the Twentieth Regiment United States Colored Troops, No. 350 Fourth Street, New York, announcing that the regiment had reached its maximum strength—1,000 men. He requested the Secretary to allow the regiment to remain in camp for thirty days or more, that the men might have an opportunity to perfect themselves in tactics and the general duties of soldiers. The officers had been selected from the army in the field; the men were physically the equals of any; and he predicted that when the regiment should depart for the seat of war it would be better drilled than any thus far sent from the State of New York. He spoke of the men as being intelligently enthusiastic in the performance of their duties. He suggested that when the regiment should leave its camp on the Island for the city, on its way to the front, it should be landed up-town and march down Broadway. He told the Secretary it was his desire to have the men armed with Springfield muskets of the pattern of 1861, and expressed the belief that the Government would thus convince the Negroes of the North that it was ready to put the best arms into their hands.

This letter was taken to the War Office by ex-Governor E. D. Morgan, and, being unable to see the Secretary, he wrote a letter on a sheet of paper with the official heading of the Department printed upon it. The letter was dated at "War Department, Washington, D. C., Wednesday, January 6, 1864." He indorsed the letter of Colonel Bliss, and urged Mr. Stanton to grant the requests made.

The wives of the members of the Union League Club were deeply interested in the work of the Club's Committee on the Recruiting of Negroes, and issued a circular calling a meeting in the club-house, January 5, 1864, at 2 P.M., to appoint a committee to secure a stand of colors for the Twentieth Regiment. Among the signers of the call were the following ladies: Mrs. Charles King, Mrs. Henry Van Rennselaer, Mrs. Samuel Wetmore, Mrs. George B. De Forrest, Mrs. John Jay, Mrs. U. A. Murdock, Mrs. Richard M. Hunt, Mrs. J. J. Astor, Mrs. D'Oremieux, Mrs. Samuel Bridgham, Mrs. William Dodge, Jr., Mrs. Jackson S. Schultz, Mrs. Frank E. Howe, Mrs. George Bliss, Jr., Mrs. L. G. B. Cannon.

There were 9,000 men in the Negro population of New York eligible by age—from eighteen to forty-five—and 2,300 of them enlisted in less than sixty days. The committee raised their first regiment in two weeks, and by the 27th of January, 1864, another regiment, which was also accepted by the Government and mustered into the service. This was the extent of the recruitment of Negroes in New York, but many left the State and enlisted elsewhere. The State of New York never enlisted Negroes, as the following statement from Major-general John G. Farnsworth shows:

"Adjutant-general's Office, Albany,
"*December* 17, 1885.

"This State did not organize any colored troops. Three regiments were recruited by authority of the United States in this State. The State received credit for enlistments made, but the credit was given by the United States, and how many of that class were received is not known here, as no detailed accounts are on file.

"There are no records of these regiments in this office from which the information you desire could be obtained."

In Pennsylvania there was deep interest manifested in the employment of Negroes as soldiers. Soon after the Government had committed itself to the policy of arming Negroes, a committee of patriotic gentlemen of Philadelphia secured authority to recruit Negroes for the army. The committee was organized, with Thomas Webster as chairman, Cadwalader Biddle as secretary, and S. A. Mercer as treasurer. The sum of $33,388 was speedily raised to promote the work. The two regiments of Negroes raised in Massachusetts had cost about $60,000, but the committee intended to raise three or four regiments at $10,000 each. A camp was laid out at Shelton Hill, near to the city, and named "Camp William Penn." On the 26th of June, 1863, the camp was inaugurated by a squad of eighty men. On the 3d of February the committee made the following statement respecting its work:

"On the 24th July, 1863, the first (Third United States) regiment was full.

"On the 13th September, 1863, the second (Sixth United States) regiment was full.

"On the 4th December, 1863, the third (Eighth United States) regiment was full.

"On the 6th January, 1864, the fourth (Twenty-second United States) regiment was full.

"On the 3d February, 1864, the fifth (Twenty-fifth United States) regiment was full.

"August 13, 1863, the Third United States Regiment left Camp William Penn, and was in front of Fort Wagner when it surrendered.

"October 14, 1863, the Sixth United States Regiment left for Yorktown.

"January 16, 1864, the Eighth United States Regiment left for Hilton Head.

"The Twenty-second and Twenty-fifth regiments are now at Camp William Penn, awaiting orders from the Government."

The regiments that went from this camp were among the best in the army. Their officers had been carefully selected and specially trained in a military school under competent teachers, and the troops themselves were noted for intelligence, proficiency, and pluck.

In accordance with the order establishing recruiting stations in Tennessee, published on the 13th of October, 1863, an office was opened at Nashville. George L. Stearns, Esq., of Medford, Massachusetts, was chosen by the War Department "Commissioner for the Organization of United States Colored Troops." His commission was issued June 6, 1863. He was given the rank of major with the powers of an assistant-adjutant-general. He was independent of the general in command of the Army of the Cumberland, and received his orders direct from the War Department. The selection of Major Stearns was a very happy one. He was an abolitionist of the most pronounced type. He had laid a large fortune on the altar of liberty, and consecrated himself to the disinthralment of bleeding Kansas. He had furnished John Brown with Sharp's rifles in the "Border Ruffian War," and his heart was in the war that he believed would inevitably put an end to slavery. He knew the Negro, believed in his manhood, and was proud to place muskets in his waiting and willing hands. He began his work with characteristic vigor and business skill. The few months he gave to the work were memorable. It is seldom the Government can command such talents and experience, such patriotism and patience, as Major Stearns brought to bear in his peculiarly trying and unique work.

The first work that Major Stearns did in raising colored troops was for Massachusetts; but he subsequently extended his labors into Pennsylvania and New York, at the same time despatching agents through nearly all of the free States. General Couch was in charge of all the troops in the State of Pennsylvania, and when Major Stearns offered him colored troops he refused to accept them. The Major immediately appealed to the War Department, and the Secretary sent the following telegram:

"War Department, *June* 18, 1863.

"*Major George L. Stearns,*
    "*Continental Hotel, Philadelphia:*
 "This morning I saw the despatch referred to in your telegram, and immediately telegraphed General Couch that he was authorized to re-

ceive troops without regard to color; but if there is likely to be any dispute about the matter, it will be better to send no more. It is well to avoid all controversy in the present juncture, as the troops can be used elsewhere. EDWIN M. STANTON,
"Secretary of War."

He took in the situation at Nashville at once, and met the exigencies of every day. He found that the men whom he was enlisting were being sent out to the front to perform fatigue duty. He felt that his honor was involved in this matter, since he had enlisted them to be soldiers, not laborers. He expressed some plain truths to the War Department about this matter. He suggested that Negro troops should be put in camps of instruction and prepared for the duties of the field. He felt that it was only justice to troops of this character to give them fair opportunities to compete with their white compatriots in camp, and successfully contend with the enemy in the field. Major-general George H. Thomas had ordered six companies of the Fourteenth Regiment of Negro troops from Gallatin, Tennessee, to Bridgeport, Alabama, to do fatigue duty. This was on the 20th of November, 1863. Major Stearns felt that he could not endure this, and remonstrated against it.

Major Stearns was a man of strong personality. He could not endure shams, and on all occasions and in all places spoke the truth without wincing. The wholesale system of impressment of Negroes in Nashville was demoralizing, and he threw himself at once into the breach. He called a meeting of the Negroes of the city in one of the largest churches. He told this people that rather than be dragged into the trenches and fortifications, they had better volunteer, and he pledged himself to pay their wages out of his private funds. The Negroes believed him, and the next day three hundred responded to his call for volunteers. It is not necessary to state that he kept his promise with these men.

Kentucky was not included in the Emancipation edict, and the Secretary of War had repeatedly requested Major Stearns to return fugitive slaves. To such a request this stalwart New England abolitionist turned a deaf ear. He could give his money and his energy; he could consecrate his talents, and even immolate his life upon the altar of humanity in the interest of the Negro, but he could not turn slave-catcher. The conservatism of the War Department was trembling lest Major Stearns should come in conflict with the military governor of Tennessee, Andrew Johnson, and day after day telegrams poured in upon him urging him not to quarrel with Governor Johnson. With characteristic dash and boldness he took a bundle of these telegrams, and walking into the presence of Andrew Johnson, asked him what quarrel he had with him. He was so intensely earnest, charged with such wonderful personal magnetism, that to know him was to love him, and Johnson found himself confronted by a friend and not a foe. Thenceforward these two men worked in harmony while Stearns remained. He was too radical for executive work of this character.

The following telegrams show the mind of the Secretary of War respecting Major Stearns's authority in the organization of Negro troops in this Department:

"War Department, *September* 18, 1863.
"*Brigadier-general Andrew Johnson,*
"*Military Governor, Nashville:*

"Your telegram just received. Major Stearns was sent to Nashville to aid in the organization of Colored troops under your directions and the directions of General Rosecrans. To prevent any possible misunderstanding, he was directed to report to you and the Commanding General. He is, while in your State, your subordinate, bound to follow your directions, and may be relieved by you whenever his action is deemed by you prejudicial. Upon your judgment in matters relating to the State of which you are Governor the Department relies in respect to whatever relates to the people, whether white or black, bond or free. No officers of Colored troops will be appointed but in accordance with your views as the Chief State Executive. If Major Stearns can be of no aid, and his presence is obnoxious, he will of course be removed, whether relieved by you or not.

"EDWIN M. STANTON,
"Secretary of War."

"War Department, *September* 18, 1863.
"*Major Stearns, Nashville:*

"If any difference of opinion exists or shall arise between Governor Johnson and yourself respecting the organization and employment of Colored men in the State of Tennessee, he being the State Executive, you will conform your action to his views. All dissension is to be avoided, and if there is any want of harmony between you, you had better leave Nashville and proceed to Cairo to await orders, reporting by telegraph your departure from Nashville and your arrival at Cairo.

"EDWIN M. STANTON,
"Secretary of War."

He was not sustained by the War Department in his methods, and in December, 1863, resigned. The work was continued under the temporary care of Captain R. D. Mussey, who was subsequently—June 14, 1864—appointed colonel of the One Hundredth Regiment of "United States Colored Troops."

In December, 1863, Colonel Augustus L. Chetlain was promoted to the rank of brigadier-general of volunteers. Colonel Chetlain had entered the war as captain of a company which he had assisted in raising at Galena, Illinois. On the 2d of May, 1861, he was appointed lieutenant-colonel of the Twelfth Illinois Infantry, and "won his spurs" and the command of the regiment at Fort Donelson. General Grant had known him well, and upon his promotion to a brigadier-generalship, urged his appointment, upon the ground of his special fitness, as chief of the recruitment and organization of Negro troops in Tennessee.

The following order from the War Department assigned him to special work:

"Nashville, Tennessee, *February* 6, 1864.
"*Special Orders No.* 14 [Extract].

"II. . . . Brigadier-general Augustus L. Chetlain, United States Volunteers, is hereby assigned to the command of all the Colored Troops now in the State of Tennessee, and that may hereafter be raised and stationed in that State. He will locate his Headquarters in the city of Memphis.

"The Officers superintending the organization of Colored Troops in Tennessee will report to Brigadier-general Chetlain, weekly, the result of their operations. Commanders of Regiments and Detachments of Troops of African Descent will furnish the General regular Regimental returns of their commands on the last day of every month, and in like manner General Chetlain will forward a complete return of his command monthly to Brigadier-general L. Thomas, U.S.A., at Vicksburg, Mississippi. Nominations for appointments in Regiments already organized will be forwarded through General Chetlain to the above-named officer. . . .

"By order of the Secretary of War.

"L. THOMAS,
"Adjutant-general."

In a conversation with General Grant, just before the publication of the above order, General Chetlain was given to understand that the work he was about to undertake would be arduous, and in some respects unpleasant. "But," continued General Grant, "*if you make a success* of it, as you can, it will be greatly to your credit."

General Grant had not made a mistake in the selection of General Chetlain for a work that was not only novel, but by some considered odious—a work that demanded patriotism, zeal, large humanity, and an unfaltering confidence in the Negro.

General Chetlain established his headquarters at Memphis, and began the recruiting of Negro troops with conspicuous ability. On the 13th of June, 1864, in General Orders No. 20, the sphere of his influence was extended in some proportion to his abilities, and he was charged with similar work in the State of Kentucky. The order concluded as follows:

"Brigadier-general A. L. Chetlain, United States Volunteers, is charged with the immediate supervision of the organization of Colored Troops in Kentucky, as authorized herein, subject to such instructions as he may receive from Brigadier-general L. Thomas, Adjutant-general United States Army.

"The assignment of Brigadier-general Chetlain to this duty will in no way interfere with his present position as commander of the Colored Troops in West Tennessee.

"General Chetlain will establish his headquarters without delay at Louisville, Kentucky.

"All commanders in Kentucky will afford General Chetlain every facility for carrying out the instructions contained in this order.

"As early as possible, Colored Troops will be used by General Chetlain for recruiting purposes, and will be distributed among the different camps of reception.

"By order of the Secretary of War.
"L. THOMAS,
"Adjutant-general."

A high standard of physical, mental, and moral excellence was required of persons seeking commands in organizations of this character. The records show that not more than one-third of the applicants before the boards charged with examination of candidates for commissions in Negro regiments were passed. In General Orders No. 24, published at Memphis, December 12, 1864, among many excellent things were the following:

"No person is wanted as an officer in a Colored Regiment who feels that in accepting the position he is making a sacrifice, or who desires appointment simply for higher rank and pay—it being the aim of those having charge of the organization of Colored Troops to have them officered, drilled, and disciplined equal to the best of white troops.

"Colored troops will, without doubt, form a large portion of the permanent army of the United States, and it should be the aim of every officer to fit himself and men for such an honorable position.

"Up to the date of this order the record of Colored Troops in battle and campaign is untarnished. Their stubborn bravery and gallant conduct has gained for them the respect even of bitter and prejudiced enemies, and given to their organization that dignity and stability which the faithful and fearless performance of duty will never fail to secure.

"It can but be an honor to any man to command in a service which, while it gives liberty to slaves and manhood to chattels, furnishes reliable and efficient soldiers for the Union.

"By order of Brigadier-general A. L. Chetlain.
"CHARLES P. BROWN,
Official. "Assistant Adjutant-general."

Eight months of the most heroic and indefatigable labor were bestowed upon the great enterprise of securing black levies for the United States Army.

General Chetlain made a tour of inspection in which he must have found great satisfaction in examining the work which he had inaugurated. The regiments organized and inspected by General Chetlain were as follows:

KENTUCKY.
At Louisville.

Fourth Regiment Heavy Artillery: from June 16 to April 19, 1863; Colonel James N. McArthur.

One Hundredth Regiment Infantry [at large]: from May 3 to June 1, 1864; Colonel Reuben D. Mussey.

One Hundred and Seventh Regiment Infantry: from May 3 to September 15, 1864; Colonel William H. Revere, Jr.

One Hundred and Eighth Regiment Infantry: from June 20 to August 22, 1864; Colonel John S. Bishop.

One Hundred and Ninth Regiment Infantry: on July 5, 1864; Colonel Orion A. Bartholomew.

[Besides the above regiments there were nearly three thousand soldiers partly organized whose officers had not yet been appointed.]

TENNESSEE.

At Nashville.

Twelfth Regiment Infantry: from July 24 to August 14, 1863; Colonel Charles R. Thompson.

Thirteenth Regiment Infantry: on November 19, 1863; Colonel John A. Hottenstein.

Fifteenth Regiment Infantry: from December 2, 1863, to March 11, 1864; Colonel William Innes.

Sixteenth Regiment Infantry: from December 4, 1863, to February 13, 1864; Colonel William B. Gaw.

Seventeenth Regiment Infantry: from December 12 to 21, 1863; Colonel William R. Shafter.

At Chattanooga.

Forty-second Regiment Infantry: from April 20, 1864, to July 6, 1865; Lieutenant-colonel J. R. Putnam.

Forty-fourth Regiment Infantry: from April 7 to September 16, 1864; Colonel Lewis Johnson.

At Pulaski.

One Hundred and Tenth Regiment Infantry: from November 20, 1863, to January 14, 1864; Lieutenant-colonel Dedrick F. Tiedemann.

One Hundred and Eleventh Regiment Infantry: from January 13 to April 5, 1864; Lieutenant-colonel William H. Scroggs.

At Gallatin.

Fourteenth Regiment Infantry: from November 16, 1863, to January 8, 1864; Colonel Thomas J. Morgan.

At La Grange.

Fifty-ninth Regiment Infantry: from June 6 to 27, 1863; Colonel Edward Bouton.

In January, 1865, General Chetlain had under his command 17,000 Negro troops, while his tour of inspection was not entirely confined to troops of this character in Tennessee and Kentucky. His work in the organization of Negro troops is without parallel in the late war, and his services were rewarded by a brevet major-generalship. The Adjutant-general of the Army, in his report to the

War Department in the summer of 1865, made the following recognition of the services of General Chetlain:

"Brigadier-general Chetlain reported to me, and I assigned him as superintendent of the recruiting service in Tennessee. He proved a most valuable officer, for I found him to possess both intelligence and zeal, with a rare qualification for the organization of troops. He never failed in any duty he was assigned, either as superintendent or as an inspector, to which latter duty I assigned him, and I am gratified that he was subsequently rewarded by a brevet major-general."

On the 22d of January, 1864, in Special Orders No. 18, Lieutenant-colonel Thomas J. Morgan, of the Fourteenth United States Colored Troops, stationed at Gallatin, Tennessee, was ordered to Knoxville to consult with General Davis Tillson as to raising a regiment of heavy artillery. Under date of February 3, 1864, from Chattanooga, Colonel Morgan reported the result of his visit; and referring to the feeling in the army respecting the military employment of Negroes, he wrote:

"There is an excellent state of feeling in the Department of the Ohio touching colored troops. General *Tillson* and staff, General *Cox*, commanding Twenty-third North Carolina, General *Haskell*, commanding divisions in Twenty-third Artillery Corps, and others high in rank, are warm friends of the move. The officers and men of the Ninth Artillery Corps look with favor upon it, and many excellent men are asking positions in the regiments now being formed. Commissioned officers of old regiments are asking to be transferred with same rank from white regiments to the black ones."

Perhaps there was not a finer specimen of a Christian soldier in the Western army than Thomas J. Morgan. He had enjoyed academic training, was deeply religious, and entertained positive ideas respecting the war and the Negro. A sort of spiritual valor marked all his actions. He reversed the Napoleonic idea that soldiers should be simply machines, and that the officers should do all the thinking. He cared for the moral and intellectual growth as well as the improvement his men made in drill and the duties of soldiership. He strove to make every man an intelligent unit. His views were grateful to the men under his immediate command, and were highly appreciated by such general officers as at that time comprehended the questions involved in the war. It was natural that, in looking for an officer to gather, by truth and personal magnetism, Negro recruits about the standards of the Union, General George H. Thomas should choose Colonel Morgan. The following order was issued placing him in charge of the recruiting of Negro troops in the Department of the Cumberland:

"Headquarters Department of the Cumberland,
"Chattanooga, Tennessee, *February* 29, 1864.
"*General Orders No.* 39.

"The raising of two Regiments of Infantry of African descent will be commenced at this place without delay, under the direction of Colonel T. J. Morgan, commanding Fourteenth United States Colored Troops.

"Colonel Morgan will receive all recruits enlisted by Mr. J. A. Spooner, agent for recruiting of Colored Troops, as well as those recruited at such other stations as he may establish, and organize them into companies under command of the officers of his regiment, until officers are appointed.

"One of these Regiments will be composed of such men only as can pass the physical examination required of all men enlisting in the military service of the United States. The other will be composed of the classes of colored men capable of performing the ordinary fatigue duties of a military depot; and as soon as companies are organized they will be subject to such details for fatigue duty as the Commanding General of the Department may direct.

"William W. Wright, Chief Engineer United States Military Railroad Division of Mississippi, has been appointed Colonel of the second regiment named above.

"The Major-general commanding the Department will nominate for appointment the additional field and staff officers, selecting such as he may deem best fitted for the service. Their names will be reported to the Bureau of Colored Troops at Washington, D. C., through Captain R. D. Mussey, Nineteenth United States Infantry, Acting Commissioner Organizing United States Colored Troops, when the appointments will be forwarded and the regiments receive their designations.

"The Quartermaster's Commissary and Ordnance Departments will fill Colonel Morgan's requisitions for necessary stores.

"By command of Major-general Thomas.
   (Signed)   "WILLIAM D. WHIPPLE,
           "Ass't. Adjutant-general.
"Headquarters Org'n U. S. Colored Troops,
 "Chattanooga, Tenn., March 4, 1864.
Official.   "THOMAS J. MORGAN,
  "Colonel 14th U. S. C. T., Com'r for Org'n'g C. T."

Colonel Morgan's service in this new sphere was valuable, and the Department commander made appropriate recognition of it.

Henry Barnes, Esq., an intelligent and patriotic citizen of Detroit, Michigan, was an early and enthusiastic advocate of the military employment of Negroes. He wrote Secretary Stanton upon the subject in July, 1863, and the following letter was addressed to the Governor of Michigan. Its spirit shows how deeply interested in this matter was the great War Secretary:

      "War Department, Washington, *July* 24, 1863.
"GOVERNOR,—H. Barnes, Esq., of Detroit, has applied to this Department for authority to raise a regiment of Colored troops in your State. The Department is very anxious that such regiments should be raised, and authorizes you to raise them by volunteering under the regulations of the Department, a copy of which is transmitted to you by the Chief of the Bureau, and it would be gratifying if you should give such authority to Mr. Barnes. It seems to me that there has been some misunderstanding upon this subject, and I am informed that you were under the impression that the Department would not authorize it. Until suitable arrangements could be made for the organization of a Bureau, it was not deemed advisable to raise such troops, but the organization of Colored troops is now a distinct Bureau in the Depart-

ment, and as fully recognized as any other branch of the military service, and every encouragement is given by the Department to the raising of such troops.
Yours truly,
"EDWIN M. STANTON,
"Secretary of War.
"His Excellency, AUSTIN BLAIR, Governor of Michigan, Jackson."

The following letter of authority for the enlistment of Negro troops was sent to the governors of Michigan, Illinois, and to other governors who desired to raise regiments of this character:

"War Department, Adjutant-general's Office,
"Washington, D. C., *July* 25, 1863.
"*His Excellency, Austin Blair, Governor of Michigan, Jackson, Mich.:*

"SIR,—I am instructed by the Secretary of War to inform you that you are hereby authorized to raise one regiment of infantry, to be composed of Colored men, to be mustered into the United States service for three years or during the war.

"To these troops no bounties will be paid. They will receive ten dollars per month and one ration per day, three dollars of which monthly pay may be in clothing.

"The organization of the regiment must conform in all respects with the requirements of General Orders No. 110, War Department, 1863, a copy of which is herewith.

"The prescribed number of commissioned officers will be appointed in accordance with the provisions of General Orders Nos. 143 and 144, War Department, current series, copies of which please find inclosed. The officers thus appointed will be mustered into service on the presentation to the mustering officer of their appointments, signed by the Secretary of War. The appointments will be made to keep pace with the muster into service of the several companies. Thus, on information being received from you that the first has been mustered into service, the necessary appointments for that company will be made. When four companies have been mustered in, the Lieutenant-colonel of the regiment will be appointed, and so on in accordance with the 'Revised Mustering Regulations.'

"To facilitate the appointment of the officers, it is respectfully suggested that it would be well to forward to the Adjutant-general of the army, as early as practicable, the names of such persons as you wish to have examined for appointment, and permission will be immediately given them to appear before the examining board now in session in

Cincinnati, or the board in session in Washington, if more convenient for the parties.

"I have the honor to be, very respectfully, your obedient servant,
"C. W. FOSTER,
"Assistant Adjutant-general."

Mr. Barnes was duly authorized to raise a regiment of Negro volunteers on the 12th of August, 1863, and on the 17th of February, 1864, a regiment, 895 strong, was mustered into the service of the United States. From the "First Michigan Colored Infantry" its designation was changed to the "One Hundred and Second United States Colored Troops."

On the 24th of September, 1863, the War Department authorized Governor Richard Yates, of Illinois, to raise "one regiment infantry," to be composed of Negroes; and on the 26th of October, 1863, he issued General Order No. 44, setting forth the fact that he had received authority to raise a regiment of Negro volunteers, and giving information respecting the *modus operandi*. Six companies were mustered into the United States Army on the 24th of April, 1864; the other four companies were raised in the field from the 22d of October, 1864, to the month of January, 1865. This was the only regiment of Negro troops raised by Illinois. Its first designation was "First Regiment Illinois Volunteers;" but it was subsequently changed to the "Twenty-ninth United States Colored Troops."

Governor David Tod, of Ohio, had insisted from the first that Negro troops should receive the same pay and bounty as other troops, and waited for the Government to change its attitude on this matter. In the mean time, however, he encouraged the recruitment of colored troops in Ohio for Massachusetts. Mr. O. S. B. Wall, a citizen of Oberlin, had recruited colored troops in Ohio under the direction of Major Stearns, who had his headquarters at Buffalo, N. Y. On the morning of the 15th of June, 1863, a squad of forty-eight recruits, headed by Powhatan Beaty, arrived at Columbus, Ohio, and reported to Mr. Wall to be forwarded to Boston, Massachusetts. Just before the men arrived he received a telegram from Major Stearns announcing that the Massachusetts regiments were full, and instructed him to send forward no more recruits. He distributed his recruits among the hospitable colored citizens of Columbus, and immediately repaired to the State House to secure an interview with the Governor. He explained his dilemma; that he had forty-eight recruits on his hands whom he had promised to put in Massachusetts regiments, and besought the Governor to accept them as a nucleus of a colored regiment to be raised by the State of Ohio. The Governor explained that he had urged Stanton to accept a regiment of soldiers of this character from Ohio, but that thus far his efforts had been unavailing. However, he promised Wall to try the Department once more, and requested him to call the next morning for an answer.

On the morning of June 16th the War Department telegraphed its consent and authority for the raising of a regiment of colored troops by the State of Ohio, and Governor Tod communicated this good news to Mr. Wall, and sent him forward at the head of his recruits to locate them in the rendezvous known as Camp Delaware, but which, at this time, was not occupied by white troops. Two days later the Governor issued the following letter of instructions respecting the recruitment of colored troops:

"Columbus, Ohio, *June* 18, 1863.
"*To Capt. Lewis McCoy, Present:*

"SIR,—Having been assigned to me for duty by General Mason, I direct that you proceed without delay to Camp Delaware, and there take the general charge and supervision of the recruits for the One Hundred and Twenty-seventh O. V. I. (colored) until further ordered. You will make such requisitions upon Quartermaster Burr and Commissioner Harrington as may be necessary for the efficiency and comfort of the troops. Report to me from time to time the progress you make.

"Respectfully yours,
"DAVID TOD, Governor."

The work of recruiting colored troops in Ohio went forward with great intelligence and zeal, until two regiments had been recruited and forwarded to the field.

On the 19th of November, 1863, the War Department authorized the Governor of Connecticut to raise a regiment to be designated as the "Twenty-ninth Regiment Connecticut Volunteers" (colored), to serve three years, or during the war; on the 23d of November, in General Orders No. 17, the work of recruiting this regiment was officially begun at Hartford.

This regiment made a splendid reputation, losing nineteen enlisted men killed, two officers wounded, one hundred and twenty-one enlisted men wounded, one enlisted man missing, making the total casualties one hundred and forty-three.

On the 12th of January, 1864, in General Orders No. 1, the Governor of Connecticut began the organization of another regiment of Negro troops, designated as the "Thirtieth Regiment Connecticut Volunteers" (colored). This regiment lost in the field one officer killed; enlisted men, thirteen; wounded, one officer; wounded, enlisted men, thirty-five; missing, one officer; missing, enlisted men, twenty-five, making the total casualties seventy-six. The whole number of colored volunteers furnished by Connecticut was 1,664, although the War Department makes it a thousand more.

The War Department gave authority to the Governor

of Indiana to raise a regiment composed of Negroes on the 30th of November, 1863. The regiment raised was designated as the "Twenty-eighth Regiment," and was complete by the 31st of March, 1864. It served with distinction in the Army of the James.

In Maryland and Virginia, North and South Carolina, and throughout the entire South, wherever the Union arms had penetrated, the indefatigable Adjutant-general of the Army had his agents welcoming the Negroes within the Federal lines, and offering them the uniform of a Union soldier. From the time the Bureau for the Organization of Colored Troops was opened, in May, until December, 1863, over 100,000 Negroes had been recruited, and it was estimated that a force of 50,000 of them was armed, equipped, and in the field. Two noble spirits triumphed in this great work, and the American people owe them a debt of imperishable gratitude. It matters not who doubted, faltered, or fell back, Edwin M. Stanton, Secretary of War, and Lorenzo Thomas, Adjutant-general of the Army, kept their faces to the front. They never turned aside for doubters, but held to the policy of arming Negroes, until it was crowned with glorious success. These Negro troops were General Thomas's pets, his children, and whenever the shock of their embattled arms leaped o'er the wires his heart thrilled with pride.

Not only had Negroes been accepted as volunteers, they had been included under the "Enrolment Act," and were accordingly drafted. Of course, Negroes were not included in the first call for volunteers on the 15th of April, 1861, nor in the other calls that preceded the Conscription Act of March 3, 1863. The Negro was not mentioned in this Act, but the War Department held that he was included in its provisions. On the 17th of October,

1863, a call was made for 300,000 volunteers, to serve for three years, or to the end of the war. They were to take the places of troops whose term of service was drawing to a close; and this was supplemental to the draft that was in operation at the time. In all States that should fail to furnish their quota of men by the 5th of January, 1864, a draft was ordered for that day. Under this Act the Negro was liable to be called into military service. On the first of February, 1864, a draft for 500,000 men, to serve three years, was ordered for March 10, 1864; and on the 14th of March, 1864, a draft for 200,000 men additional for the army and marine corps was ordered for the 15th of April, 1864. Under both of these drafts the Negro was apparently included. But the Act of February 24, 1864, equalizing the draft by calculating the quota of each district or precinct, and counting the number previously furnished by it, made special provisions for enrolment of Negroes. It provided that "All able-bodied male Colored persons, between the ages of twenty and forty-five years, resident in the United States, shall be enrolled according to the provisions of this act, and of the act to which this is an amendment, and form part of the national forces; and when a slave of a loyal master shall be drafted and mustered into the service of the United States, his master shall have a certificate therefor; and thereupon such slaves shall be free, and the bounty of one hundred dollars, now payable by law for each drafted man, shall be paid to the person to whom such drafted person was owing service or labor at the time of his muster into the service of the United States. The Secretary of War shall appoint a commission in each of the slave States represented in Congress, charged to award to each loyal person to whom a Colored volunteer may owe service a just compensation, not exceeding three hundred dollars, for each such Colored volunteer, payable out of the fund derived from commutations, and every such Colored volunteer, on being mustered into the service, shall be free. And in all cases where men of color have been enlisted, or have volunteered in the military service of the United States, all the provisions of this Act, so far as the payment of bounty and compensation are provided, shall be equally applicable as to those who may be hereafter recruited. But men of color, drafted or enlisted, or who may volunteer into the military service, while they shall be credited on the quotas of the several States, or subdivisions of States, wherein they are respectively drafted, enlisted, or shall volunteer, shall not be assigned as State troops, but shall be mustered into regiments or companies as United States Colored Troops."

Long before the above Act became a law, on the 20th of August, 1863, Judge Advocate Holt, in an elaborate and able opinion upon the legality of the employment of the Negro as a soldier, said: "In the interpretation given to the Enrolment Act, free citizens of African Descent are treated as citizens of the United States, in the sense of the law, and are everywhere being drafted into the military service."

As far as the enlistment of slaves was concerned, the Judge Advocate held that the Government could accept them upon two grounds: *First*, as *property;* and *second*, as *persons*. He cited the fact that both the organic law and usages of the Government justified the appropriation of private property to the public use on making compensation therefor. As to the second ground, he held that while persons of African descent were, under the laws of several States, recognized as property, nevertheless, under the Constitution and on the floor of Congress, they were regarded as "persons."

"The obligations of all persons—irrespective of creed or color—to bear arms," the Judge Advocate maintained, "if physically capable of doing so, in defence of the Government under which they live and by which they are protected, is one that is universally acknowledged and enforced. Corresponding to this obligation is the duty resting on those charged with the administration of the Government to employ such persons in the military service whenever the public safety may demand it."

But there was already, as has been shown, ample law for the military employment of Negroes under the Act of July 17, 1862, which empowered the President to receive into the military and naval service "persons of African Descent." The Negroes, both bond and free, had been invited by the Government to share the perils and honors of civil war; it was now seen to be a war about them, and was gradually becoming a war for them. The policy of arming the Negroes was now fully established, and the earnestness of the Government was only equalled by the enthusiasm of the host of Negro volunteers that rallied to the call for defenders of the American republic. The following corrected return exhibits the number of Negro troops in the Union Army during the Civil War:

Number of Negro Troops furnished by the States and Territories during the Civil War.

Connecticut	1,764
Delaware	954
District of Columbia	3,269
Illinois	1,811
Indiana	1,537
Iowa	440
Kansas	2,080
Kentucky	23,703
Carried forward	35,558

Brought forward	35,558
Maine	104
Maryland	8,718
Massachusetts	3,966
Michigan	1,387
Minnesota	104
Missouri	8,344
New Hampshire	125
New Jersey	1,185
New York	4,125
Ohio	5,092
Pennsylvania	8,612
Rhode Island	1,837
Vermont	120
West Virginia	196
Wisconsin	165
Not credited to any State	99,337
Total	178,975

The Negro Soldiers organized under the direct Authority of the General Government, and not credited to any State, were recruited as follows:

Alabama	4,969
Arkansas	5,526
Colorado	95
Florida	1,044
Georgia	3,486
Louisiana	24,052
Mississippi	17,869
North Carolina	5,035
South Carolina	5,462
Tennessee	20,133
Texas	47
Virginia	5,723
Enlisted at large	5,896
Total	99,337
Grand total	178,975

Of the number of colored troops credited to the States, 5,052 were obtained under the provisions of section 3 Act of Congress approved July 4, 1864, from the States that had seceded.

This was the largest force of civilized Negroes ever armed and marshalled for the field. It was without parallel in the world's history—ancient or modern, Pagan or Christian; it was unique. There was a touch of poetic justice in the sight — this army of ex-slaves who were eager to establish their freedom and vindicate their manhood.

The number of Negroes who held commissions as officers in the United States Volunteer Army during the War of the Rebellion was not considerable. The strong doubt that existed as to the Negro's qualifications for military life made it difficult for persons of that race to secure commissions. But Massachusetts took the initiative, and commissioned at least ten colored officers, and Kansas three, while two regiments of the Corps d'Afrique, raised by Generals Butler and Banks, were almost entirely officered by colored men. The precise number is not even known by the War Department, but there were at least seventy-five colored men who bore commissions in the Department of the Gulf for a short period of time. Lieutenant-colonel William N. Reed, of the First North Carolina (Thirty-fifth), was supposed by the officers of his regiment and other persons to be of Negro blood. He was educated in Germany, and was a splendid soldier. He commanded his regiment at the battle of Olustee, Florida, and he is reported as having led it into action in a most gallant manner; so great was the impression of his soldiership made in this engagement that those who witnessed the inspiring scene say that a regiment was never put into action with greater skill. He received mortal wounds in this conflict, and died a few days later at Beaufort, South Carolina.

An independent battery raised at Leavenworth, Kansas, December 23, 1864, to serve three years, was officered by colored men, as follows: H. Ford Douglass, Captain; W. D. Matthews, First Lieutenant; Patrick H. Minor, Second Lieutenant. Of the One Hundred and Fourth Regiment (U. S. C. T.), the major, Martin R. De Laney, and the captain of Company K, O. S. B. Wall, were colored men, but both were detailed in the Quartermaster's Department. Major De Laney had made something of a reputation before the war as an anti-slavery orator, as an African explorer, and as an editor, and Captain Wall had, without noise or ostentation, done noble service as a recruiting officer in Ohio, where he had been a resident for a number of years. He had been a successful boot and shoe merchant at Oberlin, Lorain County, Ohio, but as soon as colored troops were accepted he was one of the first men to take the field and secure their enlistment.

Being in Washington just after the two colored regiments had been raised in Ohio, at Camp Delaware, he called upon the Postmaster-general, William Dennison, and expressed his desire to serve his country in any capacity. At a subsequent Cabinet meeting the subject of commissioning colored officers was under discussion, when ex-Governor Dennison turned to Secretary Stanton, and said that he had a colored man that he could recommend for a commission in the army. Secretary Stanton said that if he had a competent man he would certainly commission him. Mr. Wall was sent for and directed to call upon the Secretary. As soon as he had reached the Secretary's office at the War Department, Stanton turned to him and said, "Now, sir, I propose to make you a captain in the United States Army by all the powers of this Government, and you shall be entitled to and enjoy all the emoluments and dignity of that position." Mr. Wall was directed to call upon Colonel Foster, and ask an examination for the position of captain. This was an unusual proceeding, and Colonel Foster refused to examine him. On learning this fact, the Secretary sent for Colonel Foster, and asked, in the presence of Mr. Wall, "Sir, did you get my order?" Colonel Foster: "I did, sir." The Secretary: "Do you intend to obey it?" Colonel Foster: "I do, sir." The Secretary: "Very well, sir; see then that you do, and let Mr. Wall be examined at once."

After some reflection Colonel Foster thought that it would be well to have Mr. Wall appointed a major instead of a captain, but Mr. Wall was content to have the orders of the Secretary carried out. His appointment was received with acclamations of joy by his neighbors in Oberlin, where, later, he was, at a public meeting, presented with an elegant sword. He served for nearly two years as quartermaster in the Bureau for Freedmen Refugees and Abandoned Lands, with headquarters at Charleston, South Carolina, where he displayed executive ability and business habits. He heard disputes and unravelled the feuds of refugees and freedmen; and having had charge of the abandoned property of the Government at that point, when he was mustered out he was able to give a clean report of every dollar's worth of it.

There were a number of Negro surgeons and chaplains commissioned during the war. Alexander T. Augusta was surgeon of the Seventh Regiment (U. S. C. T.), his commission dating from the 2d of October, 1863, and was made Brevet Lieutenant-colonel on the 13th of March, 1865. John V. De Grassee was Assistant Surgeon of the Thirty-fifth Regiment (U. S. C. T.), but was cashiered on November 1, 1864. Charles B. Purvis, Alpheus Tucker, John Rapier, William Ellis, Anderson R. Abbott, and William Powell were Hospital Surgeons at Washington, D. C.

Of colored chaplains, the following list is as complete as possible, the nationality of men in that position not being easy to trace: Henry M. Turner, First Regiment Infantry (U. S. C. T.); William Hunter, Fourth Regiment Infantry (U. S. C. T.); James Underdue, Thirty-ninth Regiment Infantry (U. S. C. T.); William Warring, One Hundred and Second Regiment Infantry (U. S. C. T.); Samuel Harrison, Fifty-fourth Massachusetts Regiment Infantry (Colored); William Jackson, Fifty-fifth Massachusetts Regiment Infantry (Colored); John R. Bowles, Fifty-fifth Massachusetts Regiment Infantry (Colored).

CHAPTER VI.

MILITARY STATUS OF NEGRO TROOPS.

THE legal status of the Negro soldier ought never to have been a mooted question. Ancient and modern history furnished safe and noteworthy precedents for the guidance of the Government in the War of the Rebellion. Two distinct questions were forced upon the Government: First, the legal right to employ free persons of African descent in the military service; second, the Constitutional power of the Government to emancipate and arm the slaves of its enemies.

While the Constitutions of the several States excluded free Negroes from the militia establishment, there was, nevertheless, no inhibition against their enlistment in the Volunteer and Regular Army of the United States. The words of the Constitution descriptive of persons eligible to military service are clear. On April 30, 1790, the words were: "able-bodied, of at least five feet six inches in height, and not under the age of eighteen, nor above the age of forty-six years." On March 3, 1795, the same description was adopted. March 3, 1799: "able-bodied, and of a size and age suitable for the public service, according to the directions which the President of the United States shall and may establish." March 16, 1802: "effective, able-bodied citizens of the United States, of at least five feet six inches high and between the ages of eighteen and forty-five years." In the Acts of December 24, 1811, January 11, 1812, January 20, 1813, and January

27, 1814: "effective, able-bodied men." In the Act of December 14, 1814: "free, effective, able-bodied men, between the ages of eighteen and forty-five years." June 12, 1847: "able-bodied men."

It is unnecessary to cite the law in support of the claim of free Negroes to citizenship since the adoption of the Constitution. During the war with Great Britain officers of the United States Army were regularly detailed by the War Department to recruit Negroes for military service. On the 21st of September, 1814, the free Negroes of Louisiana were invited to enlist in the United States Army by Andrew Jackson in special orders. There was no legal bar to the employment of troops of this character, and the right to incorporate them in the national military service was never challenged. But when the War of the Rebellion confronted the Government the question of arming free Negroes was opposed on prudential and political rather than upon legal grounds. Race prejudice proved to be more potent than law, and the war was well advanced before the military employment of Negroes received serious official consideration.

It was not the free Negro, however, who presented a problem so difficult of solution, but his brother in Southern bondage.

As to the second question, involving the Constitutional right of Congress to emancipate and arm the slaves of the enemies of the United States, there were grave doubts expressed. And yet a thousand facts of history for five thousand years were flashing their certain light on the path of a bewildered nation. Abraham had armed his own slaves in his war with the herdsmen. Greece and Rome had armed their slaves and rewarded their valor with citizenship. England had armed the slaves of her North American colonies, and henceforth they were free

British subjects. France, finding that Spain was about to wrest from her Hayti, converted her insurgent slaves into French soldiers. During the Revolutionary War the military commanders of the British forces and the leaders of the Continental troops appealed to the slaves to take up arms in their cause, offering them freedom as a reward. Each cause secured black levies, and the pledges of the military commanders in each case were ratified by their respective governments.

But it must not be overlooked that during the War of the Rebellion the case was somewhat different from any thus far cited. Slavery occupied an unique position in the United States; for while it existed perforce of custom in other countries, the foundations of the institution in America rested upon Constitutional law. And in the seat of Government slaves were bought and sold under the dome of the Capitol. This crime, this national disgrace, embarrassed every attempt of the Government to deal with slavery.

However, there was ample power under the Constitution to abolish the institution the moment the slave-holders' rebellion was begun. On the 26th of May, 1836, John Quincy Adams delivered a speech in the House of Representatives, in which he ably set forth the war powers of the Government: "There are, then, Mr. Chairman, in the *authority of Congress and of the Executive, two classes of powers, altogether different in their nature, and often incompatible with each other — the war power and the peace power.* The peace power is limited by regulations and restricted by provisions prescribed within the Constitution itself. *The war power* is limited only by the laws and usages of nations. This power is tremendous; *it is strictly constitutional, but it breaks down every barrier so anxiously erected for the protection of liberty, of property, and of life.* This, sir, is the power which authorizes you to pass the resolutions now before you, and, in my opinion, no other.

"But the war power of Congress over the institution of slavery in the States is yet far more extensive. Suppose the case of a servile war, complicated, as to some extent it is even now with an Indian War; suppose Congress were called to raise armies, *to supply money from the whole union to suppress a servile insurrection;* would they have no authority to interfere with the institution of slavery? The issue of a servile war may be disastrous; it may become necessary for the master of the slave to recognize his emancipation by a treaty of peace; can it for an instant be pretended that Congress, in such a contingency, would have no authority to interfere with the institution of slavery in any way in the States? Why, it would be equivalent to saying the Congress has no Constitutional authority to make peace. I suppose a more portentous case, certainly within the bounds of possibility— I would to God I could say, not within the bounds of probability.

"Do you imagine that your Congress will have no Constitutional authority to interfere with the institution of slavery, in any way, in the States of this Confederacy? Sir, they must and will interfere with it—perhaps to sustain it by war, perhaps to abolish it by treaties of peace; and they will not only possess the Constitutional power so to interfere, but they will be bound in duty to do it by the express provisions of the Constitution itself. From the instant that your slave-holding States become the theatre of a war, *civil, servile, or foreign war,* from that instant the war powers of Congress extend to interference with the institution of slavery, in every way by which it can be interfered with, from a claim of indemnity for slaves taken or destroyed, to the cession of States burdened with slavery to a foreign power."

In the annals of this young nation were just such precedents as the statesmen of the time needed for citation; but few thought of them. In December, 1814, General Jackson impressed a large number of slaves for the construction of fortifications, behind which he won the battle of New Orleans on the 8th of January, 1815. Many of these slaves were killed by the enemy's guns, and the owners, being loyal, applied to General Jackson for compensation. He would not recognize the claim, and the masters went before Congress; but the President and Congress sustained the decision of General Jackson.

During the Seminole War in Florida General T. S. Jesup secured the services of several Negro slaves as guides upon the condition that if they were faithful he would set them and their families at liberty. This was on the 25th of September, 1837. He kept faith with the slaves, and the War Department, the President, and Congress sustained his action. During the following year General Z. Taylor captured some Negroes near Tampa, Florida. The masters came to his camp to secure their slaves, and General Taylor told them that he had only prisoners of war. The masters desired to enter his camp for the purpose of identifying their property, but General Taylor ordered them away, with the observation that no citizens should ever search his camp for alleged property. He subsequently sent the Negroes to the West and gave them their liberty. The owners appealed to the War Department, and the President sustained General Taylor.

However, no man is so blind as the man who will not see. Few men cared to know the truth of history during the early part of the war. If there had been no warrant of law for the employment of the Negro as a soldier at the beginning of the war, sufficient authority was guaranteed by the several Acts of Congress and orders of the War Department. There were the Confiscation Act, August 6, 1861, and the following order of the War Department to General W. T. Sherman, October 14, 1861: "You will, however, in general, avail yourself of the services of any persons, whether fugitives from labor or not, who may offer themselves to the National Government. You will employ such persons in such services as they may be fitted for, either as ordinary employés, or, if 'special' [the word *special* interlined by President Lincoln, and in his own handwriting] circumstances seem to require it, in any other capacity, with such organization in squads, companies, or otherwise as you may deem most beneficial to the service. This, however, not to mean a general arming of them for military service.[1] You will assure all loyal masters that Congress will provide just compensation to them for the loss of the services of the persons so employed. And you will assure all persons held to involuntary labor, who may be thus received into the service of the Government, that they will under no circumstances be again reduced to their former condition, unless, at the expiration of their respective terms of service, they freely choose to return to the service of their former masters.

"It is believed that the course thus indicated will best secure the substantial rights of loyal masters, and the proper benefits to the United States of the services of all disposed to support the Government, while it will avoid all interference with the social systems or local institutions of every State, beyond that which insurrection makes unavoidable, and which a restoration of peaceful relations to

---

[1] This sentence interlined by the President.—G. W. W.

the Union under the Constitution will immediately remove."[1]

Then followed the amended Militia Law of July 17, 1862, the Confiscation and Emancipation Act of July 17, 1862, the War Department order to General Rufus Saxton, August 25, 1862, and the opinion of Judge Advocate Holt, August 20, 1863.

In the matter of the pay and bounty of Negro soldiers the action of the Government was manifestly unwise and unjust. In every army the Negro had served in—ancient and modern, Christian and Pagan—he had always received the same pay and allowances awarded to other soldiers. In the Revolutionary War it was sometimes said that slaves made expensive soldiers because they were purchased at public expense, and were then paid the same as white soldiers. General Jackson promised, "To every noble-hearted, generous freeman of color volunteering to serve during the present contest with Great Britain, and no longer, there will be paid the same bounty in money and lands now received by the white soldiers of the United States, viz., one hundred and twenty-four dollars in money and one hundred and sixty acres of land. The non-commissioned officers and privates will also be entitled to the same monthly pay and daily rations and clothes furnished to any American soldier."

When the war was over, these Negro soldiers applied for their bounty, and the matter was referred to the Attorney-general for his opinion. The Hon. William Wirt, of Virginia, was at the head of the Department of Justice, and he promptly rendered an opinion allowing that "colored troops were entitled to bounty and land."[2]

---

[1] Taken from the original draft, with the President's interlineation, in possession of the Hon. Simon Cameron.—G. W. W.

[2] "Opinions of Attorneys-general," vol. i., pp. 602, 603.

Two important decisions were rendered by Attorney-general Bates, one on the 23d of April, 1864, in the case of the Rev. Samuel Harrison, chaplain of the Fifty-fourth Massachusetts Volunteer Infantry, in which the question of his pay was raised on the ground of his nationality; the other opinion was rendered on the 14th of July, 1864, on the pay and bounty of colored soldiers. Both opinions were in favor of equal pay and bounty.[1]

On the 15th of June, 1864, the Army Appropriation Bill passed, with amendments, designed to do tardy justice to the Negro volunteer in the matter of pay and subsistence. The following are the sections of the bill relating to the matter:

"2. All persons of color who have been, or may be, mustered into the military service of the United States, shall receive the same uniform, clothing, arms, equipments, camp equipage, rations, medical and hospital attendance, pay, and emoluments, other than bounty, as other soldiers of the regular or volunteer forces of the United States of a like arm of the service, from and after the 1st of January, 1864. And every person of color who shall hereafter be mustered into the service shall receive such sums in bounty as the President shall order in the different States, not exceeding one hundred dollars.

"3. All persons enlisted and mustered into the service as volunteers under the call dated October 17, 1863, for three hundred thousand volunteers, who were at the time of enlistment actually enrolled and subject to draft in the State in which they volunteered, shall receive from the United States the same amount of bounty, without regard to color.

"4. All persons of color who were free on the 19th day

---

[1] "Opinions of Attorneys-general," vol. xi., pp. 37–43, 53–57.

of April, 1861, and who have been enlisted and mustered into the military service of the United States, shall from the time of their enlistment be entitled to receive the pay, bounty, and clothing allowed to such persons by the laws existing at the time of their enlistment; and the Attorney-general of the United States is hereby authorized to determine any question of law arising under this provision; and if the Attorney-general aforesaid shall determine that any such enlisted persons are entitled to receive any pay, bounty, or clothing, in addition to what they have already received, the Secretary of War shall make all necessary regulations to enable the pay department to make payment in accordance with such determination." [1]

Shortly after the above Act became a law, the Secretary of War issued an order to have Negro soldiers paid six months' full wages for the period embraced between January 1 and July 1, 1864. In August the Attorney-general rendered a decision in accordance with Section 4 of the above Act, that all Negroes volunteering prior to 1864 were entitled to the same pay, bounty, and clothing as other volunteers. By an Act of July 4, 1864, the widows and children of Negro soldiers dying in battle, or of wounds, or disease contracted in the military service, were declared entitled to pensions, provided such widows and children were free persons. The status of the Negro soldier up to this time had been equivocal. He had been called upon as a volunteer to defend the National Government against armed rebellion. He had been drafted into the army of

---

[1] Adjutant-general Thomas had repeatedly urged the increase of the compensation allowed Negro soldiers, and the Secretary of War recommended it in his report to Congress in October, 1863. "As soldiers of the Union," he wrote, "fighting under its banner, exposing their lives to uphold the Government, Colored Troops are entitled to enjoy its justice and beneficence."—G. W. W.

the United States. His obligations, responsibilities, and duties to, as well as his perils for, the Government were equal to those of his white comrade in arms. But his valor was doubted, and his right to bear arms in the public defence was sharply disputed. He was an experiment. The Act of the 17th of July, 1862, amending the Act of 1795, prescribing the manner of calling forth the militia, empowered the President to employ " persons of African Descent for the purpose of constructing intrenchments or performing camp service, or *any* war service for which they may be found competent." These persons of "African Descent" were to be enrolled and organized under regulations not inconsistent with the Constitution and the laws. They were to be compensated at the rate of ten dollars per month, with one ration per day, of which monthly pay three dollars might be in clothing. A stereotyped phrase in all orders issued by the War Department for the recruitment of Negro troops ran, "*To these troops no bounties will be paid. They will receive ten dollars per month and one ration per day, three dollars of which monthly pay may be in clothing.*" The War Department had employed the Negro as a soldier under the Act of the 17th of July, 1862, and was compelled to pay him according to the provisions of the same law. There was at the time no other way out of this difficulty. And while it was true that the proper interpretation of the law gave contrabands ten dollars per month, the Negro regiments for Massachusetts had the promise of the Government that they should receive the same pay as other troops. Major Geo. L. Stearns, accidentally learning that the Government had failed to keep faith with the Negro volunteers, hastened to Boston. Secretary Stanton had said, in his letter of the 26th January, 1863, granting Governor Andrew permission to raise these troops, that they should be included with other troops. Major Stearns headed a subscription list with two thousand dollars, and within three days raised fifty thousand dollars to make good the dishonored faith of the Government. His energy and skill, his humanity and benevolence, were positively without a parallel during the struggle for human liberty. He was almost ubiquitous in space, and with marvellous instinct knew every weak place along the lines of the cause of freedom. Wherever and whenever there was a gap in the line he was there, and from his marvellous resources commanded such remedies as were necessary for the exigencies of the case.

The enemies of the Negro and the obstructionists in Congress sought by every means and upon all occasions to prevent the passage of every appropriation bill that contained an item for the maintenance of the Negro troops already accepted by and in the service of the Government. And so the friends of the Negro had to be patient until a lagging public sentiment came up to a sense of the obligation of a great government to its loyal defenders.

Under date of the War Department, 25th of August, 1862, General Saxton was authorized and instructed to raise Negro troops. He was "to instruct them in military drill, discipline, and duty, and to command them." As to their compensation, the Secretary of War said: "The persons so received into the service and their officers to be entitled to and receive the same pay and rations as are allowed by law to volunteers in the service."[1] The regiment recently disbanded, and another one soon entered the service under this agreement of the War Department. Colonel T. W. Higginson, of the First South Carolina Volunteers, says: "The story of the attempt to cut down the pay of the Col-

---

[1] "Official Records of the War of the Rebellion," vol. xiv., pp. 377, 378.

ored Troops is too long, too complicated, and too humiliating to be here narrated. In the case of my regiment, there stood on record the direct pledge of the War Department to General Saxton that their pay should be the same as that of whites. So clear was this that our kind paymaster, Major W. J. Wood, of New Jersey, took upon himself the responsibility of paying the price agreed upon for five months, till he was compelled by express orders to reduce it from thirteen dollars per month to ten dollars, and from that to seven dollars, the pay of quartermaster's men and day-laborers. At the same time the 'stoppages' from the pay-rolls for the loss of all equipments and articles of clothing remained the same as for all other soldiers; so that it placed the men in the most painful and humiliating condition. Many of them had families to provide for; and between the actual distress, the sense of wrong, the taunts of those who had refused to enlist from the fear of being cheated, and the doubt how much further the cheat might be carried, the poor fellows were goaded to the utmost. In the Third South Carolina Regiment, Sergeant William Walker was shot, by order of court-martial, for leading his company to stack arms before their captain's tent, on the avowed ground that they were released from duty by the refusal of the Government to fulfil its share of the contract. The fear of such tragedies spread a cloud of solicitude over every camp of colored soldiers for more than a year; and the following series of letters will show through what wearisome labors the final triumph of justice was secured. In these labors the chief credit must be given to my admirable adjutant, Lieutenant G. W. Dewhurst. In the matter of bounty, justice is not yet obtained; there is a discrimination against those colored soldiers who were slaves on April 19, 1861. Every officer who, through indolence or benevolent design, claimed on his muster-rolls that all his men had been free on that day, secured for them the bounty; while every officer who, like myself, obeyed orders and told the truth in each case, saw his men and their families suffer for it, as I have done. A bill to abolish this distinction was introduced by Mr. Wilson at the last session, but failed to pass the House. It is hoped that next winter may remove this last vestige of the weary contest.

"To show how persistently and for how long a period these claims had to be urged on Congress, I reprint such of my own printed letters on the subject as are now in my possession. There are one or two of which I have no copies. It was especially in the Senate that it was so difficult to get justice done; and our thanks will always be especially due to Hon. Charles Sumner and Hon. Henry Wilson for their advocacy of our simple rights. The records of those sessions will show who advocated the fraud:

"'*To the Editor of the New York Tribune:*

"'SIR,—No one can overstate the intense anxiety with which the officers of Colored regiments in this Department are awaiting action from Congress in regard to arrears of pay of their men.

"'It is not a matter of dollars and cents only, it is a question of common honesty, whether the United States Government has sufficient integrity for the fulfilment of an explicit business contract.

"'The public seems to suppose that all required justice will be done by the passage of a bill equalizing the pay of all soldiers for the future. But, so far as my own regiment is concerned, this is but half the question. My men have been nearly sixteen months in service, and for them the immediate issue is the question of arrears.

"'They understand the matter thoroughly, if the public do not. Every one of them knows that he volunteered under an explicit *written assurance* from the War Department that he should have the pay of a white soldier. He knows that for five months the regiment received that pay, after which it was cut down from the promised thirteen dollars per month to ten dollars, for some reason to him inscrutable.

"'He does *not* know—for I have not yet dared tell the men—that the Paymaster has been already reproved by the Pay Department for fulfilling even in part the pledges of the War Department; that at the next payment the ten dollars are to be further reduced to seven; and that, to crown the whole, all the previous overpay is to be again deducted or "stopped" from the future wages, thus leaving them a little more than a dollar a month for six months to come, unless Congress interfere!

"'Yet so clear were the terms of the contract that Mr. Solicitor Whiting, having examined the original instructions from the War Department issued to Brigadier-general Saxton, Military Governor, admits to me (under date of December 4, 1863) that "the faith of the Government was thereby pledged to every officer and soldier enlisted under that call."

"'He goes on to express the generous confidence that "the pledge will be honorably fulfilled." I observe that every one at the North seems to feel the same confidence, but that, meanwhile, the pledge is unfulfilled. Nothing is said in Congress about fulfilling it. I have not seen even a proposition in Congress to pay the Colored soldiers, *from date of enlistment,* the same pay with white soldiers; and yet anything short of this is an unequivocal breach of contract, so far as this regiment is concerned.

"'Meanwhile, the land sales are beginning, and there is danger of every foot of land being sold from beneath my soldiers' feet, because they have not the petty sum which Government first promised, and then refused to pay.

"'The officers' pay comes promptly and fully enough, and this makes the position more embarrassing. For how are we to explain to the men the mystery that Government can afford us a hundred or two dollars a month, and yet must keep back six of the poor thirteen which it promised them? Does it not naturally suggest the most cruel suspicions in regard to us? And yet nothing but their childlike faith in their officers, and in that incarnate soul of honor, General Saxton, has sustained their faith, or kept them patient, thus far.

"'There is nothing mean or mercenary about these men in general. Convince them that the Government actually needs their money, and they would serve it barefooted and on half rations, and without a dollar—for a time. But, unfortunately, they see white soldiers beside them whom they know to be in no way their superiors for any military service, receiving hundreds of dollars for re-enlisting from this impoverished Government, which can only pay seven dollars out of thirteen to its black regiments. And they see, on the other hand, those Colored men who refuse to volunteer as soldiers, and who have found more honest paymasters than the United States Government, now exulting in well-filled pockets, and able to buy the little homesteads the soldiers need, and to turn the soldiers' families into the streets. Is this a school for self-sacrificing patriotism?

"'I should not speak thus urgently were it not becoming manifest that there is to be no promptness of action in Congress, even as regards the future pay of Colored soldiers—and that there is especial danger of the whole matter of *arrears* going by default. Should it be so, it will be a repudiation more ungenerous than any which Jefferson Davis advocated or Sydney Smith denounced. It will sully with dishonor all the nobleness of this opening page of history, and fix upon the North a brand of meanness worse than either Southerner or Englishman has yet dared to impute. The mere delay in the fulfilment of this contract has already inflicted untold suffering, has impaired discipline, has relaxed loyalty, and has begun to implant a feeling of sullen distrust in the very regiments whose early career solved the problem of the nation, created a new army, and made peaceful emancipation possible. T. W. HIGGINSON,

"'Colonel commanding First South Carolina Volunteers.
"'Beaufort, South Carolina, January 22, 1864.'"

"'Headquarters First South Carolina Volunteers,
"'Beaufort, South Carolina, Sunday, *February* 14, 1864.
"'*To the Editor of the New York Times:*

"'May I venture to call your attention to the great and cruel injustice which is impending over the brave men of this regiment?

"'They have been in military service for over a year, having volunteered, every man, without a cent of bounty, on the written pledge of the War Department that they should receive the same pay and rations with white soldiers.

"'This pledge is contained in the written instructions of Brigadier-general Saxton, Military Governor, dated August 25, 1862. Mr. Solicitor Whiting, having examined those instructions, admits to me that "the faith of the Government was thereby pledged to every officer and soldier under that call."

"'Surely, if this fact were understood, every man in the nation would see that the Government is degraded by using for a year the services of the brave soldiers, and then repudiating the contract under which they were enlisted. This is what will be done should Mr. Wilson's bill, legalizing the back pay of the army, be defeated.

"'We presume too much on the supposed ignorance of these men. I have never yet found a man in my regiment so stupid as not to know when he was cheated. If fraud proceeds from Government itself, so much the worse, for this strikes at the foundation of all rectitude, all honor, all obligation.

"'Mr. Senator Fessenden said, in the debate on Mr. Wilson's bill, January 4, that the Government was not bound by the unauthorized promises of irresponsible recruiting officers. But is the Government itself an irresponsible recruiting officer? and if men have volunteered in good faith on the written assurances of the Secretary of War, is not Congress bound, in all decency, either to fulfil those pledges or to disband the regiments?

"'Mr. Senator Doolittle argued in the same debate that white soldiers should receive higher pay than black ones, because the families of the latter were often supported by Government. What an astounding statement of fact is this! In the white regiment in which I was formerly an officer (the Massachusetts Fifty-first) nine-tenths of the soldiers' families, in addition to the pay and bounties, drew regularly their "State aid." Among my black soldiers, with half-pay and no bounty, not a family receives any aid. Is there to be no limit, no end to the injustice we heap upon this unfortunate people? Cannot even the fact of their being in arms for the nation, liable to die any day in its defence, secure them ordinary justice? Is the nation so poor, and so utterly demoralized by its pauperism, that after it has had the lives of these men, it must turn round to filch six dollars of the monthly pay which the Secretary of War promised to their widows? It is even so, if the excuses of Mr. Fessenden and Mr. Doolittle are to be accepted by Congress and by the people.

"'Very respectfully, your obedient servant,
"'T. W. HIGGINSON,
"'Colonel commanding First South Carolina Volunteers.'"

But there was another phase of this question of inequality between white and black troops. The policy of arming Negroes was never contemplated by the Government until military necessity lifted her stern voice, and political evolution brought the Negro forward as *the* problem of the war. General Hunter's idea in organizing Negro troops was to use them in taking possession of the island plantations in South Carolina, and holding these as a basis of supply for an operating army. Nevertheless, it is due to the memory of this grand military character to record that from the first he entertained the highest ideas of the Negro, both as a man and a soldier. The authority granted Governor Andrew, of Massachusetts, to raise companies of troops, including Negroes, contemplated using such troops to garrison "the forts of Massachusetts and elsewhere." Adjutant-general Thomas, in a speech to the army in Mississippi, April 8, 1863, said he would take the Negro "regiments and put them in the rear." In concluding his speech he emphasized his plan. "Recollect," he said, "for every regiment of blacks I raise, I raise a regiment of whites to face the foe in the field." This seemed to be the policy of the Government, and General Thomas was fully authorized to speak and act for both the Secretary of War and the President. This was after the battles of Port Hudson and Milliken's Bend; and this was practically the end of the fighting of Negro troops in the Department of the Gulf. These troops, both under Generals Butler and Banks, were consigned to garrison duty. In the army of the Cumberland Negro troops had the same misfortune; they were used in garrison and upon fatigue duty almost exclusively.

The parent of this policy was the cruel doubt that lurked in every quarter lest the Negro would not fight in the open field. His military employment was apologized for in some quarters upon the ground that he was to be the merest servant to the white soldier. The idea was dangerous and degrading from the first. The difference in pay between the white and black troops was no less damaging to the Government than it was unjust to the Negro. It made an unnatural distinction among patriots enlisted in the same sacred cause, and it impaired the usefulness of a class of troops who were on trial before a doubting, sneering world. The extraordinary amount of fatigue duty required of these troops seriously detracted from their military character. Frequently entire regiments were excused from drill, and were abandoned to almost total ignorance of the simplest duties of a soldier. In a letter to the officer in charge of the organization of Negro troops at Nashville, Tennessee, Colonel Thomas J. Morgan, of the Fourteenth United States Colored Troops, said, under date of December 6, 1863, from Gallatin, Tennessee, "I feel so great an interest in the success of the regiment which I have the honor to command, and of the entire corps 'd'Afrique,' that I cannot refrain from making another effort to secure the return of the Fourteenth Regiment to this point. I send you a communication which I desire to be forwarded to Major-general *Thomas*, asking that the regiment be ordered back to Gallatin. And I would most earnestly ask that Major *Stearns* be urged to use his influence with the Secretary of War to secure this point. The raising of Negro Regiments in this Department is an experiment as yet, and its success depends largely upon the impression made upon the public mind by those Regiments now formed and organizing during the present winter." After making some observations about public sentiment concerning troops of this character, he continued: "It behooves the friends of this movement to secure a favorable decision from the great tribunal—public opinion. This cannot be done by making laborers of these Troops. The best of soldiers must needs work; and commanders of Negro Regiments are willing that the Troops under their command shall do their part in all Army labor incident to Camp life, or required by the exigencies of the hour. But they feel it to be degrading to single out Colored Troops for fatigue duty, while white soldiers stand idly by. Such treatment savors too much of the old *régime*, and if persisted in will utterly ruin the prospects of the work of here making soldiers of black men. Negroes will not enlist for this purpose, nor will efficient officers enter the service. The class of men who are willing to take hold, with all their energies, to drill and discipline a body of soldiers will not, for any consideration, consent to become overseers for black men. Rather would they carry their rifles in the ranks of fighting men."

No response came, and Colonel Morgan, nothing daunted, wrote a letter to Major-general Reynolds, at Washington, D. C., bearing date of December 6, 1863:

"Allow me to ask that, if not inconsistent with the public service, the six companies of the Regiment I have the honor to command, which are now at Bridgeport, Alabama, doing fatigue duty, be ordered back to Gallatin for the purpose of drill, discipline, and the legitimate duties of the soldier, for the work which the Government expects the soldier to perform.

"The Government, through its executive, has said that it knows no distinction among its soldiers arising from Color. It was with the clear understanding that the officers and men of Colored Regiments were to be treated in every respect as white soldiers that I and those officers with me accepted the positions we now hold. We are proud of such places, and are willing to devote all our energies to drill, discipline, and instruct Colored men in their duty as *soldiers;* but rather would I carry my rifle in the ranks of fighting men than hold any position as overseer of black laborers.

"I will very cheerfully perform my proportion of the labor required by the exigencies of the hour, but I do not feel that it is just, either to officers or men, to require Colored Regiments to perform fatigue duty for other troops.

"The Government is in need of fighting men, and it proposes to form Regiments of such out of the numerous able-bodied black men in the enemy's land. To make these men efficient soldiers will require rigid discipline, careful instruction, and untiring drill. This will be impossible so long as they are used as common laborers."

No officer of Negro troops ever entertained loftier sentiments or sounder views of their military status than Colonel Morgan. He had sounded the key-note; and other white officers in these organizations, although lacking his moral and intellectual breadth, saw at once that the brave men they commanded were not fairly dealt with. The discrimination became notorious in every department where Negro troops were stationed, and the newspaper correspondents joined in an earnest protest against the injustice. Public sentiment was changing all the time. Adjutant-general Thomas became convinced at last that the policy of converting Negro regiments into squads of laborers was unjust and detrimental, and issued the following order:

"The incorporation into the army of the United States of Colored Troops renders it necessary that they should be brought as speedily as possible to the highest state of discipline.

"Accordingly, the practice which has hitherto prevailed, no doubt from necessity, of requiring these troops to perform most of the labor on fortifications, and the labor and fatigue duties of permanent stations and camps, will cease, and they will be only required to take their fair share of fatigue duty with white troops. This is necessary to prepare them for the higher duties of conflicts with the enemy.

"By order of the Secretary of War.
"L. THOMAS,
"Adjutant-general."

In the Department of the South the Negro soldier was often used to do fatigue duty for white troops, and this became so notorious that it called forth the following order:
"Department of the South, Headquarters in the Field,
"Morris Island, South Carolina, *September* 17, 1863.
"*General Orders No.* 77.
"I. It has come to the knowledge of the Brigadier-general Commanding that detachments of colored troops, detailed for fatigue duty,

have been employed, in one instance at least, to prepare camps and perform menial duty for white troops. Such use of these details is unauthorized and improper, and is hereafter expressly prohibited. Commanding Officers of colored regiments are directed to report promptly to these Headquarters any violations of this order which may come to their knowledge."

And the following order was subsequently issued, showing that General Gillmore intended to put a stop to this abuse of colored troops:

> "Department of the South, Headquarters in the Field,
> "Folly Island, South Carolina, *November* 25, 1863.

"*General Orders No.* 105.

"I. The Major-general Commanding has heretofore had occasion to rebuke officers of this command for imposing improper labors upon colored troops. He is now informed that the abuses sought to be corrected still exist. Attention is called to General Order No. 77, current series, from these Headquarters, and commanding officers are enjoined to its strict enforcement. Colored troops will not be required to perform any labor which is not shared by the white troops, but will receive in all respects the same treatment, and be allowed the same opportunities for drill and instruction."

On the 1st of January, 1863, Horace Greeley wrote the following admirable views respecting the use of Negro troops in garrison:

"It has been supposed that these black troops would prove fitter for garrison duty than active service in the field. No impression could be more mistaken. Their fidelity as sentinels adapts them especially, no doubt, to garrison duty, but their natural place is in the advance. There is an inherent dash and fire about them which white troops of more sluggish Northern blood do not emulate, and their hearty enthusiasm shows itself in all ways. Such qualities are betrayed even in drill, as anybody may know who has witnessed the dull, mechanical way in which ordinary troops make a bayonet charge on the parade-ground, and contrasts it with the spirit of those Negro troops in the same movement. They are to be used, moreover, in a country which they know perfectly. Merely from their knowledge of wood-craft and water-craft, it would be a sheer waste of material to keep them in garrison. It is scarcely the knowledge which is at once indispensable and impossible to be acquired by our troops. See these men, and it is easier to understand the material of which the famous Chasseurs d'Afrique are composed."

Garrison life is trying and tempting to the best troops, and it is not infrequently positively demoralizing. The largest portion of these troops had been recruited from the plantations; they were enthusiastic and eager to enter upon the active service and practical duties of military life. It was natural, therefore, that they should be restive, sullen, and sometimes insubordinate — for their officers were not exempt from the insidious influences of the permanent camp. It is a mournful fact that the Fourth Regiment of the Corps d'Afrique, garrisoning Fort Jackson, on the Mississippi River, was guilty of many a wide breach of military discipline. But even in this most notable case the cause was the inefficiency of officers. There were other cases of lax discipline among these troops, but the order of the Adjutant-general sent them to the drill-ground, and within one hundred days they were absolutely transformed. Elevated by the majesty of law to the actual position of soldiers of a proud republic, receiving the same amount of remuneration in bounty, wages, rations, and clothing, and equally and unreservedly intrusted with the national honor and charged with the public defence, the heart of the Negro army was instinct with gratitude, pride, and martial valor.

CHAPTER VII.

NEGRO IDIOSYNCRACIES.

The Negro is a strong man physically; Nature has endowed him with marvellous strength of limb and constitution. The color of skin, texture of hair, solidity of cranium, and perfect teeth are his safeguards against the malignant forces of the climate of Africa. Transplanted, he bears well the semi-tropical climate of the Southern United States.

Generations of servitude did not impair his physical virtues, but rather enhanced them. He was proof against the intensest heat and most deadly fevers, and could endure the pangs of hunger and thirst with peerless fortitude. His teeth were representative of unusually sound bones throughout a massive body. Nature gave him clear and sharp eyes for nature. His acute hearing warned him of danger and devoured every strain of music, whether in the sublime disturbance of the elements or in the touching, pathetic song or story of his fellows.

To the physical perfections of the Negro were added mental endowments not to be despised. The Negro has an amiable disposition, a sunny nature, and a happy-go-lucky spirit under the most trying circumstances. He is gentle, submissive, teachable, and strongly attached to those who treat him with kindness. But he is no coward. He is not easily provoked into violent exhibitions of temper, but when aroused cannot easily be soothed. He is thoroughly unselfish, and is constant as a friend. He is patient and docile in suffering and in loss, and his spirit is one of resignation and contentment. His domesticity is proverbial, and his affection for persons and places has often worn the charm of genuine poetry. His bright fancy and romantic thoughts lead him to the enjoyment of fiction and poetry; and if to his rare native ability had been added the culture of the academy, both fiction and poetry would have been his debtors. His devotion to an interest he espouses is absolute. His service to a sentiment, whether of friendship, love, or religion, is enthusiastic and noble. He is sentimental in the best sense. Like all unlettered races, the Negro as a slave was very superstitious, especially in matters which philosophy and science explain to educated races. In religious matters he was the trustful child, grasping eagerly the great primal truths—man a sinner, Christ a savior. His orthodoxy may not have been up to the standard of the schools, but he believed unhesitatingly in the impotency of man and the omnipotence of God.

Unable to harness his thoughts to the polished and balanced phrases of refined expression, the Negro turned the impetuous current of his feeling into rhyme. He did not speak, he gurgled, cried, and sang out of his soul. A peculiar intonation held fellowship with his verse—pleading, tender, pathetic, heroic, and sometimes sublime—always interesting. His rich voice could mount the highest scale and reach the deepest note. It had a tremulous sweetness in it that revealed its kinship to sorrow, but at times it rang with a hope and spiritual valiancy. His unique proverbs and quaint sayings are pregnant with meaning, wit, and philosophy; they will occupy a curious and interesting place in the folk-lore of the world.

The Negro's love of music and song taught him the poetry of movement, and his grace, under the influence of music, was quite captivating in a laborer. His movement in field or cabin, at toil or in recreation, marked him as alert and full of fine spirit.

That the Negro had blemishes upon his body and character history does not assume to deny. Overworked, poorly fed, partially clothed, wretchedly housed, and cruelly treated, his body grew ill-shaped.

Petty stealing and persistent prevarication were prompted by hunger and fear, and not by the Negro's normal moral nature. The apparent wanton violation of the seventh commandment was traceable to the demolition of the family altar by the slave-holders. If he were cruel to his offspring at times, it was but under the occasional influence of the organized cruelty of a most cruel institution. It was sporadic, not generic; the exception and not the rule of his conduct. But his genuine religious bias helped him over many difficult places, stayed his hand, checked his temper, and turned his feet from temptation when, otherwise, he would have succumbed to his trials and dangers. His obedience to law was unquestioning and uncomplaining.

Taken for all in all, the Negro slave was a remarkable personage. His powerful physique, his celerity and poetry of movement, his sentiment and love of music, his firm attachment to friends, his deep longing for freedom, his splendid courage and power of endurance, his patience in suffering and hope in despair, his trust in God and instinct for the right, his cunning aptitude and perfect obedience eminently qualified him for military service in the imperilled cause of the Union in the War of the Rebellion.

CHAPTER VIII.

THE OUTLOOK.

Even after the Negro had obtained the uniform and musket of a Union soldier he was persistently denied public confidence. His enslavement by the dominant race for centuries furnished no illustration of racial valor. A few irascible Negroes had inaugurated puny insurrections, but they were destitute of that element of enlightened courage which invests revolutions for liberty with invincible power. It was asked if the Negro have courage why has he not shown it during the last two centuries? There was no room for defence, little for apology. It was true that their numbers were inconsiderable and their leaders few. As rapidly as leaders developed they disappeared. The Underground Railroad was the safety-valve to the institution of slavery, else it would have been blown into atoms. These fugitive slaves became agitators at the North, and assisted in bringing about the condition of affairs in which bullets took the place of books, and cannon supplanted counsel.

Even the most advanced leaders on the Union side, the antislavery friends of the Negro, were neither willing to affirm nor deny the Negro's courage in a military encounter. A very few well-informed persons felt quite sure of the Negro's fighting qualities under any circumstance. They knew the past, and were enabled to predicate their belief upon incontestable historical data. But the Negro was a soldier now, and there was but one thing left to do, and that was to try his mettle under fire. On the 16th of February, 1863, the *New York Times*, in a careful and conservative editorial, expressed the doubt that seemed to oppress the public mind:

"Whether they are or are not, by nature, by law, or by usage, the equals of the white man, makes not the slightest difference in this respect. Even those at the North who are so terribly shocked at the prospect of their being thus employed confine their objections to grounds of expediency. They urge,

"1st. That the Negroes will not fight. This, if true, is conclusive against their being used as soldiers. But we see no way of testing the question except by trying the experiment. It will take but a very short time and but very few battles to determine whether they have courage, steadiness, subjection to military discipline, and the other qualities essential to good soldiership or not. If they have, this objection will fall; if not, then beyond all question they will cease to be employed.

"2d. It is said that the whites will not fight with them, that the prejudice against them is so strong that our citizens will not enlist, or will quit the service if compelled to fight by their side, and that we shall thus lose two white soldiers for one black one that we gain. If this is true they ought not to be employed. The object of using them is to strengthen our military force, and if the project does not accomplish this it is a failure. The question, moreover, is one of fact, not of theory. It matters nothing to say that it *ought* not to have this effect, that the prejudice is absurd and should not be consulted. The point is not what men *ought* to do, but what they will *do*. We have to deal with human nature, with prejudice, with passion, with habits of thought and feeling, as well as with reason and sober judgment and the moral sense. Possibly the Government may have made a mistake in its estimate of the effect of this measure on the public mind. The use of Negroes as soldiers may have a worse effect on the army and on the people than they have supposed.

"But this is matter of opinion upon which men have differed. Very prominent and influential persons—Governors of States, Senators, popular editors, and others—have predicted the best results from such a measure, while others have anticipated the worst. The President has resolved to try the experiment. If it works well, the country will be the gainer. If not, we have no doubt it will be abandoned. If the effect of using Negroes as soldiers upon the army and the country proves to be depressing and demoralizing, so as to weaken rather than strengthen our military operations, they will cease to be employed. The President is a practical man, not at all disposed to sacrifice practical results to abstract theories.

"3d. It is said we shall get no Negroes—or not enough to prove of any service. In the free States very few will volunteer, and in the slave States we can get but few, because the Rebels will push them southward as fast as we advance upon them. This may be so; we confess we share with many others the opinion that it will.

"But we may as well wait patiently the short time required to settle the point. When we hear more definitely from Governor Sprague's black battalions, and Governor Andrew's Negro brigades, we shall know more accurately what to think of the measure as one for the free States; and when we hear further of the success of General Banks and General Saxton in enlisting them at the South, we can form a better judgment of the movement there. If we get very few, or even none, the worst that can be said will be that the project is a failure, and the demonstration that it is so will have dissipated another of the many delusions which dreamy people have cherished about this war.

"4th. The use of Negroes will exasperate the South, and some of our Peace Democrats make that an objection to the measure. We presume it will; but so will any other scheme we may adopt which is warlike and effective in its character and results. If that consideration is to govern us, we must follow Mr. Vallandigham's advice and stop the war entirely, or, as Mr. McMasters puts it in his Newark speech, go ' for an immediate and *unconditional* peace.' We are not quite ready for *that* yet.

"The very best thing that can be done under existing circumstances, in our judgment, is to possess our souls in patience while *the experiment* is being tried. The problem will probably speedily solve itself—much more speedily than heated discussion or harsh criminations can solve it."

But this was not all—this cold, silent doubt—that confronted the Negro. This was but the negative side of the obstacles that obstructed his way to the battle-fields of the Republic. The mobocratic element in the larger cities was always at the service of Negro-haters who violently opposed the military employment of Negroes. Up to the breaking out of the Rebellion, Negroes had not only been sold at the South, but freely mobbed in the North; along with Abolitionists they were despised, proscribed, and assaulted. So when the exigencies of a great civil war seemed to call the Negro from obscurity and the dark places assigned him by race prejudice, he was confronted by intense malevolence. It was indeed a strange spectacle to see a regiment of Negro soldiers guarded by a municipal police force! When the Fifty-fourth Massachusetts Volunteer Infantry was ready to leave the Commonwealth for the seat of war, it was determined to have it pass through New York City; but the "Chief of the Metropolitan Police Force" telegraphed Governor Andrew, of Massachusetts, that he would be unable to protect this regiment of loyal Negroes against mob violence. The regiment did not pass through New York City, but went from Boston to the scene of war in South Carolina by water.

The Draft Riots had occurred in New York and elsewhere while the recruitment of Negro troops was in a tentative form in the Eastern and Middle States, and the objects of the rioters' special wrath were inoffensive Negro men, defenceless women, and helpless children. The Draft Riots in New York City began on Monday morning, July 13, 1863. There will be no attempt here to describe the infuriated mobs that destroyed human life and property in their resistance to the draft, but only so much of the bloody drama must be told as affects the Negro martyrs. Nowhere did the fury of the mob flame more furiously than in the abodes of Negroes. Restaurants and hotels and other places where this unhappy people were employed were visited with fell destruction. The furniture and tableware were destroyed, while the Negroes were driven before a storm of oaths, bludgeons, and brickbats. From place to place where Negroes were known to be employed the mob swayed and swaggered with increasing insolence and cruelty. Negroes were constrained to run for their lives, leap into the river, and cast themselves from their hiding-places on roofs of houses. A Negro residing in Carmine Street was seized by a mob of above four hundred persons as he was leaving his stables on Clarkson Street. He was beaten and kicked upon the ground until life was almost extinct; he was then hung upon a tree, and a fire was built under him, which revived his consciousness, while the smoke strangled him.

In the afternoon an up-town mob was destroying every building where Negroes were known to be employed. In the midst of their diabolical work some human fiend cried, "To the Colored Orphan Asylum!" Celtic malice and religious intolerance led the way with frantic glee. The asylum was a handsome and substantial structure, having been erected in 1858. It was located on Fifth Avenue, between Forty-third and Forty-fourth streets, and gave shelter to nearly eight hundred children. The mob fell upon this building with fury untempered by mercy. The rooms were sacked, the spoils thrown out to a multitude of Irishwomen, who, amid wild cheers, bore them away in triumph. The inmates were beaten most cruelly, and even the little children were kicked and ruthlessly trampled upon. To crown this inhuman crime, arson was added to murder, and the building was fired. The gallant Chief Decker resisted the mob with martial spirit. He extinguished the flames and threw his stalwart person into the door-way to check the mob. His noble remonstrance was in vain; he was overpowered, and again the fire-fiends applied the torch, and the building perished in the flames.

Among the ignorant and prejudiced whites the Negro was regarded as the real cause of the draft, and this demonstration of murderous violence against him was as hurtful to a patriotic war sentiment as it was perilous to the Negro himself; and it was especially unfortunate that it came at a time when the Negro had just been called to the bar of public sentiment. The Emancipation Proclamation of September 22, 1862, which was preliminary in character, had made the Negro problem more prominent than ever, and provoked public criticisms. The probationary period had elapsed, and the final Emancipation Proclamation had been issued on the 1st of January, 1863.

It was midsummer now, and these bloody riots told how deeply rooted and inveterate were race malice, and party grudges. These were not manifested exclusively by the mobs, not alone by the ignorant, foreign-born population. Men born and educated under the influence of the beneficent institutions of the great republic here and in the West; men who owed their preferment and commanding positions to the simplicity and genuine democracy of the Government, were either the hired enemies of the Union or the willing assassins of the national life. Too cowardly to stake their convictions upon the chances of honorable warfare, they lurked in the rear to plot. They hissed the Union soldier, despised the Union flag, and, as copperheads, crawled upon their stomachs, hissing and biting at the heels of Union men and Union measures. No language was too strong to express their hatred of the Negro and their opposition to his enrolment in the army of the United States. These men, like the serpent in Eden, were very plausible, and the field in which they operated was at a safe distance from the contending armies. Even the home of the President contained many of these plotters. In responding to an invitation of unconditional Union men of Illinois, the President made the following reference to the enemies of the Negro: "You say you will not fight to free Negroes. Some of them seem to be willing enough to fight for you. But no matter; they fight, then, exclusively to save the Union. I issued the Proclamation on purpose to aid you in saving the Union. Whenever you shall have conquered all resistance to the Union, if I shall urge upon you to continue fighting, it will be an apt time then for you to declare that you will not fight to free Negroes. I thought that in your struggle for the Union, to whatever extent the Negroes should cease helping the enemy, to that extent it weakened the enemy in their resistance to you.

"Do you think differently? I thought that whatever Negroes can be got to do as soldiers leaves just so much less for white soldiers to do in saving the Union. Does it appear otherwise to you? But Negroes, like other people, act upon motive. Why should they do anything for us, if we will do nothing for them? If they stake their lives for us, they must be prompted by the strongest motive, even the promise of freedom, and the promise being made, must be kept."

This was written on the 26th of August, 1863, just after the Draft Riots. The President goes on in his letter to recount the victories of the Union arms in the Mississippi, and makes felicitous mention of the glorious part borne by Negro soldiers who were severely tested at Port Hudson. The President then concludes in this homely manner, referring to the early restoration of peace:

"It will then have been proved that among freemen there can be no successful appeal from the ballot to the bullet, and that they who take such appeal are sure to lose their case and pay the costs; and then there will be some black men who can remember that, with silent tongue, and with clinched teeth, and with steady eye and well-poised bayonet, they have helped mankind on to this great consummation, while I fear that there will be some white men unable to forget that, with malignant heart and deceitful speech, they have striven to hinder it."

But the feeling against the Negro as a man and a soldier was not confined to the blatant assistant—rebels in the rear. There was a bitter feeling in the Border State regiments and among troops from the populous Atlantic seaboard cities. Complexional prejudice and social caste were eating like cankers into the good-sense and patriotism of the rank and file of the army; and it was not a cheerful outlook for the Negro volunteer to feel that his white comrades in arms looked down upon him, distrusted him, disliked him. The cold fact was there, however, and the Negro sometimes encountered it to his hurt. But the Negro soldier was patient; all he asked was safe passage to the battle-field, and once in conflict with the enemy he would win for himself a new name by desperate deeds of valor.

On the 8th of December, 1863, in a message to the Congress, the President referred to the Negro question in his usual solemn manner: "The preliminary emancipation proclamation issued in September was running its assigned period to the beginning of the new year. A month later the final proclamation came, including the announcement that colored men of suitable condition would be received into the war service. The policy of emancipation and of employing black soldiers gave to the future a new aspect, about which hope and fear and doubt contended in uncertain conflict. According to our political system, as a matter of civil administration, the General Government had no lawful power to effect emancipation in any State, and for a long time it had been hoped that the rebellion could be suppressed without resorting to it as a military measure. It was all the while deemed possible that the necessity for it might come, and that, if it should, the crisis of the contest would then be presented. It came, and, as we anticipated, it was followed by dark and doubtful days."

But there was a gradual change all the time for the better in public sentiment regarding the Negro. Even New York City was susceptible to the widening influences of humanity and patriotism. A short time after the riots Negroes were recruited in the metropolis, and by the spring of 1864 were quite tolerable to the late rioters. When the Twentieth Regiment United States Colored Troops was ready to leave its rendezvous on Riker's Island, it was proposed by its friends—chiefly members of the Union League

Club—to tender it a public reception in New York City. Some members of the committee on recruitment of Negro troops were unwilling to expose the regiment to the rancorous hate of the mobocratic element of New York City, and protested against any demonstration. The committee wrote the commander of the regiment, Colonel Nelson B. Bartram, asking if he thought his regiment could get through all right. Colonel Bartram sent back a soldierly answer: "Give me room to land my regiment, and if it cannot march through New York it is not fit to go into the field." The question of the regiment coming was settled. The police cleared a space for it to disembark at Thirty-sixth Street, and with loaded muskets and fixed bayonets, with company front and martial music, the first regiment of Negro soldiers marched through New York City. The magnificent bearing of the men extorted the wildest enthusiasm and cheers among the very persons who had participated in the Draft Riots.

"The scene of yesterday," says a New York paper, " was one which marks an era of progress in the political and social history of New York. A thousand men with black skins, and clad and equipped with the uniforms and arms of the United States Government, marched from their camp through the most aristocratic and busy streets, received a grand ovation at the hands of the wealthiest and most respectable ladies and gentlemen of New York, and then moved down Broadway to the steamer which bears them to their destination—all amid the enthusiastic cheers, the encouraging plaudits, the waving handkerchiefs, the showering bouquets, and other approving manifestations of a hundred thousand of the most loyal of our people.

"In the month of July last the homes of these people were burned and pillaged by an infuriated political mob; they and their families were hunted down and murdered in the public streets of this city, and the force and majesty of the law were powerless to protect them. Seven brief months have passed, and a thousand of these despised and persecuted men march through the city in the garb of United States soldiers, in vindication of their own manhood, and with the approval of a countless multitude—in effect, saving from inevitable and distasteful conscription the same number of those who hunted their persons and destroyed their homes during those days of humiliation and disgrace. This is noble vengeance—a vengeance taught by Him who commanded, 'Love them that hate you; do good to them that persecute you.'"

But the most appalling fact that stared the Negro soldier in the face was an Act of the Confederate Congress denying him the immunity of a prisoner of war. He was threatened with summary vengeance. He had enemies in his rear and enemies in his front. When asked if, in their opinion, the Negro soldier would fight, the men who were forced to accept his enlistment as a heroic war measure damned him with faint praise—with elevated eyebrows and elaborate pantomime. The good words of the conscientious few who felt all the time that he would fight were drowned by a babel of wrathful depreciation of him as a man and as a soldier. The outlook for the Negro soldier was certainly unpromising at first blush; but he knew how to be patient, and with intensest longing listened for the call to battle, where he hoped to command the respect of the enemy and the admiration of the Government. The days of hope and fear, of distrust and discontent, of discussion and detraction, soon swept by in the wild current of war events; the hour for the trial of the Negro volunteer in the fire of civil war came. No one welcomed it more sincerely than the Negro himself, and history shall record his splendid bearing, his heroic deeds, his proud achievements.

CHAPTER IX.

NEGRO TROOPS IN BATTLE.—DEPARTMENT OF THE SOUTH (1862-1865).

SOUTH CAROLINA had set the other States a dangerous example in her attempts at nullification under President Jackson's administration, and was not only first in seceding, but fired the first shot of the slave-holders' rebellion against the laws and authority of the United States Government. It was eminently fitting, then, that the first shot fired at slavery by Negro soldiers should be aimed by the ex-slaves of the haughty South Carolina rebels. It was poetic justice that South Carolina Negroes should have the priority of obtaining the Union uniform, and enjoy the distinction of being the first Negro soldiers to encounter the enemy in battle. And the honor belongs to Massachusetts in furnishing a graduate of Harvard College, Thomas Wentworth Higginson, as the first colonel to lead the First South Carolina Negro Regiment of Volunteers.

Before Colonel Higginson assumed command of this regiment, in fact before it was organized as a regiment, Company A did its first fighting on Saint Helena Island.[1] From the 3d to the 10th of November, 1862, Company A, under Captain Trowbridge, participated in the expedition along the coasts of Georgia and East Florida. The expedition was under the command of Lieutenant-colonel

---

[1] "Official Records of the War of the Rebellion," vol. xiv., p. 189.

Oliver T. Beard, of the Forty-eighth New York Infantry. Of their fighting quality Colonel Beard in his report says:

"The colored men fought with astonishing coolness and bravery. For alacrity in effecting landings, for determination, and for bush-fighting I found them all I could desire—more than I had hoped. They behaved bravely, gloriously, and deserve all praise."[1]

From the 13th to the 18th of November three companies of the First South Carolina Colored Volunteers participated in an expedition from Beaufort, South Carolina, to Doboy River, Georgia. In his report of the expedition General Rufus Saxton says:

"It gives me pleasure to bear witness to the good conduct of the Negro troops. They fought with the most determined bravery. Although scarcely one month since the organization of this regiment was commenced, in that short period these untrained soldiers have captured from the enemy an amount of property equal in value to the cost of the regiment for a year. They have driven back equal numbers of rebel troops, and have destroyed the salt-works along the whole line of this coast."[2]

On the 23d of January, 1863, by order of Major-general Hunter, Colonel Higginson sailed in transports from Beaufort, South Carolina, to make a raid into Georgia and Florida. No strategic blow was to be struck, no important manœuvre was to be executed. But there were two objects in view. Negro regiments were to be recruited in the Department, but the enemy, in retiring before the Union forces, had taken with him all effective Negroes. It was one of the objects of the expedition to secure Ne-

---

[1] "Official Records of the War of the Rebellion," vol. xiv., pp. 189, 190, 191, 192.

[2] Ibid., vol. xiv., p. 192.

gro recruits in the enemy's country. The second object of the expedition was to obtain the far-famed lumber which was to be had by a bold dash into the enemy's country. These two objects were of sufficient importance to justify the expedition, but Colonel Higginson cherished another idea that had not been canvassed at headquarters. This First South Carolina Volunteers was the only organized regiment of Negro troops in the army of the United States at this time. The tentative effort of General Hunter in raising this regiment the year before had met the inexorable disapproval of the President, and had drawn the fierce fire of the enemies of the Negro. Colonel Higginson knew that if he could get his black soldiers in battle once, the question of their employment in unlimited numbers would be finally settled. So, while he went ostensibly for recruits and lumber, his main aim was to find the enemy and engage him. His force consisted of four hundred and sixty-two officers and men. The vessels that bore the expedition were the *Ben de Ford*, Captain Hallet, carrying several six-pound guns; the *John Adams*, an army gun-boat, carrying a thirty-pound Parrott gun, two ten-pound Parrotts, and an eight-inch howitzer; the *Planter*, carrying a ten-pound Parrott gun and two howitzers. The *Ben de Ford* was the largest, and carried most of the troops. It was the "flag-ship" of the expedition, in a manner. Major John D. Strong was in command on the *John Adams*, and Captain Charles T. Trowbridge commanded the troops on the *Planter*. For prudential reasons, each vessel sailed at a different hour for St. Simon's, on the coast of Georgia.

On the night of the 26th of January Colonel Higginson found himself on the right track; the enemy he was looking for was not far away. Of his purpose Colonel Higginson says: "That night I proposed to make a sort of trial trip up stream as far as Township Landing, some fifteen miles, there to pay our respects to Captain Clark's company of cavalry, whose camp was reported to lie near by. This was included in Corporal Sutton's programme, and seemed to me more inviting and far more useful to the men than any amount of mere foraging. The thing really desirable appeared to be to get them under fire as soon as possible, and to teach them, by a few small successes, the application of what they had learned in camp."[1]

Back from the river and five miles from Township Landing the much-desired enemy was bivouacked. A troop of skirmishers was landed behind the bend below the landing, with orders to march upon the town and surround it. When the troops arrived by water the town was in possession of the force that had proceeded by land. Colonel Higginson had brought along a good supply of the Emancipation Proclamation to distribute among the Negroes, and these were rather assuring to many who had been led to believe that the "Yankees would sell them into Cuba."

After making a selection of one hundred of the best soldiers in the expedition, Colonel Higginson took up his line of march for the enemy's camp shortly after midnight. The moon shone brightly, but the command soon reached the resinous pines, and clouds of shadows hid it. The column moved on in silence until, when about two miles from its base, the advance-guard came suddenly upon the rebel cavalry and exchanged shots. Colonel Higginson gave orders to fix bayonets, and prepared to receive the enemy kneeling, and the enemy delivered his fire over the heads of the intrepid black soldiers. "My soldiers," says Colonel

---

[1] "Army Life in a Black Regiment," p. 70.

Higginson, "in turn fired rapidly—too rapidly, being yet beginners—and it was evident that, dim as it was, both sides had opportunity to do some execution.

"I could hardly tell whether the fight had lasted ten minutes or an hour, when, as the enemy's fire had evidently ceased or slackened, I gave the order to cease firing. But it was very difficult at first to make them desist: the taste of gunpowder was too intoxicating. One of them was heard to mutter indignantly, 'Why de cunnel order *cease* firing, when de Secesh blazin' away at de rate of ten dollar a day?'"

The enemy beat a precipitate retreat, and left Colonel Higginson's Negro troops in undisputed possession of the field. The dead and wounded were tenderly taken up by their more fortunate comrades, and the command returned to Township Landing without being again assailed by the enemy. Of the wounded, Surgeon Seth Rogers wrote: "One man killed instantly by a ball through the heart and seven wounded, one of whom will die. Braver men never lived. One man with two bullet-holes through the large muscles of the shoulders and neck brought off from the scene of action, two miles distant, two muskets, and not a murmur has escaped his lips. Another, Robert Sutton, with three wounds—one of which, being on the skull, may cost him his life—would not report himself till compelled to do so by his officers. While dressing his wounds he quietly talked of what they had done and of what they yet could do. To-day I have had the colonel *order* him to obey me. He is perfectly quiet and cool, but takes this whole affair with the religious bearing of a man who realizes that freedom is sweeter than life. Yet another soldier did not report himself at all, but remained all night on guard, and possibly I should not have known of his having had a buckshot in his shoulder if some duty requiring a sound shoulder had not been required of him to-day." [1]

The engagement in which Colonel Higginson's Negro soldiers had courageously and unflinchingly met and returned the enemy's fire was called the *"Battle of the Hundred Pines."* It decided no important military question, but, under the circumstances, it was of great importance to Negro soldiership throughout the entire country. It was one of the first stand-up fights that ex-slaves had had with their late masters, and their splendid bravery was at once a vindication and a prophecy of valor upon other fields that were yet to be fought for freedom.

But this was not the end of the practical military experiences of this Negro regiment during the expedition up the St. Mary's River. The coveted lumber was secured, brick and railroad iron were obtained, and some "contrabands." The return trip of the expedition was signalized by a number of sharp contests with the enemy. The captain of the *John Adams* was killed in the first river engagement, but there was not the least demoralization among the troops. A Negro corporal took the wheel and guided the vessel through a hail-storm of bullets, occasionally taking a shot at the enemy from the pilot-house. The men who were detailed to man the guns fought them with the coolest courage, although they were exposed to the musket and artillery fire of the enemy.

As musketry service was valueless against the enemy upon the high bluffs, most of the troops were confined in the hot and disagreeable hold of the vessel. When the firing began it required great firmness on the part of the officers to keep the men from rushing on deck. A safety-valve to their overflowing martial zeal was permitted by

---

[1] "Army Life in a Black Regiment," pp. 76, 77.

the use of the port-holes under deck, through which they discharged their pieces at will. So eager were they to do service that they fought each other to secure control of the port-holes. Others begged to be put ashore, and exclaimed that it was "mighty mean" to be shut down in the hold when they might be "fightin' de Secesh in *de clar field.*"

The expedition was in every way a success; and while it reflected great credit upon the commanding officer, it demonstrated the fact that Negroes well led make capable and reliable soldiers. The country was waiting for just such evidence, and Colonel Higginson's Negro soldiers furnished it. War correspondents who accompanied the expedition or received their information from the officers hurried the news to the rear, and the country was thrilled at learning that its Negro defenders had justified its hopes and disarmed all fear.

During the same week that this expedition was testing the Negro's valor another expedition from the same regiment was performing a perilous march into Georgia. On the 30th of January, 1863, Captain Charles T. Trowbridge, with the small force of thirty men, set out to destroy a rebel salt-works on the coast of Georgia. His Negro troops were familiar with the country and delighted with their military mission. The swamps were numerous and almost impassable, but they heroically dragged a boat over the country in order to cross them, and endured the fatigue, privations, and perils of the undertaking with the fortitude of veterans. They finally reached their objective point, and found thirty-two large boilers, two store-houses, and a large quantity of salt. Captain Trowbridge was a good engineer officer, and the work of destruction[1] was complete. The com-

---

[1] "Rebellion Record," vol. vi., D, p. 41.

manding officer of the Department of the South was highly gratified with the results of the expedition under Colonel Higginson and that under Captain Trowbridge. Although of no great military moment, the war correspondents were easily impressed with the value of the whole affair. The *New York Times* said concerning the expedition:

"THE NEGROES IN BATTLE.

"Colonel Higginson, of the First South Carolina Volunteers, furnishes an entertaining official report of the exploits of his black regiment in Florida. He seems to think it necessary to put his case strongly and in rather exalted language, as well as in such a way as to convince the public that Negroes will fight. In this expedition his battalion was repeatedly under fire—had rebel cavalry, infantry, and, says he, 'even artillery' arrayed against them, yet in every instance came off with unblemished honor and undisputed triumph. His men made the most urgent appeals to him to be allowed to press the flying enemy. They exhibited the most fiery energy, beyond anything of which Colonel Higginson ever read, unless it may be in the case of the French Zouaves. He even says that 'it would have been madness to attempt with the bravest white troops what he successfully accomplished with black ones.' No wanton destruction was permitted, no personal outrages desired, during the expedition. The regiment, besides the victories which it achieved, and the large amount of valuable property which it secured, obtained a cannon and a flag, which the Colonel very properly asks permission for the regiment to retain. The officers and men desire to remain permanently in Florida, and obtain supplies of lumber, iron, etc., for the Government. The Colonel puts forth a very good suggestion, to the effect that a 'chain of such posts would completely alter the whole aspect of the war in the seaboard slave States, and would accomplish what no accumulation of Northern regiments can so easily effect.' This is the very use for Negro soldiers suggested in the proclamation of the President. We have no doubt that the whole State of Florida might easily be held for the Government in this way by a dozen Negro regiments."[1]

The official account is excellent.[2]

---

[1] *Times*, February 10, 1863.
[2] "Official Records of the War of the Rebellion," vol. xiv., pp. 194–198.

In March, 1863, Colonel Higginson was in command of an expedition up the St. John's River, consisting of the First and Second South Carolina Volunteer Negro regiments. He reoccupied Jacksonville, and held it against the enemy until ordered to evacuate the place. In July, 1863, Colonel Higginson was placed in command of another expedition, this time ordered up the South Edisto. Like the previous expeditions, this one was composed of Negro troops; and this one, while less imposing in numbers, was charged with a most arduous and perilous undertaking. The infantry force consisted of two hundred and fifty men of Colonel Higginson's First South Carolina Regiment; and besides these there was one section of the First Connecticut Battery, Lieutenant Clinton. There were two twelve-pound Armstrong guns, three Parrott guns, and one of twenty and two of ten pound calibre, and several howitzers. The war correspondent with the expedition gave a most graphic and succinct account of the fighting, and he may relate the affair again:

"A NATIONAL ACCOUNT.
"Camp First Regiment South Carolina Volunteers,
"Beaufort, South Carolina, *July* 16, 1863.

"Thinking, perhaps, that you would like to hear of an expedition made by a detachment of the First South Carolina Volunteers, I will proceed to give you a few items.

"The expedition left Beaufort on the 9th of July, at 4 P.M., and arrived at Wiltown Bluff next morning about 3 A.M. The expedition was composed of four companies of the First Regiment South Carolina Volunteers — Companies A, B, G, and K — with a detachment of twenty men from Company C, who nobly and fearlessly worked the guns on board the gun-boat *Enoch Dean*. The little steamer *Governor Milton*, commanded by Major Strong, First South Carolina Volunteers, was armed with two brass twelve-pounder Armstrongs from the Connecticut Battery, commanded by Lieutenant Clinton, First Connecticut Battery. The *John Adams* had on board two twenty-four pounder rifles and two twenty-four pounder howitzers, commanded by Mr. Edward

Herron and Lieutenant Walker, First South Carolina Volunteers. The *Enoch Dean* had two guns, one ten-pounder Parrott and one six-pounder howitzer, commanded by Captain George Dally, First South Carolina Volunteers. On arriving near the bluff a contraband was seen on shore, and a boat sent for him. He reported a battery of three guns on the bluff. The *John Adams* fired one gun, and was answered by one gun from the bluff, when the rebels retired. Companies K, Captain Whitney, and G, Lieutenant Sampson, landed at the bluff and deployed their companies as skirmishers. After marching about one mile they encountered about one company of cavalry and a company of sharpshooters, when they had a brisk skirmish, and succeeded in driving the rebel cavalry and infantry, capturing one lieutenant and one private belonging to the Sixth South Carolina. While the skirmishing was going on, the *John Adams* was employed in removing some spiling that extended across the river. The work was done under the supervision and engineering of Captain Trowbridge, First South Carolina Volunteers, and was done with despatch—opening a breach wide enough for the boats to pass up the river. The little *Milton* and the *Dean* passed through the breach, and proceeded up the river for about a mile and a half, and encountered a battery of two guns. The *Dean* exchanged a few shots with the battery, when the battery retired. The *Milton* meanwhile got aground, when the rebels posted a battery of two guns on the opposite bank and commenced a brisk fire on the *Milton*. A few well-directed shots from Lieutenant Clinton's guns on board the *Milton* caused them to retire. The *Dean* went on about a mile farther, and encountered two more rebel guns, one on each side of the river. A few shots drove them back. Owing to the draft of the *Dean* she was obliged to return to the spiling. I almost forgot to mention a detachment of Captain Rogers's company (F) who accompanied the expedition, and were landed below the bluff, and proceeded about a mile to some extensive rice-mills, containing about fifteen thousand bushels of rice, and burned them all. We were detained about two hours for the tide to rise, so that we could fulfil the object of our mission. We then weighed anchor, and the *Milton* and the *Dean* proceeded up the river to burn the bridge, about fifteen miles from the spiling. When about six miles from the spiling the *Dean* got aground, and Colonel Higginson ordered the *Milton* to proceed up the river; but when about twenty rods from the *Dean* the *Milton* was fired at from the shore by a three-gun battery. One shell hit the *Milton* about amidships, and exploded, injuring her machinery and killing her engineer. The *Milton* was obliged to turn back, leaving the *Dean* aground and exposed to two batteries—one on each side of the river. The *Dean* was hit with eleven shots from the rebels while aground. One shell burst quite near Colonel Higginson, injuring him severely by the concussion; another shell passed through the bows of the *Dean*, killing one gunner and injuring three deck-hands severely. Captain Dolly expended all his ammunition for his ten-pounder rifle, and had only his six-pounder howitzer to fight with. The *Dean* managed to get afloat by using tar to get up steam, and proceeded down the river and encountered a battery of five guns about four miles from the piles, which riddled the *Dean* completely with shot and canister. The *Milton* had meanwhile run down the river, and by mistake run headlong on the spiles. Being unable to get her off, she was abandoned and burned. The machinery of the *Dean* was now disabled, and she was taken in tow by the *John Adams*.

"We then proceeded down the river; but it would be well to mention another brisk skirmish which occurred before embarking, between the rebels and Company K, Captain Whitney, and Company G, Lieutenant Sampson, with a detachment of Company B, under Lieutenant Parker, and a detachment of Company A, under Lieutenant Trowbridge. As they were about to embark, the rebels dashed down upon them with a force five hundred strong, consisting of cavalry and infantry. A brisk skirmish ensued, and braver men never used a musket than our boys proved themselves to be on that occasion. They fought with admirable bravery, and the rebels fled before them. The extent of the damage to the rebel side is not yet known. Our troops then embarked, and we proceeded down the river about a mile and a half, and then encountered another battery of four guns, which opened a brisk fire upon us. Two balls struck the *John Adams*, one of which killed two men. The *Enoch Dean* was struck seventeen times with shot and shell, beside the grape and canister. The boats then proceeded back to Beaufort. The rebel lieutenant who was captured was taken by a Negro, who, after firing his gun without effect, seized the horse by the bridle, and with his other hand grasped firmly the rebel, who was armed with sabre and carbine, and pulled him off his horse."

While Colonel Higginson's South Carolina Negro troops were fighting their way among the rebel batteries which lined the banks of the Edisto, a regiment of Northern Negroes was learning its first lessons in the practical school of war. The Fifty-fourth Massachusetts Volunteer Infantry had already joined General A. H. Terry on James Island, and on the 16th of July, 1863, while on picket, was surprised by the enemy and hurled back upon Terry's main line. The enemy, a body of Georgians, more numerous than the Union force, was nevertheless driven off. Although the attack was a morning surprise, the black soldiers had what Napoleon styled "Two-o'clock-in-the-morning courage." Although confronted by a superior force, the Negro regiment recoiled in good order, delivering a deliberate fire. After this engagement the Fifty-fourth Regiment started the same day for Morris Island, in order to participate in a meditated assault upon Fort Wagner.

The Department of the South up to this time had done little effective military service. Most of the Sea Islands had fallen into the control of the Union forces, but the way to Charleston, both by land and water, was guarded by forts, fortifications, and torpedoes. Fort Wagner was a strongly mounted and thoroughly garrisoned earthwork extending across the north end of the island; it was within twenty-six hundred yards of Fort Sumter. The reduction of this fortress left but little work to subdue Cumming's Point, and thus siege guns could be brought within one mile of Fort Sumter, and the city of Charleston — the heart of the rebellion—would be within extreme shelling distance. In this assault the Fifty-fourth Massachusetts was to participate. It had sustained a loss of fourteen killed, seventeen wounded, and thirteen missing while on James Island, and having had a taste of war, was eager for more. It was eminently proper, too, that this Northern Negro regiment from stalwart old Massachusetts should have its fighting qualities tested in South Carolina before a haughty and formidable fortress, from under whose guns the most splendid valor of white troops had recoiled. Before the trying hour they had been subjected to tests not only of martial pluck, but of endurance, hunger, heat, and thirst. At the close of the engagement on the morning of the 16th these Negro soldiers were set in motion from James to Morris Island. The first shock of battle had burst upon them in the ominous silence of the early morning. All day they marched over the island under the exhausting heat of a July sun in Carolina, with the uncertain sand slipping under their weary tread. All night the march was continued through darkness and rain, amid thunder and lightning, over swollen streams, broken dikes, and feeble, shuddering, narrow causeways. Now a halt for no apparent reason, and then the column moved forward to lead in the dance of death. This dreary, weary, and exhausting march was continued till six o'clock in the morning of the 18th, when the Fifty-fourth reached Morris Island.

General Quincy A. Gillmore, an excellent engineer officer, had carefully matured his plans for the proposed assault upon Fort Wagner. It was intended to open a preliminary bombardment at daylight on the 18th, and having by heavy ordnance tranquillized Wagner, to effect its reduction by the bayonet. But a tempest came on suddenly and delayed the cruel ingenuity of war. The thunder roared, the lightning flashed, and the rain fell in torrents. The military operations were suspended in the presence of Nature's awful spectacle. About eleven o'clock aides-de-camp and mounted couriers sped in different directions, and the force on land and its naval support upon the sea began to exhibit signs of preparation for the impending conflict. The pale face and steady look of officers as they transmitted their weighty orders told the nature of their mission here and there on the island. At 12.30 P.M. a flash of fire leaped from the mouths of batteries that were ranged in semicircle for a mile across the island, and the bombardment was formally opened. The naval vessels came into action also, within a few hundred yards of the fortress, and the enemy replied promptly from Wagner, Sumter, and Cumming's Point. A storm of fire and whirring missiles was kept up all the afternoon. The enemy did not serve all his guns in Wagner, but the two operated were fought with admirable skill and daring. The infantry support clung to the bomb-proofs all the afternoon, for the commanding officer evidently knew what the Union troops would attempt at nightfall. At least one hundred great guns were engaged in an attempt to batter down this rebel fortress, and the work of destruction went on all the afternoon. Great clouds of sand were thrown into the air by the tons of metal that struck inside. A shot cut the halyards on the flag-staff, and the rebel banner went fluttering to the earth like a stricken bird.

Some of the Union officers thought the garrison was about to capitulate, but Sumter fired a shot over the fort, as much as to say, "I protest." Out from their bombs rushed a squad of men, and, with the rebel yell, hauled their colors to their place again.

As the day wore away it seemed certain, from the Union stand-point, that the garrison must yield or perish. Through a field-glass Wagner seemed little less than an unrecognizable mass of ruins, a mere heap of sand. It seemed as if the approaches to the bomb-proofs were choked with sand, and that most of the heavy guns were disabled and the fort practically dismantled. Its reduction seemed now near at hand, and the bombardment had facilitated the work of the infantry who were to consummate its reduction by a dash at the point of the bayonet. Towards evening the breaching siege guns and monitors slacked their fire. Soon the beach was filled with life. Couriers dashed in every direction, and the troops were now being disposed for an assault. At 6 P.M. the Fifty-fourth Regiment reached General Geo. C. Strong's headquarters, about the middle of the island, wet and weary, hungry and thirsty; but there was no time for rest or refreshments. Onward the Negro regiment marched several hundred yards farther, and proudly took its place at the head of the assaulting column. General Strong and Colonel Shaw addressed it briefly, and with burning words of eloquent patriotic sentiment urged the men to valorous conduct in the approaching assault. Both officers were inspired; the siren of martial glory was sedulously luring them to the bloody and inhospitable trenches of Wagner. There was a tremor in Colonel Shaw's voice and an impressiveness in his manner. He was young and beautiful, wealthy and refined, and his heroic words soon flowered into action—bravest of the brave, leader of men! The random shot and shell that screamed through the ranks gave the troops little annoyance. The first brigade consisted of the Fifty-fourth Massachusetts, Colonel Robert Gould Shaw; the Sixth Connecticut, Colonel Chatfield; the Forty-eighth New York, Colonel Barton; the Third New Hampshire, Colonel Jackson; the Seventy-sixth Pennsylvania, Colonel Strawbridge; and the Ninth Maine, Colonel Emory. After about thirty minutes' halt, General Strong gave the order for the charge, and the column advanced quickly to its perilous work. The ramparts of Wagner flashed with small-arms, and all the large shotted guns roared with defiance. Sumter and Cumming's Point delivered a destructive cross-fire, while the howitzers in the bastions raked the ditch; but the gallant Negro regiment swept across it and gained the parapet. Here the flag of this regiment was planted; here General Strong fell mortally wounded; and here the brave, beautiful, and heroic Colonel Shaw was saluted by death and kissed by immortality. The regiment lost heavily, but held its ground under the most discouraging circumstances. The men had actually gained the inside of the fort, where they bravely contended with a desperate and determined enemy. The contest endured for about an hour, when the regiment, shattered and torn, with nearly all of its officers dead or wounded, was withdrawn under the command[1] of Captain Luis F. Emilio. He formed a new line of battle about seven hundred yards from the fort, and awaited orders for another charge. He despatched a courier to the commanding officer of the second brigade that had gone to the front, stating that he was in supporting position, and was ready and willing to do what he could. Word came that the enemy was quiet and that the Fifty-fourth was not needed. Captain Emilio then occupied the rifle-pits flanking the Union artillery which he found unoccupied, and being out of musket range, organized his men as best he could. The national colors of the regiment which he had brought back from the scene of the battle he sent to the rear with the wounded color-sergeant, William H. Carney, as they could not serve as a rallying point in the deep darkness. The following extracts from a letter written by a late sergeant of the Fifty-fourth to Captain Luis F. Emilio gives personal observations during this action that are not without their value:

"Regarding the assault on Fort Wagner, I recollect distinctly that when our column had charged the fort, passed the half-filled moat, and mounted to the parapet, many of

---

[1] Several histories of the war have given Lieutenant Higginson the honor of leading the regiment from the parapets of Wagner. This is an error. Lieutenant Higginson was not in this action, but on detail at the other end of the island. *Captain Luis F. Emilio* was the officer who commanded at the close of the battle.—G. W. W.

the men clambered over and some entered by the large embrasure in which one of the big guns was mounted, the firing substantially ceased there by the beach, and the rebel musketry firing steadily grew hotter on our left. An officer of our regiment called out, 'Spike that gun.' Whether this was done I do not know, for we fired our rifles and fought as hard as we could to return the fire on our right.

"But the rebel fire grew hotter on our right, and a field-piece every few seconds seemed to sweep along our rapidly thinning ranks. Men all around me would fall and roll down the scarp into the ditch. Just at the very hottest moment of the struggle a battalion or regiment charged up to the moat and halted, and did not attempt to cross it and join us, but from their position commenced to fire upon us. I was one of the men who shouted from where I stood, 'Don't fire on us! We are the Fifty-fourth!' I have heard it was a Maine regiment. This is God's living truth! Immediately after I heard an order, 'Retreat!' Some twelve or fifteen of us slid down from our position on the parapet of the fort.

"The men-of-war seemed to have turned their guns on the fort, and the fire of the Confederates on the right seemed to increase in power. The line of retreat seemed lit with infernal fire; the hissing bullets and bursting shells seemed angry demons.

"I was with Hooker's division, cooking for Colonel B. C. Tilghman, of the Twenty-sixth Pennsylvania Regiment, in the battle of Fredericksburg, when General Burnside commanded. I traversed the Hazel Dell Marr, the Stone House, when all the enemy's artillery was turned upon it; but hot as the fire was there, it did not compare to the terrific fire which blazed along the narrow approach to Wagner.

"I care not who the man is who denies the fact, our

regiment did charge the fort and drove the rebels from their guns. Many of our men will join me in saying that in the early stages of the fight we had possession of the sea end of Battery Wagner. Indeed, most of the colored prisoners taken there were captured inside the battery.

"When we reached the Gatling Battery drawn up to repel the counter-attack, I remember you were the only commissioned officer present, and you placed us indiscriminately—that is, without any regard to companies—in line, and prepared to renew the charge. The commanding officer, whom I do not know, ordered us to the flanking rifle-pits, and we there awaited the expected counter-charge the enemy did not make."

Captain Emilio, who was an intelligent and experienced officer, thought that in all probability the enemy would make a counter-assault, having driven the Negro troops from the fort, and in forming a new line of battle, he was preparing for such a contingency. Fortunately for the Union forces no counter-assault was delivered, although a desultory firing was maintained nearly all night. Some time after midnight General Thomas G. Stevenson called upon Captain Emilio, where he held the front line, and personally thanked him for the dispositions he had made, and promised to relieve his gallant but weary command. Accordingly, the Tenth Connecticut relieved the Fifty-fourth Massachusetts at two o'clock the next morning, July 19th. Captain Emilio had rallied the stragglers of other regiments on the front line, and now that he was relieved he sent these men to the rear by detachments to join their regiments. With the remnant of the Fifty-fourth he went into bivouac for the night a short distance to the rear, where also some officers and men of this regiment had been swept by the tide of battle, which unfortunately had gone the wrong way that night. On the following morning Captain Emilio, still being in command of the regiment, led it to an old camp formerly occupied by the command near the south end of Morris Island.

The appalling list of casualties shows how bravely this Negro regiment had done its duty, and the unusually large number of men missing proves that the regiment had fought its way into the fort, and if properly supported, Wagner would have been captured. Colonel Shaw led about six hundred enlisted men and twenty-two officers into this action. Of the enlisted men thirty-one were killed, one hundred and thirty-five wounded, and ninety-two missing. Of the twenty-two officers participating three were killed and eleven were wounded. Nearly half of the enlisted men were killed, wounded, or missing, while more than one-half of the officers were either killed or wounded.

From a purely military stand-point the assault upon Fort Wagner was a failure, but it furnished the severest test of Negro valor and soldiership. It was a mournful satisfaction to the advocates of Negro soldiers to point the doubting, sneering, stay-at-home Negro-haters to the murderous trenches of Wagner. The Negro soldier had seen his red-letter day, and his title to patriotic courage was written in his own blood. Pleased with the splendid behavior of the regiment in particular and the special courage of several enlisted men, General Gillmore awarded a medal to the following soldiers of the Fifty-fourth: Sergeant Robert J. Simmons, Company B; Sergeant William H. Carney, Company C; Corporal Henry F. Peal, Company F; and Private George Wilson, Company A.

But it would be unjust to forget the gallant color-sergeant John Wall who fell in the outer trench. He was a brave and competent soldier, but after the United States colors had been taken up and borne to the top of the parapet, henceforth history seems to have kept her jealous eye upon Sergeant William H. Carney, the heroic self-appointed successor to Sergeant John Wall. Sergeant Carney planted his flag upon the ramparts of the rebel fort, and after having received three severe wounds, brought it to the rear stained with his own blood—

>"Glares the volcanic breath,
> Breaks the red sea of death,
> From Wagner's yawning hold,
> On the besiegers bold.
>   Twice vain the wild attack,
>   Inch by inch, sadly slow,
>   Fights the torn remnant back,
>   Face to the foe.
>
>"Yet free the colors wave,
> Borne by yon Afric brave,
> In the fierce storm wind higher;
> But, ah! one flashing fire:
>   He sinks! the banner falls
>   From the faint, mangled limb,
>   And droop to mocking walls
>   Those star-folds dim.
>
>"Stay, stay the taunting laugh!
> See! now he lifts the staff,
> Clinched in his close-set teeth,
> Crawls from dead heaps beneath,
>   Crowned with his starry robe,
>   Till he the ranks has found:
>   'Comrades, the dear old flag
>   Ne'er touched the ground.
>
>"O man so pure, so grand,
> Sidney might clasp thy hand!
> O brother! black thy skin,
> But white the pearl within!
>   Man, who to lift thy race
>   Worthy, thrice worthy art,
>   Clasps thee, in warm embrace
>   A Nation's heart."

The State colors were lost in the unequal struggle at the beach end of the fort. The rebel general Ripley took them to England with him, saying that whenever Massachusetts should elect a Democrat as governor he would return the flag. Twelve years later William Gaston, the candidate of the Democratic party of the Commonwealth, was chosen governor. True to his resolve, General Ripley returned the flag to the State Government, accompanied by a polite note, and after an absence of nearly thirteen years the beautiful banner came back to Boston, that had witnessed its presentation on the Common; and on the 17th of June, 1875, on the Centennial celebration of the battle of Bunker Hill, it was borne in the imposing procession by an ex-member of the Fifty-fourth who had fought under its folds Saturday night, July 18, 1863! Its wanderings are ended forever, and now it hangs permanently in its appointed place among the regimental flags of the troops of Massachusetts. Like many of the other flags it is rent by bullets and faded by a Southern sun, but it will tell to generation after generation the matchless story of Negro patriotism and valor.

General Ripley's generous and noble letter deserves a place in history:

"8 Stanhope Terrace, Gloster Road, South Kensington,
"London, *January* 12, 1875.

" *To his Excellency the Governor of Massachusetts:*

"I have the honor to forward to your Excellency the Regimental color for the Fifty-fourth Massachusetts Volunteers, which was taken in action on the evening of the 18th of July, 1863, by the garrison of Battery Wagner, under General Taliaferro, being a part of the forces defending Charleston, South Carolina, under my command, when that work was assaulted by the Federal troops under General Gillmore.

"Since the close of the Civil War in America I have been generally absent from the country, and I have seen with regret the failure of expedients attempted to restore peace and content to the Southern States.

"It seems to me, however, that the lapse of time and the course of events have produced a less imbittered state of public feeling than that which existed just after the close of the strife. Under the existing state of things I deem it decorous, if not a positive duty, to promote the oblivion of the animosities which led to and were engendered by the war.

"Such being the case, I prefer to look upon trophies of the character of the color in question as mementos of the gallant conduct of men who like Shaw, Putnam, and other sons of Massachusetts sealed their devotion to the cause which they adopted with their lives, rather than as evidences of prowess on the one side or the other. The custodians of such a memento, I think, should be the authorities of the State served by these gallant men, and I therefore transmit the flag to your Excellency for such disposition as the authorities of Massachusetts shall determine. Very respectfully,

"Your obedient servant,

(Signed) "R. S. RIPLEY."

At the battle of Thermopylæ three hundred Spartans held the pass against an enormous army, and yet history has made Leonidas representative of them all. Many brave soldiers fell in the forlorn assault upon Fort Wagner, but when some great painter has patriotic inspiration to give this battle an immortal representation, Colonel Shaw will be the central figure; and America will only remember one name in this conflict for all time to come—Colonel Robert Gould Shaw! This was a noble and precious life, but it was cheerfully consecrated to human freedom and the regeneration of the nation. He had good blood, splendid training, wide experience for one so young, and had inherited strong antislavery sentiments. When he had fallen, a flag of truce called for his body. A rebel officer responded, "We have buried him with his niggers." It was thought thus to cast indignity upon the hero dead, but it was a failure. The colonel and his men were united in life, and it was fitting that they should not be separated in death. In this idea his father joined, and the following letter exhibits his feelings:

"*Brigadier-general Gillmore, commanding Department of the South:*

"Sir,—I take the liberty to address you because I am informed that efforts are to be made to recover the body of my son, Colonel Shaw, of the Fifty-fourth Massachusetts Regiment, which was buried at Fort Wagner. My object in writing is to say that such efforts are not authorized by me or any of my family, and that they are not approved by us. We hold that a soldier's most appropriate burial-place is on the field where he has fallen. I shall therefore be much obliged, General, if, in case the matter is brought to your cognizance, you will forbid the desecration of my son's grave, and prevent the disturbance of his remains or those buried with him. With most earnest wishes for your success, I am, sir, with respect and esteem,

"Your most obedient servant,
"Francis George Shaw.

"New York, *August* 24, 1863."

Instead of dishonoring the remains of Colonel Shaw by burying him with his brave black soldiers, the intended ignominy was transformed into a beautiful bow of promise that was to span forever the future of the race for which he gave his life. He was representative of all that was good in American life; he had wealth, high social position, and the broadest culture. From his exalted station he chose to fight with and for Negro troops —not only to lead them in conflict, but to die for them and the Republic; and although separated from them in civil life, nevertheless he united the rich and the poor, the learned and the unlearned, the white and black, in his military apotheosis.

"'They buried him with his niggers!'
Together they fought and died;
There was room for them all where they laid him
(The grave was deep and wide),

For his beauty and youth and valor,
     Their patience and love and pain;
   And at the last day together
     They shall all be found again.

   "'They buried him with his niggers!'
     Earth holds no prouder grave;
   There is not a mausoleum
     In the world beyond the wave
   That a nobler tale has hallowed
     Or a purer glory crowned,
   Than the nameless trench where they buried
     The brave so faithful found.

   "'They buried him with his niggers!'
     A wide grave should it be.
   They buried more in that shallow trench
     Than human eye could see.
   Ay, all the shames and sorrows
     Of more than a hundred years
   Lie under the weight of that Southern soil
     Despite those cruel sneers.

   "'They buried him with his niggers!'
     But the glorious souls set free
   Are leading the van of the army
     That fights for liberty.
   Brothers in death, in glory
     The same palm-branches bear,
   And the crown is as bright o'er the sable brows
     As over the golden hair."

In the recklessly fought battle of Olustee the left wing of General Seymour's little army was composed of three Negro regiments—the Eighth United States Colored Troops, the First North Carolina,[1] and the Fifty-fourth Massachusetts Volunteers. This battle, fought on the 20th of Feb-

---

[1] Subsequently the Thirty-fifth United States Colored Troops.—G. W. W.

ruary, 1864, was one of the severest of the war; and had it not been for the stubborn fighting of these Negro troops Seymour would have been routed and annihilated.

During the closing weeks of 1863 the Government was somewhat moved by rumors that Florida might be restored to the Union under certain contingencies. General Q. A. Gillmore proposed an expedition into that State, and the President approving it, sent one of his secretaries to join it. It was placed under the command of General Truman Seymour, and set sail from Hilton Head February 6, 1864. Jacksonville was occupied the next afternoon, and two days later a small cavalry force under Colonel Guy V. Henry, Fortieth Massachusetts, moved westward along a road running parallel to the railroad, with the intention of surprising a force of the enemy. The movement was successful, resulting in the capture of a large amount of stores and four guns. Emboldened by this success, Henry pushed forward to Baldwin, where he beat off the enemy and captured valuable property. Gillmore had accompanied Seymour thus far, and having cautioned him not to make any hostile demonstration for the present, returned thence to Hilton Head.

On the 17th he received a despatch from Seymour that he was proposing to push forward to the Suwannee River. Gillmore sent a despatch of even date disapproving the proposed expedition, but the next news he received was of the disaster at Olustee.

With a force short of five thousand men, of all arms, Seymour broke camp at Barber's Station at 7 A.M. Saturday, February 20, 1864, and moved westward towards Lake City, parallel to the railroad. The force consisted of two brigades. Colonel J. R. Hawley commanded the First Brigade, with his own regiment, the Seventh Connecticut; Eighth United States Colored Troops, Colonel Charles W.

Fribley; Fortieth Massachusetts Mounted Infantry, Colonel Guy V. Henry; and the Seventh New Hampshire, Colonel Joseph C. Abbott; Independent Battalion of Massachusetts Cavalry, Major Atherton H. Stevens; and the Artillery, twenty guns, being Captain Hamilton's, Captain Langdon's, Captain Elder's batteries, and one section of the Third Rhode Island Artillery. The Second Brigade was commanded by Colonel William H. Barton, and consisted of the Forty-seventh, Forty-eighth, and One Hundred and Fifteenth New York, the Fifty-fourth Massachusetts, and First North Carolina Volunteers. Of this force three regiments were Negroes—the Eighth, Fifty-fourth Massachusetts, and First North Carolina.

The column moved steadily forward, with the cavalry in front and the artillery distributed along the line of infantry, from 7 A.M. till 2 P.M., when an outpost of the enemy was encountered. For some reason not revealed in his report Seymour used no flankers, and the enemy drew him into ambush before he was aware of his immediate presence. Besides, the Union force was weary and hungry, having marched sixteen miles over heavy roads and through numerous swamps. The enemy was quietly awaiting the assault, confident of success, behind earthworks extending through heavy timber and his flanks covered by impassable swamps.

One section of Elder's battery was brought into action right, but the enemy made no response. The Seventh Connecticut and the Seventh New Hampshire were ordered to assault the enemy's right, and moved into action with spirit and gallantry. The enemy now opened a terrific fire. It was soon discovered that the enemy's right lapped Seymour's left, and that an engagement was in progress wherein the Union forces were outnumbered by about five to one. The remainder of Hawley's brigade was at once brought into action. The enemy held his fire in the centre and on the left until Hamilton's battery was brought into action, when the musketry fire was severe; many men and horses were killed or disabled before the guns could be unlimbered and served. Langdon's battery now came into action on the extreme left amid a shower of rebel musket-balls, and four guns were fought with skill within about one hundred yards of the enemy's lines. Amid the roar of battle Seymour gave an order contracting the left flank of his infantry line, which left the artillery without support. In about thirty minutes forty-five of the eighty-two men in the artillery, and forty out of the fifty battery horses, were killed and wounded. The two regiments on the right began to give way, recoiling slowly and stubbornly before a fierce fire. They were ordered to the rear, and the Eighth United States Colored Troops charged in on the right, led by that gallant officer Colonel Charles W. Fribley. Next came Barton's brigade, splendidly led to the conflict; but the enemy was yet unmoved behind his cover, whence he delivered a destructive fire.

Seymour now ordered the Fifty-fourth Massachusetts to relieve Colonel Fribley's regiment, and the men double-quicked to their work with hearty cheers.

The First North Carolina Volunteers was ordered into action on the extreme right, and Barton's brigade, marching in columns *en echelon*, moved steadily to the assault. Lieutenant-colonel William N. Reed, splendidly mounted, with drawn sword, led the First North Carolina against the enemy's left. It was reported of Reed that he was bound to both races by the ties of consanguinity; that he was educated in Germany, and that in the army of that empire he had reached the *état-major*, having graduated from the military school at Keil. He was an able officer, whose conspicuous gallantry attracted the attention of the officers of other troops who saw the First North Carolina led thus splendidly to battle.

However, unable to drive back the enemy's left, Seymour's right recoiled; but the centre held its ground until the troops were withdrawn in excellent order.

Seymour was almost recklessly brave, exposing himself at every point along his entire line of battle, but his troops could not successfully contend with such an enemy in such a place. Colonel Fribley was now dead on the field; Captain Hamilton, with a broken arm and a bullet in his thigh, was still the inspiring presence on the left. Lieutenant-colonel Reed, already wounded, and his major, Archibald Bogle, now stretched upon the field severely injured, hearing that his brave and accomplished adjutant, William C. Manning, had been struck, embraced the young lieutenant and implored him to leave the field; but Manning, a born soldier, with all the noble instincts of an educated New England gentleman, would not leave his regiment at such a critical moment, and in remaining he fell wounded again at the moment Colonel Reed received a mortal hurt.

Taking advantage of a slight diversion, Seymour, almost with superhuman energy and tact, re-established his batteries in the centre, and in withdrawing his decimated forces delivered some effective parting shots at the victorious enemy.

Had the advance been conducted with the same cautious, soldierly calculations which characterized the retreat the conflict would have ended in a victory for the Union. However, when he reached Baldwin and Jacksonville, Seymour again lost his head; for having lost about 250 killed and 1,200 wounded, he now destroyed over one million dollars' worth of Government stores.

Although the battle of Olustee was not a victory, yet it furnished an opportunity for martial valor of the highest order, and the opportunity was fully appreciated and employed by all the troops, but by none more than the gallant Negro regiments.

It seemed to be the fate of the Negro troops in the Department of the South to lead a forlorn hope. First came the bold and perilous stroke of the South Edisto Expedition to burn a bridge fifteen miles above Wiltown Bluff to aid General Sherman; then came the assault upon Fort Wagner, next the bloody and fruitless action at Olustee; and on the 30th of November, 1864, came the battle of Honey Hill, in which several regiments of Negroes added to the laurels they had won on other fields. General Halleck had instructed General J. G. Foster, commanding the Sea Islands, to make a demonstration by land to aid General Sherman, who was expected to make his appearance near Pocotaligo towards the close of November. General Foster found that he could spare about five thousand men for this purpose, and at the head of this force he ascended Broad River by transports and landed at Boyd's Neck. General J. P. Hatch was pushed forward to seize and destroy the Charleston and Savannah railroad near Grahamsville, in the Beaufort district. General Hatch missed his way and failed to reach the railroad that day, and on the following morning, November 30th, he found himself confronted by a powerful enemy intrenched upon Honey Hill. His advance-guard felt the foe and drew his fire, but he warily fell back, leading the Union troops into a very death-trap. The fortified position of the enemy was about two miles and a half from Grahamsville. There was a semicircular line of light earthworks forming the centre of the enemy's lines; his left extended far out into pine lands and his right along a substantial fence that skirted a swamp. His batteries commanded a narrow road, and even this was overflowed at times for many yards by the swamp that was swollen by an overflowing creek near by. A few yards beyond the swamp the main road turned off to the left, making an obtuse angle, and a smaller and less frequented road turned off to the right. By a happy coincidence the Negro brigade under Colonel A. S. Hartwell was singing a magnificent song when the enemy made his presence known by a destructive fire.

> "Ho, boys, chains are breaking,
> Bondsmen fast awaking,
> Tyrant hearts are quaking,
> Southward we are making.
>   Huzza! huzza!
>   Our song shall be
>   Huzza! huzza!
>   *That we are free!*
>
> * * * *
>
> "Our flag's Red, White, and Blue;
> We'll bear it marching through,
> With rifles swift and true,
> And bayonets gleaming too.
>   Huzza! huzza! etc.
>
> * * * *
>
> "No more for trader's gold
> Shall those we love be sold;
> Nor crushed be manhood bold
> In slavery's dreaded fold.
>   Huzza! huzza! etc.
>
> "But each and all be free
> As singing-bird in tree,
> Or winds that whistling flee
> O'er mountain, vale, and sea.
>   Huzza! huzza! etc."

As soon as the first line of battle could be formed the Thirty-second Negro Infantry was ordered to carry the enemy's earthworks with the bayonet; but the marsh was found to be impassable at the designated point of assault. This regiment was withdrawn and the Thirty-fifth Negro Infantry was gallantly led to the assault; but it was impossible to reach within effective assaulting position, and under a terrific concentric fire the regiment recoiled upon the reserve. At last the Fifty-fourth Massachusetts, holding the right of Colonel Hartwell's brigade, was ordered forward. It moved as if on dress parade, while the enemy's guns and musketry swept the narrow gap. It did not recoil, the lines merely quivered under the raking fire. In a moment the gallant Colonel Hartwell rode up and gave the order—"Follow your colors!" and led the regiment to desperate fighting. The colonel was wounded in the hand, yet he refused to leave the field; but the fighting effected nothing. Finally the Fifty-fifth was formed in line of battle, with close column on company front. These troops fought with almost reckless bravery, but it was impossible to reach the enemy's batteries. While in the midst of the swamp Colonel Hartwell's horse was torn to pieces by the explosion of a shell, and the gallant horseman was again wounded. In the fall both became involved, and it was only by the most desperate exertions that he was extricated and borne to the rear in the strong and tender arms of his own men. In this service one was killed and another severely wounded, while the colonel was again struck before he was beyond the range of the enemy's guns. A Confederate account of this engagement does not overlook or ignore the splendid fighting of the Negro troops. Early in December, 1864, *The Savannah Republican* (Confederate) gave the following account of the battle of Honey Hill:

"The Negroes, as usual, formed the advance, and had

nearly reached the creek when our batteries opened upon them down the road with a terrible volley of special case. This threw them into temporary confusion, but the entire force, estimated at five thousand, was quickly restored to order, and thrown into a line of battle parallel with our own, up and down the margin of the swamp. Thus the battle raged from eleven in the morning till dark. The enemy's centre and left were most exposed and suffered terribly. Their right was posted behind an old dam that ran through the swamp, and it maintained its position till the close of the fight. Our left was very much exposed, and an attempt was once or twice made by the enemy to turn it by advancing through the swamp and up the hill, but they were driven back without a prolonged struggle.

"The centre and left of the enemy fought with a desperate earnestness. Several attempts were made to charge our batteries, and many got nearly across the swamp, but were in every instance forced back by the galling fire poured into them from our lines. We made a visit to the field the day following, and found the road literally strewn with their dead. Some eight or ten bodies were floating in the water where the road crosses, and in a ditch on the roadside just beyond we saw six Negroes piled one on top of the other. A colonel of one of the Negro regiments, with his horse, was killed while fearlessly leading his men across the creek in a charge. With that exception, all the dead and wounded officers were carried off by the enemy during the night. Many traces were left where they were dragged from the woods to the road and thrown into ambulances or carts. We counted some sixty or seventy bodies in the space of about an acre, many of which were horribly mutilated by shells, some with half their heads shot off, and others completely disembowelled. The artillery was served with great accuracy, and we doubt if any battle-field of the war presents such havoc among the trees and shrubbery. Immense pines and other growth were cut short off or torn into shreds."

In many other engagements in the Department of the South Negro troops maintained their reputation for steadiness and courage so dearly earned at Wagner and Olustee. Their officers had unbounded confidence in them, and the white troops, who at first shrank from their comradeship, soon esteemed it an honor to be associated with them in camp and in battle. Every duty was discharged joyfully, every privation and pain endured heroically, and but one thought animated them from first to last, the preservation of the national life with the death of slavery. To compass this end there were no trials too severe, no duties too arduous, no death too bitter. In all the engagements in which they participated, as far as it was possible, their officers sought for them the posts of danger and honor. Danger never awed them and honor never spoiled them. They were equal to every military contingency, and neither General Hunter nor the Government ever had occasion to regret the military employment of Negroes in the Department of the South.

CHAPTER X.

IN THE MISSISSIPPI VALLEY (1863).

By some fateful fortuitous circumstance the first fighting of Negro troops in the Mississippi Valley was as severe and fruitless as that of their brethren and comrades in the Department of the South. Port Hudson and Fort Wagner, where the Negro soldier earned his reputation for valor, were much alike. Both were strongly fortified; one was protected by a bayou under its very guns, the other had made captive the ocean in its treacherous trenches; and in each instance the service to be performed demanded the highest qualities of courage, steadiness, endurance, and prompt obedience.

General Grant was busy with the work of reducing Vicksburg. He had proposed to General N. P. Banks, who held the lower Mississippi, to join their forces for the reduction of Port Hudson or Vicksburg first, and then to assault the other position vigorously. General Banks could not well leave New Orleans to the mercy of General Richard Taylor, who, the moment he should learn of Banks's absence up the river, would move into Louisiana from Texas with a fresh army. On the 12th of May, 1863, General Grant had crossed the Mississippi and entered upon his siege against Vicksburg. General Banks, who had been on the Atchafalaya, landed at Bayou Sara at two o'clock on the morning of the 21st of May, and immediately proceeded to embark a portion of his force on steamers, and the remainder moved up the west bank of the river. On the 23d he formed a junction with the forces under Major-general Auger and Brigadier-general Sherman, who had advanced within five miles of Port Hudson. General Gardner, commanding the rebel forces at Port Hudson, despatched Colonel Miles to defeat the proposed junction of Union troops behind his fastness. Colonel Miles attempted to strike Auger's flank while on the march, but was assaulted vigorously and driven back' with severe loss. The right wing of General Banks's army, consisting of the troops under Generals Weitzel, Grover, and Dwight, struck the enemy with vigor, and compelled him to contract his outer lines and retire within his intrenchments on the 25th. The investment of Port Hudson was now complete, and on the morning of the 27th a grand assault was ordered upon the enemy's position. During the previous night the First and Third regiments of Louisiana Native Guards, the only Negro troops under General Banks, had been on the march. They had been some months in garrison, but this was their first movement towards active military service. The dust was thick, the air heavy, and the heat oppressive. The morning of the 27th dawned upon these Negro troops with a sort of sullen silence. The sky was flushed, and Nature seemed to hold her breath in horror at the terrible slaughter that was soon to take place. The enemy's works had been constructed with skill and deliberation, at a time when the slave labor of that vicinity was placed at the disposal of the military commander. The works formed a semicircle, and both ends extended towards the river. In the disposition of the troops the two Negro regiments were posted upon the right, immediately in front of two large forts. The presence of these troops in the Mississippi Valley had caused much speculation and considerable feeling. It was coldly proposed now to subject them to the severest test; and the men themselves were not less anxious to win a name than the white soldiers were desirous to see them tried in the fires of battle. The assault was intended to be simultaneous all along the line. At 5.40 A.M. General Banks's artillery opened upon the rebel works, but the attack on the right was not ordered until ten o'clock, and the left did not assault until two o'clock in the afternoon. The First Regiment of Native Guards was composed of free Negroes of means and intelligence, and all their line officers were Negroes: the regiment was under the command of Lieutenant-colonel Chauncy J. Bassett; while the Third Regiment Native Guards, mostly ex-slaves, had white line officers, and was commanded by Colonel John A. Nelson. Colonel Nelson was placed in the position of Brigadier-general, and Lieutenant-colonel Henry Finnegas assumed command of the regiment. This Negro force numbered 1,080, and was formed in four lines. The first two lines were led by Lieutenant-colonel Bassett. When the order for the assault was given, the men moved forward in quick time, and then changed it into double-quick. The line was almost perfect, and the movement was executed with spirit and dash. The enemy held his fire until the assaulting column was within four hundred yards of the point of attack. Suddenly the earth quaked, and a sheet of fire flashed along the forts; a cloud of smoke rose over the ramparts, and the air was filled with demons of destruction and death—hissing, screaming, howling, and leaping at their black victims with the rapidity of lightning. The slaughter was dreadful, but the shattered, quivering, bleeding columns only wheeled by companies to the rear, reformed at a short distance from the foe, and again gallantly dashed down through the Valley of Death and charged for the guns on the bluff. But the sixty-two pound shot, the shell, canister, and minie-ball were more than infantry could contend with in the open field; the pierced and thinned columns recoiled before such terrible odds. Lieutenant-colonel Henry Finnegas fearlessly led his columns to the assault over the same crimson path, obstructed by the dead and wounded, ploughed by shell, but lighted forever by fadeless deeds of martial valor. The mill of death was now grinding with rapacious greed. The enemy was serving his guns with rapidity and accuracy; the Union gunboats were hurling monstrous shot and shell into the river side of the enemy's work; but all eyes, of friend and foe, were turned towards the remorseless hell of conflict, bristling with bayonets and glinting with the red flash of shotted cannon, into which Negro troops were being hurled by the inexorable orders of Brigadier-general William Dwight. It was of no avail that these troops fought like white veterans. A deep bayou ran under the guns on the bluff, and although the troops reached its edge, some fifty yards from the enemy's guns, they could not cross it. After Colonel Nelson had become convinced that his men could not carry the forts, he despatched an aide to General Dwight to report the difficulties he had to contend with. "Tell Colonel Nelson," he sternly said, "I shall consider that he has accomplished nothing unless he takes those guns!"

> "Theirs not to make reply,
> Theirs not to reason why,
> Theirs but to do and die."

Not a man faltered when the torn and decimated lines were reformed and led over the same field to the same terrible fate. Shell and solid shot severed limbs from trees, tore off tops, and, in falling, these caused the men much annoyance. The colors of the First Louisiana were pierced by bullets and almost severed from the staff. The color-sergeant, Anselmas Planciancois, was gallantly bearing the colors in front of the enemy's works when a shell cut the flag in two and carried away part of the sergeant's head. His brains and blood stained the beautiful banner, which fell over him as he embraced it in death. In a struggle for the flag the generous rivalry of two corporals was ended by the shot of a sharp-shooter which felled one of them. He dropped upon the lifeless body of the color-sergeant, while his successful rival carried the colors proudly through the conflict. Captain André Cailloux, of Company E, First Regiment Native Guards, won for himself a proud place among the military heroes of the Negro race for all time. He was of pure Negro blood, but his features showed the result of generations of freedom and culture among his ancestry. He was a man of fine presence, a leader by instinct and education. He was possessed of ample means, and yet was not alienated from his race in any interest. He loved to boast of genuine blackness, and his race pride made him an acceptable, successful, and formidable leader. It was the magnetic thrill of his patriotic utterances that rallied a company for the service of his country the previous year. Upon all occasions he had displayed talents as a commander, and gave promise of rare courage when the trying hour should come. It had come at length: not too soon for this eager soldier, if unhappily too early for the cause he loved! During the early part of this action the enemy had trained his guns upon the colors of these Negro troops, and they especially received the closest attention of the sharp-shooters. Captain Cailloux commanded the color company. It had suffered severely from the first, but the gallant captain was seen all along the line encouraging his men by brave words and inspiring them by his noble example. His left arm was shattered, but he refused to leave the field. Now in English and then in French, with his voice faint from exhaustion, he urged his men to the fullest measure of duty. In one heroic effort he rushed to the front of his company and exclaimed, "Follow me!" When within about fifty yards of the fort a shell smote him to his death, and he fell, like the brave soldier he was, in the advance with his face to the foe. It was a soldier's death, and just what he would have chosen.

> "'*Still forward and charge for the guns!*' said Cailloux,
> And his shattered sword-arm was the guidon they knew.
> But a fire rakes the flanks and a fire rakes the van;
> He is down with the ranks that go down as one man."

Six desperate charges were made by these Negro troops, and after it was evident that it was by no lack of courage on their part that the guns were not taken, they were recalled from the scene of their fierce trial. The correspondent of the *New York Times* gave the following account of the conduct of these regiments:

"During this time they rallied, and *were ordered to make six distinct charges*, losing thirty-seven killed, and one hundred and fifty-five wounded, and sixteen missing, the majority, if not all, of these being in all probability now lying dead on the gory field, and without the rites of sepulture; for when by flag of truce our forces in other directions were permitted to reclaim their dead, the benefit, through some neglect, was not extended to these black regiments.

"The deeds of heroism performed by these colored men were such as the proudest white men might emulate. Their colors are torn to pieces by shot, and literally bespattered by blood and brains. The color-sergeant of the First Louisiana, on being mortally wounded, hugged the colors to his breast, when a struggle ensued between the two color-corporals on each side of him as to who should have the honor of bearing the sacred standard, and during this generous contention one was seriously wounded. One black lieutenant actually mounted the enemy's works three or four times, and in one charge the assaulting party came within fifty paces of them. Indeed, if only ordinarily supported by artillery and reserve, no one can convince us that they would not have opened a passage through the enemy's works.

"Captain Cailloux, of the First Louisiana, a man so black that he actually prided himself upon his blackness, died the death of a hero, leading on his men in the thickest of the fight. One poor wounded fellow came along with his arm shattered by a shell, and jauntily swinging it with the other, as he said to a friend of mine, 'Massa, guess I can fight no more.' I was with one of the captains, looking after the wounded going in the rear of the hospital, when we met one limping along towards the front. On being asked where he was going, he said, 'I been shot bad in the leg, captain, and dey want me to go to de hospital, but I guess I can gib 'em some more yet.' I could go on filling your columns with startling facts of this kind, but I hope I have told enough to prove that we can hereafter rely upon black arms as well as white in crushing this infernal rebellion. I long ago told you there was an army of 250,000 men ready to leap forward in defence of freedom at the first call. You know where to find them, and what they are worth.

"Although repulsed in an attempt which, situated as things were, was all but impossible, these regiments, though badly cut up, are still on hand, and burning with a passion ten times hotter from their fierce baptism of blood."

On the 30th of May, 1863, General Banks, in an elaborate report to General Halleck, spoke thus flatteringly of the conduct of his Negro troops:

"It gives me pleasure to report that they answered every expectation. Their conduct was heroic; no troops could be more determined or more daring. They made during the day three charges upon the batteries of the enemy, suffering very heavy losses, and holding their position at nightfall with the other troops on the right of our line. The highest commendation is bestowed upon them by all the officers in command on the right. Whatever doubt may have existed before as to the efficiency of organizations of this character, the history of this day proves conclusively to those who were in a position to observe the conduct of these regiments, that the Government will find in this class of troops effective supporters and defenders.

"The severe test to which they were subjected, and the determined manner in which they encountered the enemy, leave upon my mind no doubt of their ultimate success. They require only good officers, commands of limited numbers, and careful discipline to make them excellent soldiers."

Military sentiment was completely revolutionized in the Mississippi Valley respecting the Negro as a man and a soldier; and the Negro himself, with the confidence of a child just learning to walk, was now conscious of his power, and was anxious to consecrate it with lavish generosity to the Government with whose uniform and flag he had been intrusted.

The Second Regiment Louisiana Native Guards, although not on trial at Port Hudson, had won a reputation for the coolest bravery the month before. While Brigadier-general Sherman was in command of the defences of New Orleans, in the early spring of 1863, the Second Louisiana was stationed at Ship Island, Mississippi, under the command of Colonel Naham W. Daniels. While the enemy was pushing forward all available troops from Mobile to reinforce Charleston, he decided upon several demonstrations up the Mississippi Sound by land and water. Colonel Daniels, learning that the enemy contemplated a demonstration in the direction of East Pascagoula, determined to counter this movement. Accordingly, on the 9th of April, 1863, he embarked with Companies B and C, consisting of one hundred and eighty men. At 9 A.M., the United States transport *General Banks* landed the detachment at Pascagoula, and Colonel Daniels proceeded to take possession of the hotel, and hauled his colors to the flag-staff. He immediately threw out a picket-line, the town was taken possession of, and small squads held the roads leading thereto. Colonel Daniels had scarcely made his dispositions when the enemy's cavalry, numbering over three hundred, made its appearance on the Mobile road. The Negro pickets were driven in, but the reserve met the enemy with the coolness of veterans, and after a sharp fight drove the foe off. The cavalry reformed, and made a dash upon the force holding the hotel, but met with no better success. Confederate infantry executed a movement upon the left flank. The lines were skilfully and deliberately contracted, and then the men took refuge behind an old wharf, whence they did excellent execution. He was repulsed, and retired in confusion. In a short time the enemy made a determined assault upon Colonel Daniels's centre, but the black troops, although never under fire before, stood up to their work nobly. The enemy went under cover of timber and buildings, but the gallant little Union force fought in the open field and repulsed the assaulting party.

The fighting continued from 10 A.M. till 2 P.M., when, the enemy having retreated, the Union force retired to their transport undisturbed, the undisputed victors of the battle of East Pascagoula.

The enemy's loss was heavy, both in killed and wounded, while Colonel Daniels's force sustained a loss of three killed and seven wounded. In his report to General Sherman, bearing date of the 11th of April, 1863, Colonel Daniels says:

"The expedition was a perfect success, accomplishing all that was intended, resulting in the repulse of the enemy in every engagement with great loss. . . . Great credit is due to the troops engaged for their unflinching bravery and steadiness under this their first fire, exchanging volley after volley with the coolness of veterans, and for their determined tenacity in maintaining their position, and taking advantage of every success that their courage and valor gave them; and also to their officers, who were cool and determined throughout the action, fighting their commands against five times their number, and confident throughout of success—all demonstrating to its fullest extent that the oppression which they have hitherto undergone from the hands of their foes, and the obloquy that had been showered upon them by those who should have been friends, had not extinguished their manhood or suppressed their bravery, and that they had still a hand to wield the sword and a heart to vitalize its blow."

In his masterful effort to effect the reduction of Vicksburg, General Grant was compelled to contract his long line of forts extending through the Mississippi Valley, and often to strip important posts of nearly all their effective men. He was confronted by Generals Pemberton and Johnson, two able Confederate leaders, and had all he could do to force an opening into the rebel stronghold.

Milliken's Bend was greatly exposed by the concentration of troops about Vicksburg. It was an important point on the river in the State of Arkansas. Brigadier-general E. S. Dennis was left in command with a garrison numbering one thousand and sixty-one effectives, whereof the Twenty-third Iowa, Colonel Glasgow, mustered one hundred and sixty, and the remainder of the force consisted of the Ninth and Eleventh Louisiana and the First Mississippi, all Negroes. These latter troops had been recently recruited, and had never been in conflict with the foe.

On the 6th of June, 1863, General Henry McCulloch, at the head of six regiments, moved against Milliken's Bend from Richmond, Louisiana. He struck the Ninth Louisiana Regiment, and drove it back on the earthworks, when nightfall arrested his further operations. He bivouacked for the night, intending to carry the Union position by the bayonet in the early morning. Just at dark a steamboat was passing the Bend, and General Dennis seized the opportunity to send to Admiral Porter for assistance. The *Choctaw* and *Lexington* were up the river at Helena, Arkansas, and the Admiral despatched them to the Bend at once. The *Choctaw* arrived upon the scene at 3 A. M. At this hour the enemy assaulted the Union position with great spirit, yelling "*No quarter!*" to Negroes and their officers. The gallant little force under Dennis met the enemy with dauntless courage. The rebel force was not only superior in numbers, but in military experience, for they soon swept over the fortifications and delivered a blow on Dennis's flank with deadly effect. A desperate struggle now ensued, wherein Negro recruits and veteran rebels engaged in a hand-to-hand conflict. Bayonets were freely used, and many of each force were transfixed, and hand-to-hand conflicts with clubbed muskets and swords were numerous. The Union force was pushed back against the levee, where the struggle was continued with desperation. At this point of the action the *Choctaw* opened her fire upon the enemy, who was pressing the Union troops towards the river in an unequal contest. The shelling was effective, and the enemy was compelled to retire for shelter. In the mean time McCulloch was trying to effect a movement against Dennis's right flank. The engagement had continued from 3 A.M. until 12 M., and the Negro troops had covered themselves with glory. Never had men fought with greater courage against such odds at the point of the bayonet. After all, the severest test of martial valor is the bayonet. That these Negro troops stood the test the appalling list of casualties shows. The battle ended early in the afternoon, the enemy retiring without being pursued by Dennis; yet many newspaper accounts of this engagement insist that the Negro troops were sent in pursuit, and lost heavily from the shells of the gunboats. This fact, however, is not disclosed in the report of General Dennis. He estimates the enemy's loss at one hundred and fifty killed and three hundred wounded, while he places his own loss at one hundred and twenty-seven killed, and two hundred and eighty-seven wounded, and three hundred missing, many of whom were subsequently accounted for. But the corrected list reveals these dreadful facts: "Of the officers in the Negro force, seven were killed, nine wounded, and three missing; total, nineteen. Of the enlisted men, one hundred and twenty-three were killed, one hundred and eighty-two wounded, and one hundred and thirteen missing; total, four hundred and eighteen. Officers and men, grand total, four hundred and thirty-seven." Of the three officers and one hundred and thirteen men missing, no word was ever had, and it is fair to presume they were murdered. Captain Matthew M. Miller gave the following interesting account of the battle:

"We were attacked here on June 7th, about three o'clock in the morning, by a brigade of Texas troops, about two thousand five hundred in number. We had about six hundred men to withstand them, five hundred of them Negroes. I commanded Company I, Ninth Louisiana. We went into the fight with thirty-three men. I had sixteen killed, eleven badly wounded, and four slightly. I was wounded slightly on the head near the right eye with a bayonet, and had a bayonet run through my right hand near the forefinger; that will account for this miserable style of penmanship.

"Our regiment had about three hundred men in the fight. We had one colonel wounded, four captains wounded, two first and two second lieutenants killed, five lieutenants wounded, and three white orderlies killed, and one wounded in the hand, and two fingers taken off. The list of killed and wounded officers comprised nearly all the officers present with the regiment, a majority of the rest being absent recruiting.

"We had about forty men killed in the regiment and eighty wounded, so you can judge of what part of the fight my company sustained. I never felt more grieved and sick at heart than when I saw how my brave soldiers had been slaughtered—one with six wounds, all the rest with two or three, none less than two wounds. Two of my colored sergeants were killed, both brave, noble men, always prompt, vigilant, and ready for the fray. I never more wish to hear the expression, 'The Niggers won't fight.' Come with me, a hundred yards from where I sit, and I can show you the wounds that cover the bodies of sixteen as brave, loyal, and patriotic soldiers as ever drew bead on a rebel.

"The enemy charged us so close that we fought with our bayonets, hand-to-hand. I have six broken bayonets, to show how bravely my men fought. The Twenty-third Iowa joined my company on the right, and I decláre truthfully that they had all fled before our regiment fell back, as we were all compelled to do.

"Under command of Colonel Page, I led the Ninth Louisiana when the rifle-pits were retaken and held by our troops, our two regiments doing the work.

"I narrowly escaped death once. A rebel took deliberate aim at me with both barrels of his gun, and the bullets passed so close to me that the powder that remained on them burnt my cheek. Three of my men who saw him aim and fire thought that he wounded me each fire. One of them was killed by my side, and he fell on me, covering my clothes with his blood; and before the rebel could fire again, I blew his brains out with my gun.

"It was a horrible fight, the worst I was ever engaged in, not excepting Shiloh. The enemy cried, 'No quarter!' but some of them were very glad to take it when made prisoners.

"Colonel Allen; of the Sixteenth Texas, was killed in front of our regiment, and Brigadier-general Walker was wounded. We killed about one hundred and eighty of the enemy. The gunboat *Choctaw* did good service shelling them. I stood on the breastworks after we took them, and gave the elevations and direction for the gunboat by pointing my sword, and they sent a shell right into their midst which sent them in all directions. Three shells fell there, and sixty-two rebels lay there when the fight was over.

"My wound is not serious, but troublesome. What few men I have left seem to think much of me, because I stood up with them in the fight. I can say for them that I never saw a braver company of men in my life.

"Not one of them offered to leave his place until ordered to fall back. I went down to the hospital, three miles, to-day to see the wounded. Nine of them were there, two having died of their wounds. A boy I had cooking for me came and begged a gun when the rebels were advancing, and took his place with the company; and when we retook the breastworks I found him badly wounded, with one gunshot and two bayonet wounds. A new recruit I had issued a gun to the day before the fight was found dead with a firm grasp on his gun, the bayonet of which was broken in three pieces. So they fought and died, defending the cause that we revere. They met death coolly, bravely; not rashly did they expose themselves, but all were steady and obedient to orders."

The battle of Milliken's Bend will always rank as one of the hardest fought actions of the Civil War, and the unimpeachable valor of the Negro troops engaged in it will remain a priceless heritage of the race for whose freedom they nobly contended. Although recently from the house of bondage, they knew the value of liberty, and those who fell in conflict with their old enemy did not grudge the price they paid in yielding up their lives.

The battle of Poison Springs, in the same State, Arkansas, was another of those decisive engagements wherein individual valor is severely tested and conspicuously displayed. Colonel J. M. Williams was in command of a train-guard comprising the First Kansas Negro Volunteers, the Eighteenth Iowa Infantry, and a detachment of the Second Kansas Cavalry. Six companies of the First Kansas were left at White Oak Creek as a rear-guard, in command of Major Richard G. Ward. There was also one company of the Sixth Kansas, under the command of Lieutenant Henderson, and Rabb's Battery, under Lieutenant Haines. Early on the morning of the 18th of

April, 1864, Colonel Williams was confronted by the advance-guard of General Price's army. Major Ward was ordered to the front, where skirmishing was becoming very heavy. The battery was brought into action, and Companies A, B, E, H were disposed in supporting position. The enemy soon moved against Colonel Williams's right flank, and proceeded to form a line of battle accordingly. Lieutenant Mitchell, commanding a detachment of the Second Kansas Cavalry, was driven back by the enemy, who now appeared in force. But a line of battle was now formed in almost the shape of a segment of a circle, with the convex side towards the enemy. About 11 A.M. the enemy opened the battle with a six-gun battery east of the Union line, and a four-gun howitzer battery opposite the right of the line to the South. The former battery was within a thousand yards of the Union line of battle, and the latter battery within seven hundred yards. The guns were well served, and the fire was terrific upon the exposed Negro infantry, many of whom had never seen a cannon or been in conflict. But they behaved coolly, holding their ground and obeying every order. At a little past 12 M. the artillery fire slackened and the enemy's infantry was ordered to take Rabb's Battery with the bayonet. The Negro infantry supporting it held their fire until the enemy was within one hundred yards, when it was delivered with telling effect. The columns of gray veterans recoiled from before the steady fire of ex-slaves, but charged again with perfect abandon, determined, if possible, to break the Union lines and capture the battery. Companies G and K of the Negro regiment were brought up to support the right and left wings. The Negroes were doing splendid fighting, the white cavalry having retired, but the enemy was exasperated at his failure to break the lines of the gallant black regiment, and now delivered another assault in double columns, yelling vociferously. In this charge nearly every gunner was killed or wounded in the battery, but a private served the last gun with a double load of canister, and gave the charging column a parting shot when only about three hundred yards away. The enemy was demoralized, but the Negro troops cheered at this and fought with increased enthusiasm. After sustaining most gallantly four charges of a force ten times its number, the First Kansas Negro Volunteers slowly fell back, keeping up a continual fire. The enemy had flanked the Union force, and was now pouring a hot, roaring cross-fire on the flanks. Four of the Negro companies fought their way back without a commissioned officer.

In removing the wounded great courage was displayed. The men were often constrained to abandon their wounded comrades or cast away their arms; and choosing the latter, they buried them in the swamps rather than let the enemy get them. The losses were severe, but no veteran white regiment could have made a stand-up fight against the whole of Price's army for two hours with more valor and determination. There were two officers killed and five wounded, while the enlisted men sustained a loss of one hundred and eight killed, seventy-two wounded, and fifteen missing, making a total loss of two hundred and two in a conflict of two hours' duration. This regiment saw much hard service, but on every field proved itself courageous and competent.

CHAPTER XI.

THE ARMY OF THE POTOMAC (1864).

VIRGINIA, the mother of Presidents, was the mother of slavery, and within the limits of this ancient commonwealth the principal battles of the war were fought. Its history, traditions, institutions, topography, its water-ways and magnificent resources, furnished inspiration to the embattled armies that met upon its soil. Richmond was the capital of the Confederate Government, and Petersburg was the base of supplies and the real gate-way to the heart of the rebel Civil Government. After the Mississippi had been opened to the Gulf, the next most important military move was the reduction of Petersburg. General George B. McClellan had menaced the Confederate capital with a splendid army in 1862, but most of the veterans had returned home or had gone into other Departments. Bounty men, substitutes, and conscripts were numerous. By the spring of 1864 a numerous force of Negro troops had been added to this army, and an active and brilliant military career opened up to them.

During the winter of 1863-64 a large number of Negro troops were at persistent drill in Maryland, under Burnside, and in Virginia, under Butler. The first appearance of these troops in the field was in February, 1864, when a brigade was despatched to New Kent Courthouse to reinforce Kilpatrick, who, having made a brilliant and daring dash at Richmond in recoiling before a numerous foe, had burned bridges, destroyed railroads, and made many prisoners. The timely approach of this Negro brigade checked the impetuous and impulsive pursuit of the enemy, and gave Kilpatrick's jaded animals and weary men the relief they so much needed.

On the 7th of April, 1864, General A. E. Burnside, at the head of the Ninth Army Corps, crossed the Potomac and joined General George G. Meade's army, although actual incorporation did not occur until the Rapidan had been passed. This corps contained the majority of Negro troops who had thus far made their appearance in the Army of the Potomac, while later on the Army of the James contained, first, a full division, and subsequently an entire army corps of such troops. The reputation that Negro troops had won at Port Hudson and Fort Wagner served them well in coming in contact with the white troops in the Army of the Potomac. Most of this army was from the Middle and New England States, where Negroes were scarce, and prejudice among the working classes pronouncedly against the Negro, who was by them generally regarded as the cause of the war. But whatever doubt there was concerning the military character of the Negro, it was chiefly silent. There was, therefore, no moral or sentimental proscription to overcome; the army was eager to see the Negro soldier on trial against the flower of Lee's veteran army.

Early in the spring of 1864 Lieutenant-general Grant decided to move Meade's army across the James River, and advance upon Richmond from the south. At the same time he instructed Butler to impel his Army of the James against Petersburg. General W. F. Smith, with the majority of Butler's army, had joined Meade, and the thinned condition of Butler's lines admonished him to keep quiet within his intrenchments. But a restless and ambitious foe grudged him this quiet, and his northern outposts at Wilson's Wharf were chosen as the point of attack. This position was held by Brigadier-general E. A. Wild with a small force of Negro troops, consisting of Battery B, Second Light Artillery, and the First and Tenth Infantry regiments. Fitz-Hugh Lee, at the head of his famous cavalry force, summoned Wild to surrender on the 24th of May. Wild replied that he was there to fight, not to surrender. Lee dismounted his men and assaulted Fort Powhatan about 12.30 P.M. The Negro pickets and skirmishers retired to the intrenchments. The enemy raised a yell and rushed down upon the garrison, but the Negro troops held their fire with the coolness of veterans. When the enemy was well tangled in the abatis, General Wild delivered his fire upon the foe. Confusion and consternation followed, and the enemy recoiled and sought the cover. Lee was angered at Wild's reply, but when he saw his troops shrinking from the deadly fire of ex-slaves, he set his heart on taking the fort. The enemy was determined and desperate in the next charge, but again found the Negroes cool and deliberate in their gallant defence. Lee rightly anticipated the humiliation he would suffer if beaten off by Negro troops, and was busy among the singing bullets urging his men to desperate fighting. It was now determined to impel a massed column against the stubborn fortress, and the savagery of the onslaught told that these Virginia gentlemen were deeply chagrined. But the inferior race met the superior with a steady fire, and the Southern chivalry were driven from the field, after more than five hours' fighting, by their former slaves. Thus ended the battle of Fort Powhatan, and thus the attempt of a division of the enemy's cavalry to turn Butler's flank was a failure. The Negro had fought his first battle in this Department, and exhibited a valor which no one disputed.

General Wild sustained a loss of two killed, twenty-one wounded, and three missing: a total of twenty-six. The enemy suffered a severe loss: twenty to thirty dead were left on the field and nineteen prisoners taken, and thus his casualties footed up about two hundred in the judgment of careful officers who went over the field next day. The correspondent of the *New York Times* wrote of this battle as an eye-witness:

"In Camp, Bermuda Hundred, Virginia, *May* 26, 1864.

"The chivalry of Fitzhugh Lee and his cavalry division was badly worsted in the contest last Tuesday with Negro troops composing the garrison at Wilson's Landing. Chivalry made a gallant fight, however. The battle began at 12.30 P.M. and ended at six o'clock, when chivalry retired disgusted and defeated. Lee's men dismounted far in the rear and fought as infantry. They drove in the pickets and skirmishers to the intrenchments, and several times made valiant charges upon our works. To make an assault, it was necessary to come across an 'open' in front of our position, up to the very edge of a deep and impassable ravine. The rebels with deafening yells made furious onsets, but the Negroes did not flinch, and the mad assailants, discomfited, turned to cover with shrunken ranks. The rebel fighting was very wicked; it showed that Lee's heart was bent on taking the Negroes at any cost. Assaults on the centre having failed, the rebels tried first the left and then the right flank, with no greater success. . . .

"There is no hesitation here in acknowledging the soldierly qualities which the colored men engaged in this fight have exhibited. Even the officers who have hitherto felt no confidence in them are compelled to express themselves mistaken. General Wild, commanding the post, says that the troops stood up to their work like veterans."

General Grant was now ready to turn his attention to the reduction of Petersburg, and General Gillmore, with three thousand five hundred men, crossed the Appomattox and moved on the city from the north over an admirable turnpike. General Kautz, with one thousand five hundred cavalry, went forward to charge the city from the southwest. In addition to these dispositions a battery and two gun-boats were to bombard Fort Clinton, defending the enemy's water approach. These movements were to have been executed in simultaneous harmony, but for no good reason known to military critics they utterly failed. On the 10th of June Q. A. Gillmore had reached within two miles of the city, had attracted the attention and drawn the fire of the enemy, and was competent to drive the enemy's skirmishers. Instead of following up this advantage, Gillmore judged himself unequal to a vigorous assault and retired upon his own judgment. On the other side of the city, Kautz, with the fiery impetuosity of a born cavalry officer, dashed in. The menace of Gillmore had most effectually stirred the enemy, and he was massing to receive the threatened assault. But now that Gillmore had retired, the foe turned on Kautz's command, and expelled it with little effort. The failure of this movement to be concerted had apprised the enemy of the blow that Grant was about to deliver, and hence there was the necessary massing of the Confederate army to ward it off. Grant did not turn aside from his purpose, but hurried forward W. F. Smith's corps from the Chickahominy by steamers *via* the White House. Smith crossed the Appomattox at Point of Rocks and moved southward, encountering the enemy in large numbers on the 15th of June. It was a proud moment for the division of Negro troops in his command, who were now to have the post of honor and danger, and assault the enemy in his intrenched position. A brigade of Hinck's Negro division was ordered to clear a line of rifle-pits immediately in front of Smith's corps. It was about nine o'clock in the morning when the black brigade went forward with a brilliant dash that made all Union hearts thrill with pride, while the heart of the enemy quailed before the advancing columns of Negro soldiers. They carried the rifle-pits with the bayonet. General

Smith, who watched black soldiers fight for the first time, declared that they were equal to any troops, and ordered them to carry a redoubt just ahead. On the men rushed, with "Remember Fort Pillow!" as their battle-cry, and swept the enemy out of the first redoubt. The captured guns were turned upon the enemy, who was either taken or driven off.

A very poetic and inspiring incident of the first charge was the advancing beyond a centre regiment of the national colors. The color-sergeant planted his flag on the enemy's works, and held it there until the regiment came up. One gun was captured and many prisoners taken. The brigade moved on about two miles and a half, when the defences of Petersburg were confronted. From two o'clock until evening these Negro troops reconnoitred and skirmished, at all times exposed to the shells and musketry of the enemy. At about sunset the black brigade was impelled against the intrenched enemy, and it dashed at the works so quickly that the enemy could not depress his guns sufficiently to cover the space before the charging column. In a few moments the Negro soldiers were within the enemy's works, cheering lustily. An officer in one of these regiments gives the following graphic account of the fighting:

"We charged across what appeared to be an almost impassable ravine, with the right wing all the time subject to a hot fire of grape and canister, until we got so far under the guns as to be sheltered, when the enemy took to their rifle-pits as infantrymen. Our brave fellows went steadily through the swamp and up the side of a hill at an angle of almost fifty degrees, rendered nearly impassable by fallen timber. Here again our color-sergeant was conspicuous in keeping far ahead of the most advanced; hanging on to the side of the hill till he would turn about and wave the Stars and Stripes at his advancing comrades, then steadily advancing again, under the fire of the enemy, till he could almost have reached their rifle-pits with his flag-staff. How he kept from being killed I do not know, unless it can be attributed to the fact that the party advancing up the side of the hill always has the advantage of those who hold the crest. It was in this way that we got such decided advantage over the enemy at South Mountain. We took in these two redoubts four more guns, making in all five for our regiment, two redoubts, and a part of a rifle-pit as our day's work. The Fifth, Sixth, and Seventh United States Colored Troops advanced against works more to the left. The Fourth United States Colored Troops took one more redoubt, and the enemy abandoned the other. In these two we got two more guns, which made in all seven. The Sixth Regiment did not get up in time, unfortunately, to have much of the sport, as it had been previously formed in the second line. We left forty-three men wounded and eleven killed in the ravine over which our men charged the last time. Our loss in the whole day's operations was one hundred and forty-three, including six officers, one of whom was killed. Sir, there is no underrating the good conduct of these fellows during these charges; with but a few exceptions they all went in as old soldiers, but with more enthusiasm. I am delighted that our first action resulted in a decided victory.

"The commendations we have received from the Army of the Potomac, including its general officers, are truly gratifying. Hancock's corps arrived just in time to relieve us (we being out of ammunition), before the rebels were reinforced and attempted to retake these strong works and commanding positions, without which they could not hold Petersburg one hour, if it were a part of Grant's plan to advance against it on the right here.

"General Smith speaks in the highest terms of the day's work, as you have doubtless seen, and he assured me in person that our division should have the guns we took as trophies of honor. He is also making his word good in saying that he could hereafter trust colored troops in the most responsible positions. Colonel Ames, of the Sixth United States Colored Troops, and our regiment have just been relieved in the front, where we served our tour of forty-eight hours in turn with the other troops of the corps. While out we are subjected to some of the severest shelling I have ever seen, Malvern Hill not excepted. The enemy got twenty guns in position during the night, and opened on us yesterday morning at daylight. Our men stood it, behind their works, of course, as well as any of the white troops. Our men, unfortunately, owing to the irregular features of ground, took no prisoners. Sir, we can bayonet the enemy to terms on this matter of treating colored soldiers as prisoners of war far sooner than the authorities at Washington can bring him to it by negotiation. This I am morally persuaded of. I know, further, that the enemy won't fight us if he can help it. I am sure that the same number of white troops could not have taken those works on the evening of the 15th; prisoners that we took told me so. I mean prisoners who came in after the abandonment of the fort because they could not get away. They excused themselves on the ground of pride; as one of them said to me, 'D—d if men educated as we have been will fight with niggers, and your government ought not to expect it.' The real fact is, the rebels will not stand against our colored soldiers when there is any chance of their being taken prisoners, for they are conscious of what they justly deserve. Our men went into these works after they were taken, yelling, 'Fort Pillow!' The enemy well knows what this means, and I will venture the assertion that that piece of infernal brutality enforced by them there has cost the enemy already two men for every one they so inhumanly murdered."[1]

The result of this engagement was the capture of sixteen guns and three hundred prisoners, at the cost of six hundred killed, wounded, and missing. The action was also valuable as settling the question of the valor of Negro soldiers. It was unfortunate that a campaign opened so brilliantly should have failed so signally; not, however, on account of these troops. Instead of following up the success won by his Negro troops, General Smith bivouacked for the night. Hancock, who ought to have been within supporting distance, did not arrive until late, and then disclaimed any knowledge that an assault was meditated upon Petersburg, although he must have heard Smith's guns all day. The enemy, startled at the vehement assaults of black troops, put twenty guns in position during the night, and Lee's Confederate veterans, marching at the sound of the enemy's guns, had reached the beleaguered city before sunrise next morning. With daylight came Warren and Burnside to meet the enemy. Smith's right rested on the Appomattox, while Hancock, Burnside, and Warren were disposed to the left, which was covered by Kautz's cavalry. Having returned from City Point, where he had been in consultation with General Grant, Meade ordered a general assault at 2 P.M. on the 16th of June, but it was not delivered until 6 P.M. In this assault white troops were employed mainly, but the Negro troops were despatched to Terry, who was instructed to seize Port Walthall Junction, on the Bermuda Hundred front. It was now proved that Petersburg could not be reduced by a direct assault, and the Union troops intrenched themselves and sought to subdue it by a siege.

---

[1] "Rebellion Record," vol. xi., pp. 580, 581.

"Walthall's Farm, near Petersburg,
"6 A.M. *June* 17, 1864.

"The Eighteenth Corps, under command of General W. F. Smith, which had but just returned to Bermuda Hundred, although greatly needing rest, moved out at three o'clock on the morning of the 15th on the Petersburg side of the river. They were joined by General Hinck's division, United States Colored Troops, which had crossed the pontoon bridge over the Appomattox at ten o'clock the night before. This division consisted of Samuel A. Duncan's brigade, the Fourth, Fifth, Sixth, and Twenty-second regiments, with Captain Angell's battery attached, of Colonel John H. Holman's brigade, the First Regiment, and a detachment of the Fifth Massachusetts Colored cavalry under Colonel Henry S. Russell, with Captain F. C. Choate's Colored battery attached; General Kautz's division of cavalry were also with the column.

"As the column approached the City Point and Petersburg turnpike at a right angle it was suddenly enfiladed by a battery on Baylor's farm. Kautz's cavalry was sent forward to reconnoitre, and found the rebels posted on rapidly rising ground, some four hundred yards behind an almost impenetrable thicket a quarter of a mile wide, extending to a forest on the left. The rebels had four pieces of artillery, two regiments of infantry, behind breastworks, and a small force of cavalry.

"Duncan's black brigade was formed in line on both sides of the pike as follows: the Fifth Regiment, Colonel Jas. W. Conine, on the right; the Twenty-second, Colonel Joseph B. Kiddoo, at the right centre; and the Sixth, Colonel John W. Ames, on the left. Colonel Holman's small brigade formed the second line.

"In this order the troops struggled through the swampy and tangled and almost impassable woods, the rebels shelling them furiously all the distance.

"As our line emerged irregularly from the woods the rebels threw canister with terrible effect. The Fourth received their whole concentrated fire. Captain Wm. V. King was instantly killed and Lieutenant Alfred M. Brigham mortally wounded. The whole regiment suffered severely. Both wings were forced to return and remain in cover for a short time until the lines could be reformed; but at the word the right wing charged with exultant shouts up the slope and through the murderous fire. The rebels fled in confusion to the woods in their rear, leaving one gun behind, which was instantly turned upon them by some of the Negroes of Colonel Kiddoo's regiment, under the direction of Private John Norton, of Company B, of the First District of Columbia Cavalry.

"The rebels at Baylor's farm opened fire at about six o'clock. By eight they were driven out. This affair, although attended with heavy losses, gave the black troops confidence in themselves, and prepared them for a more terrible trial in the attack upon the strong lines of rifle-pits, redoubts, and redans which ran irregularly from the Appomattox up and along the crests of hills, on several farms, two miles from Petersburg. . . .

"The Colored Troops were obliged to advance across an open field, exposed the whole distance to a deadly fire, completely enfilading their two lines of battle, to a fire from two batteries directly in front, and to a cross-fire from an intermediate battery. An hour was consumed in forming the lines of battle and advancing the first quarter of a mile. The men could move but a few rods before the rebels got range, when they were obliged to lie down and await opportunity. Soon they would rise, push forward a few rods farther, and again lie down.

"At about half-past one they gained the designated locality, and then for five mortal hours lay exposed to the strain of constant apprehension from the ceaseless shelling. Old officers declared that while they have been under a more furious cannonading, it has been under the excitement of a charge, but that they were never subjected to a severer trial under fire, considering the time during which they were exposed and the unavoidable inactivity, and add that there can be no severer test of a soldier, particularly for green troops, than Duncan's entire brigade withstood. They say that after such a long strain upon their nerves, that the troops should be able to rise, move against such a formidable line of works, and carry them triumphantly, is irresistible proof that black troops can and will fight.

"At half-past six the charge was ordered. The first plan, to advance in two lines of battle, was changed, General Smith deeming it madness to throw full lines against such strong redoubts. Half the first line was, therefore, sent forward as skirmishers, to be promptly supported if any advantage should be gained. As the skirmishers pushed on, our batteries on the right opened, and were replied to by the rebels with equal vigor.

"After half an hour of very heavy cannonading and musketry firing, a shout of victory, drowning all other sounds, and plainly to be heard for two miles away, arose from our troops as they gained and dashed into the works. These works were five formidable redans, half a mile, three-quarters, and a mile, severally, distant, on the other side of a deep and difficult ravine, and in a very commanding position. Colonel Kiddoo's regiment gained the hill. In support of this general flank movement of the first line, the second line, consisting of the Fifth and Sixth regiments of Duncan's brigade, were swung round and moved against the front of the remaining works. The rebels, assailed in flank and front, fought to the last moment, and then so precipitately withdrew that but few were captured.

"It was now nine o'clock in the evening. Immediate pursuit was impossible, and General Smith deemed it prudent to rest and await reinforcements. The Second Army Corps, which had made a forced march, began arriving two hours later. General Smith showed his appreciation of the day's work by remarking that 'it was one of the greatest of the war.' He said, 'It will make the old Army of the Potomac open its eyes wide.' The earthworks so successfully carried are regarded as the most formidable the army has encountered during the present campaign.

"The success has a peculiar value and significance from the thorough test it has given of the efficiency of Negro troops. Their losses were heavy. In the thickest of the fight, and under the most trying circumstances, they never flinched. The old Army of the Potomac, so long prejudiced and so obstinately heretical on this subject, stand amazed as they look on the works captured by the Negroes, and are loud and unreserved in their praise. As near as I can make it out, Duncan's brigade alone took six redoubts or redans, with their connecting rifle-pits, and captured seven pieces of artillery. General Smith, speaking of their conduct, said, 'No nobler effort has been put forth to-day, and no greater success achieved, than that of the Colored Troops.' From so reticent an officer this testimony is invaluable. Subjoined is his order of the day, just issued:

"'*To the Eighteenth Army Corps:*

"'. . . To the Colored Troops comprising the division of General Hinks, the General commanding would call the attention of his command. With the veterans of the Eighteenth Corps they have stormed the works of the enemy and carried them, taking guns and prisoners, and in the whole affair they have displayed all the qualities of good soldiers.

"'By command of   W. F. SMITH, Major-general.'

"WILLIAM RUSSELL, Jr., Assistant Adjutant-general."[1]

From June 15th to June 30th the losses of the Negro troops in front of Petersburg were as follows:

---

[1] "Rebellion Record," vol. xi., Doc., pp. 570, 571, 572.

NEGRO DIVISION, FIELD AND STAFF.

Killed—Officers	4
" Enlisted Men	58
Wounded—Officers	27
" Enlisted Men	417
Missing—Officers	—
" Enlisted Men	69
Aggregate	575

From this time (June 16th) until the explosion of the mine (July 30th) the Negro troops participated in the various duties of building fortifications, skirmishing, picket-duty, and sharp-shooting. In all these they did their duty cheerfully, and won the entire confidence of the army. There were other Negro troops arriving daily, and they were distributed through the Ninth, Tenth, and Eighteenth corps—in the Army of the Potomac and in the Army of the James. The Ninth Corps, containing a division of Negro troops, had secured in the last assault a position immediately in front of Petersburg, distant only about one hundred and fifty yards from the enemy. A fort projecting some distance beyond the enemy's main line did the Union lines and forces great damage. Moreover, its position was so commanding that if it were once in the possession of the besiegers the capture of the city could speedily be effected. To compass this end it was decided to mine this fort. A ravine extending through the lines screened the operations of the Forty-eighth Pennsylvania infantry from the enemy, and furnished a convenient place in which to deposit the earth, borne out patiently in cracker-boxes. The mine completed, the two galleries charged, the morning of the 30th of July, 1864, was determined upon as the time to fire it. Some consideration had been given to the question which division should charge through the crater, gain the elevated ground, and hold this gate open, while Meade's army should rush through.

The inspecting officer of the Ninth Corps, Lieutenant-colonel Charles G. Loring, in obedience to orders had inspected the four divisions comprising the corps, and had reported that the "Black Division" was the fittest for the perilous work in hand. They had an alertness and dash which made them equal to the task.

Colonel Loring gives the following reasons for the selection of the Black Division:

"Some time previous to the intended assault I officially informed General Burnside that, in my opinion, the white troops of his corps were not in a fit condition to make the assault; that many of them had been for six weeks in close proximity to the enemy's lines—within one hundred and thirty yards; that all of them had been very near the enemy's fire; and that when troops are exposed, as they were, day and night for six weeks to an incessant fire, it is impossible that they should have the same spirit as fresh troops. In addition to that, before sitting down before the enemy's lines, they had been very much worn by the long and arduous campaign, in which, as I considered, the Ninth Corps had performed more arduous services than the other corps. But even if they had been fresh when they had arrived before Petersburg, the experience of those six weeks—during which they had been under fire day and night without cessation, so that it was impossible to go to the rear, even to attend to the calls of nature, without being exposed to being killed on the spot; during which period their losses had averaged over thirty (30) per day, amounting in the whole to one man in eight—was enough at least to weaken the zeal of the men. For this reason, principally, General Burnside selected to lead the assault the colored division, which up to that time had never been under any serious fire. Parts of it had been engaged in one or two little skirmishes, but the division had never been under any serious fire. That division was therefore selected upon the principle that fresh troops are much better to make an assault than old but worn-out troops. This plan was changed at noon of the day previous to the assault, and the first division of white troops, under General Ledlie, was selected to lead the attack the next morning."

Under date of July 26, 1864, General Burnside submitted his plan of battle to General Meade, and in referring to the use of the Black Division said:

"My plan would be to explode the mine just before daylight in the morning, or at about five o'clock in the afternoon; mass the two brigades of the colored division in the rear of my first line in columns of division 'double columns closed in mass,' 'the head of each brigade resting on the front line,' and as soon as the explosion has taken place, move them forward with instructions for the division to take half distance, and as soon as the leading regiments of the two brigades pass through the gap in the enemy's line, the leading regiment of the right brigade to come into line perpendicular to the enemy's line by the 'right companies on the right into line, wheel,' the 'left companies on the right into line,' and proceed at once down the line of the enemy's works as rapidly as possible; and the leading regiment of the left brigade to execute the reverse movement to the left, moving up the enemy's line. The remainder of the columns to move directly towards the crest in front as rapidly as possible, diverging in such a way as to enable them to deploy into columns of regiment, the right column making as nearly as possible for Cemetery Hill. These columns to be followed by the other divisions of the other corps as soon as they can be thrown in."

On the 28th General Burnside called upon Meade at his headquarters. General Burnside says of this visit:

"A long conversation ensued, in which I pointed out to General Meade the condition of the three white divisions, and urged upon him the importance, in my opinion, of placing the colored division in the advance, because I thought it would make a better charge at that time than either of the white divisions. I reminded him of the fact that the three white divisions had for forty days been in the trenches in the immediate presence of the enemy, and at no point of the line could a man raise his head above the parapet without being fired at by the enemy. That they had been in the habit, during the whole of that time, of approaching the main line by covered ways, and using every possible means of protecting themselves from the fire of the enemy. That their losses had been continuous during that time, amounting to from thirty to sixty men daily. That the men had had no opportunity of cooking upon the main line, everything having been cooked in the rear, and carried up to them. That they had had very few, if any, opportunities of washing; and that, in my opinion, they were not in condition to make a vigorous charge. I also stated that I was fortified in this opinion, which had been formed from personal observation, by the report of my inspector-general, who had taken occasion to look at the troops with a view to making up his mind as to their effectiveness for a work of that kind.

"General Meade still insisted that the black troops should not lead; that he could not trust them, because they were untried, and probably gave other reasons which do not occur to me at this moment. But he said that, inasmuch as I was so urgent in the matter, he would refer it to General Grant, whom he expected to visit that afternoon, and his decision, of course, would be final. I said to him that I would cheerfully abide by any decision that either one of them would make, but I must still urge upon him that I thought it of the utmost importance that the colored troops should lead.

"General Meade did go to see General Grant that day, and I think returned the same afternoon, but I did not hear from him. During the next forenoon (Friday) General Wilcox and General Potter, commanding two of my white divisions, came to my headquarters to talk over the attack, which it was understood would be made the next morning. I told them that I had been very much exercised the day before lest that portion of my plan which contemplated putting the colored division in advance should be changed by General Meade, but that I was pretty well satisfied he had given it up, because I had heard nothing further from him about it.

"While in the midst of this conversation, or very soon after, General Meade came to my headquarters, and there told me that General Grant agreed with him as to the disposition of the troops, and that I would not be allowed to put the colored division in the advance. I asked him if that decision could not be reconsidered; he replied, 'No, general, the order is final; you must detail one of your white divisions to take the advance.' I said, 'Very well, general, I will carry out this plan to the best of my ability.'"

General Grant said of this change of plan: "General Burnside wanted to put his colored division in front,[1] and I believe if he had done so it would have been a success. Still I agreed with General Meade in his objection to that plan. General Meade said that if we put the colored troops in front (we had only that one division), and it should prove a failure, it would then be said, and very

---

[1] In his "Personal Memoirs" (vol. ii., p. 313) Grant says, "Meade interfered with this."—G. W. W.

properly, that we were shoving those people ahead to get killed because we did not care anything about them, but that could not be said if we put the white troops in front. That is the only point he (General Meade) changed after he had given his orders to General Burnside."

Burnside ordered the commanders of the three divisions composed of white troops to draw lots—a curious way of deciding such an important question. The lot fell to Brigadier-general J. H. Ledlie of the first division. Grant had rejected the opinions of nearly all the military critics of Europe, who maintain that the troops on the ground are fittest for such work. It has been said that Ledlie was the poorest choice that could have been made in the army in front of Petersburg, but it is an unfair statement. He did the best he could under the circumstances.

The mine was to be fired at 3.30 A.M., but an obstruction in the train, extending through the gallery, prevented an explosion. Lieutenant Jacob Douty and Sergeant Henry Rees, of the Forty-eighth Pennsylvania, volunteered to remove the obstruction, and at 4.45 A. M. the fuse did its work, and the enemy's fort was blown up, with over three hundred picked men. When the air was clear again, where the fort had stood but a few moments before was now a yawning crater one hundred and fifty feet in length, sixty feet in width, and thirty feet in depth. It was through this crater of loose earth that Ledlie was to charge. The guns along the line had opened upon the enemy, and the very earth shook and rocked to their roar. Ledlie led his division to the appointed task, but there was neither method nor martial spirit in his charge. The Tenth New Hampshire broke into the shape of a V, and the other troops fell into disorder, and once in the crater the confusion was indescribable. Two other white divisions were sent in, but they only added to the confusion, for Ledlie's men merely blocked the way. For two hours—ages on the battle-field —no fighting was done, but the enemy, although unnerved at first, had recovered, and was preparing for desperate resistance. He planted guns on each side of the crater, and threw forward infantry to strike the assaulting column on the flanks, while his guns could sweep the crater, now turned into a very death-trap for the brave men whose brawn had made it. At the critical moment, when the enemy could not only hold this opening in his works, but threatened to sweep through and rout Meade, the Black Division was ordered to charge and gain the crest beyond the crater. Three veteran white divisions had been hurled back in confusion, but these Negro troops were sent forward to contend with an infuriated, brave, and numerous foe. They were gallantly led, and nobly followed where duty and devotion were terribly tested. Obstructed at first by the disorganized and distracted white troops, who, raked front and rear, could neither advance nor retreat, they subsequently charged farther to the right. They were met with a destructive enfilading and cross-fire. Again and again they charged for the ridge, but it was now too firmly held by the enemy, and after exhibiting great courage and sustaining severe loss, these Negro troops were recalled. They had borne themselves with conspicuous gallantry, and having done all that was required of them were withdrawn to their works. An officer of the Black Division said, after the engagement was concluded, " Our men went forward with enthusiasm equal to anything under different circumstances; but in going through the fort that had been blown up, the passage was almost impeded by obstacles thrown up by the explosion. At the same time we were receiving a most deadly cross-fire from both flanks. At this time our lieutenant-colonel, W. E. W. Ross, fell, shot through the left leg, bravely leading his men. I immediately assumed command, but only to hold it a few minutes, when I fell, struck by a piece of shell in the side."

Another officer in this division testified: "In regard to the bravery of the Colored Troops, although I have been in upward of twenty battles, I never saw so many cases of gallantry. The 'crater,' where we were halted, was a perfect slaughter-pen. Had not 'some one blundered,' but moved us up at daylight instead of eight o'clock, we should have been crowned with success, instead of being cut to pieces by a terrific enfilading fire. . . .

"I was never under such a terrific fire, and can hardly realize how any escaped alive. Our loss was heavy. In the Twenty-eighth (colored), for instance, commanded by Lieutenant-colonel Russell (a Bostonian), he lost seven out of eleven officers, and ninety-one men out of two hundred and twenty-four; and the colonel himself was knocked over senseless for a few minutes by a slight wound in the head. Both his color-sergeants and all his color-guard were killed. . Lieutenant-colonel Bross, of the Twenty-ninth (colored), was killed outright, and nearly every one of his officers hit. This was nearly equal to Bunker Hill. Colonel Ross, of the Thirty-first (colored), lost his leg. The Twenty-eighth, Twenty-ninth, and Thirtieth (colored) all charged over the works, climbing up an earthwork six feet high, then down into a ditch, and up on the other side, all the time under the severest fire in front and flank. Not being supported, of course the storming party fell back."

The Negro soldiers' valor was, after this engagement, no more questioned than his loyalty, and the reputation secured at such a high price was kept untarnished to the end of the campaign.

In the action at Deep Bottom, Virginia, enduring from the 14th until the 18th of August, 1864, Negro troops fought the enemy behind his intrenchments, contended with cavalry and sharp-shooters, and met his veteran infantry in the open field. In every conflict with the enemy they behaved like veterans, and exhibited enthusiasm and endurance wonderful in raw troops. It was Grant's purpose, not at all dismayed by his discomfiture in front of Petersburg, to impel a considerable force against the enemy's left facing Deep Bottom. In this force, incorporated with the Tenth Corps, under General Birney, were a number of Negro troops, and holding the right of the Union line on the river side, the enemy thought to dash through and turn Grant's flank. Accordingly, on the night of the 18th of August, 1864, the enemy assaulted Birney vigorously; but his Negro soldiers were cool and determined, meeting the blow with courage. Next day General Birney made the following report of the assault:

"Headquarters Tenth Army Corps, *August* 19, 1864.
" *Major-general Butler, commanding Department:*
"The enemy attacked my lines in heavy force last night, and was repulsed with great loss. In front of one Colored regiment eighty-two dead bodies of the enemy are already counted. The Colored troops behaved handsomely, and are in fine spirits. The assault was in columns a division strong, and would have carried any works not so well defended. The enemy's loss was at least one thousand.
"Respectfully,
(Signed) "D. B. BIRNEY, Major-general."

On the 29th of September, 1864, General Butler despatched the Tenth Corps, under Birney, and the Eighteenth Corps, under Ord, across the James, intending to find and turn the enemy's left flank, while Warren and Hancock were engaged in a similar movement at Hatcher's Run. Here again the Negro troops under Birney added to their well-earned reputation for gallantry. The country through which they passed was heavily wooded and broken by numerous hills. The enemy's outposts were struck and hurled back in confusion, and the white troops were ordered to assault the enemy in his fortified position on Chaffin's farm, where also he commanded Fort Harrison. The white troops moved forward to the work with courage and coolness, but the assaulting column was again and again smitten with shot and shell, grape and canister, and at length was beaten back with loss and confusion. General Butler addressed the Negro troops and ordered them to take the fort at the point of the bayonet. With a yell that told the enemy his position was untenable the Negro division sprang forward and charged down a hill, through a tortuous stream, and up a hill again to the abatis. Preceded by pioneers, they never flinched under the terrific fire while a way was being cut for them. The enemy, emboldened by the apparent hesitancy of the dark warriors, sprang upon his works and exultingly called out, "Come on, darkies, we want your muskets!" The troops rushed forward, crying, *"Remember Fort Pillow!"* The enemy retired without taking their guns, but the contents cut short the precipitous retreat of many. A considerable number of prisoners and fifteen guns were taken, and the Union flag was planted on Fort Harrison by Negro troops. It was a brilliant and daring piece of work, securing the New Market Road and a strong line of intrenchments. Fort Harrison occupied a commanding position overlooking the James River, and but five miles from Richmond. North of this, one half mile, but a little farther back, was Fort Gilmer, and this also was assaulted by Birney's intrepid Negro soldiers. It was a beautiful autumn afternoon, and a cornfield, free of all obstruction, was the ground to be passed over in the charge. It was, indeed, an inspiring sight to see these troops charge Fort Gilmer. Shotted cannon blazed and smoked and hurled grape and canister at the assaulting columns. But on they went, and many of the Negro soldiers actually crawled up to the mouth of the cannon. A sergeant of one of these regiments planted his flag on the fort, but was blown to atoms the next moment by a cannon discharged when he was but two feet from its mouth. Several charges were made, but all in vain. Gilmer was an impregnable fortress; and, after a severe loss, the troops were withdrawn.

But the capture of Fort Harrison was too great a menace to Richmond, and the enemy determined to retake it. Major-general C. W. Field hurled three brigades against Fort Harrison on one side, while General Hoke charged on the other side, the next morning, the 30th of September. The Negro troops held their ground and inflicted great punishment upon the enemy. He was routed and beaten off with severe loss. The position thus gained was held till the close of the war; and the campaign of 1864 in Virginia, opened so brilliantly and successfully by Negro troops, was closed with equal valor and prowess. The following general order testifies to the courage of these troops:

"Headquarters, Third Division, Eighteenth Army Corps,
"Before Richmond, Virginia, *October* 7, 1864.

"*General Orders No.* 103.

"OFFICERS AND SOLDIERS OF THIS DIVISION,—General D. B. Birney, commanding the Tenth Army Corps, has desired me to express to you the high satisfaction he felt at your good conduct while we were serving with the Tenth Corps, September 29 and 30, 1864, and with your gallantry in storming New Market Heights.

"I have delayed issuing this order, hoping for an opportunity to say this to you in person.

"Accept, also, my own thanks for your gallantry on September 29, and your good conduct since. You have won the good opinion of the whole Army of the James, and every one who knows your deeds.

"Let every officer and man, on all occasions, exert himself to increase your present deserved reputation.
"C. J. PAINE,
"Brigadier-general.
(Signed) "S. A. CARTER,
"Assistant Adjutant-general."

More than ten years after this campaign, General B. F. Butler, advocating in Congress the passage of a bill giving civil rights to the Negro race, said, "I went myself with the Colored troops to attack the enemy at New Market Heights, which was the key to the enemy's flank on the north side of James River. That work was a redoubt built on the top of a hill of some considerable elevation, then running down into a marsh; in that marsh was a brook; then rising again to a plain which gently rolled away towards the river. On that plain, when the flash of dawn was breaking, I placed a column of three thousand Colored troops, in close column by divisions, right in front, with guns at 'right shoulder shift.' I said, 'That work must be taken by the weight of your column; no shot must be fired;' and to prevent their firing I had the caps taken from the nipples of their guns. Then I said, 'Your cry, when you charge, will be, "Remember Fort Pillow!"' and as the sun rose up in the heavens the order was given, 'Forward!' and they marched forward, steadily as if on parade, went down the hill, across the marsh; and as they got into the brook they came within range of the enemy's fire, which vigorously opened upon them. They broke a little as they forded the brook, and the column wavered. Oh, it was a moment of intensest anxiety; but they formed again as they reached the firm ground, marching steadily on with closed ranks under the enemy's fire, until the head of the column reached the first line of abatis some one hundred and fifty yards from the enemy's work. Then the axe-men ran to the front to cut away the heavy obstructions of defence, while one thousand men of the enemy, with their artillery concentrated, poured from the redoubt a heavy fire upon the head of the column hardly wider than the clerk's desk. The axe-men went down under that murderous fire; other strong hands grasped the axes in their stead, and the abatis is cut away. Again, at double-quick, the column goes forward to within fifty yards of the fort, to meet there another line of abatis. The column halts, and there a very fire of hell is pouring upon them. The abatis resists and holds; the head of the column seems literally to melt away under the rain of shot and shell; the flags of the leading regiments go down, but a brave black hand seizes the colors; they are up again, and wave their starry light over the storm of battle; again the axe-men fall, but strong hands and willing hearts seize the heavy, sharpened trees and drag them away, and the column rushes forward, and with a shout which now rings in my ear, go over the redoubt like a flash, and the enemy never stopped running for four miles.

"It became my painful duty, sir, to follow in the track of that charging column, and there, in a space not wider than the clerk's desk, and three hundred yards long, lay the dead bodies of five hundred and forty-three of my Colored comrades, slain in the defence of their country, who had laid down their lives to uphold its flag and its honor as a willing sacrifice; and as I rode along among them, guiding my horse this way and that way, lest he should profane with his hoofs what seemed to me the sacred dead, and as I looked on their bronzed faces upturned in the shining sun as if in mute appeal against the wrongs of the country for which they had given their lives, and whose flag had only been to them a flag of stripes on which no star of glory had ever shone for them—feeling I had wronged them in the past, and believing what was the future of my country to them—among my dead comrades there I swore to myself a solemn oath: 'May my right hand forget its cunning, and my tongue cleave to the roof of my mouth, if I ever fail to defend the rights of those men who have given their blood for me and my country this day and for their race forever;' and, God helping me, I will keep that oath." [1]

The armies in Virginia now went into winter-quarters, and the same zeal manifested in the field characterized the Negro troops in camp. They were patient and persevering in drill, and vigilant on picket; and their high character for soldiership, won on the battle-field, entitled them to and secured for them the cordial comradeship of their white compatriots.

---

[1] The incident and sentiment are beautiful; and the story has been told with telling effect in several political campaigns.—G. W. W.

CHAPTER XII.

THE FORT PILLOW MASSACRE (1864).

Fort Pillow was in Tennessee, about forty miles from Memphis. It occupied a high bluff overlooking the Mississippi River, flanked by two deep and precipitous ravines slightly fringed with light timber. The garrison consisted of two hundred and ninety-five men of the Thirteenth Tennessee Union Cavalry, under command of Major W. F. Bradford, and two hundred and sixty-two men of the Sixth United States Heavy Artillery (Negroes), making five hundred and fifty-seven men, all under the command of Major L. F. Booth, of the Artillery. The slave system made the entire South brutal, and many soldiers of the Confederate army were exceedingly cruel to prisoners. There were two classes of troops in the Union army against whom the rebels manifested at all times the most bitter feeling. They were Union white Southerners and ex-slaves. They despised the latter for fighting against their old masters and for their freedom; they hated the former on account of their loyal sentiments and association with Negroes in arms. One of the most cruel exhibitions of Confederate malice was the massacre of the garrison of Fort Pillow after it had surrendered.

On the 12th of April, 1864, Major-general N. B. Forrest, at the head of a division of cavalry, appeared before Fort Pillow and demanded its surrender. The fort mounted six guns, and the gunboat *New Era* rendered the beleaguered garrison excellent support. Forrest's summons was declined, and the battle opened some time before sunrise, and progressed with great zeal on both sides until 9 A.M., when the gallant Major Booth fell. The command now devolved upon Major Bradford, and he immediately withdrew the strong skirmish line that, up to this time, had fearlessly held an outer line of intrenchments. The Negroes fought their guns with coolness and skill, and the *New Era* shelled the ravines as best she could. But owing to the height of the embankments the work of the gunboat was not very effective. As fast as the enemy was shelled out of one ravine he sought shelter in the other. Between twelve and one o'clock there was a lull in the fighting on both sides, when the *New Era* backed into the centre of the river to cool and clean her guns. Forrest seized this opportunity to summon the garrison to surrender. First-lieutenant Mack J. Leaming, adjutant of the Thirteenth Tennessee Cavalry, met the enemy's flag of truce about three o'clock, and conveyed to Major Bradford General Forrest's summons, which was declined. Meanwhile, in violation of the truce, Forrest's men were stealing the horses of the garrison, and crawling to the shelter in both ravines. The summons, as recalled by Lieutenant Leaming, was as follows:

"Headquarters Confederate Cavalry, near Fort Pillow,
"*April* 12, 1864.

"As your gallant defence of the fort has entitled you to the treatment of brave men [or something to that effect], I now demand an unconditional surrender of your force, at the same time assuring you that they will be treated as prisoners of war. I have received a fresh supply of ammunition, and can easily take your position.

"N. B. FORREST.

"Major L. F. BOOTH,
"Commanding United States Forces."

Major Bradford replied that he desired an hour for consultation with his officers and the officers of the gunboat.

Captain Young, provost-marshal of the post, and Lieutenant Leaming went and delivered this message to the Confederate flag of truce. In a very short time another flag of truce appeared, and a Confederate officer handed a message to Lieutenant Leaming, saying, "That gives you twenty minutes to surrender; I am General Forrest." Lieutenant Leaming conveyed the message to Major Bradford. The substance of Forrest's summons was: "Twenty minutes will be given you to take your men outside of the fort. If in that time they are not out I will immediately proceed to assault your works." Major Bradford's reply was despatched to Forrest: "I will not surrender." When this message was handed to Forrest he read it, and saluting Leaming, turned away in silence. Leaming had scarcely returned to the fort when the firing began. During the parleying a large force of the enemy's dismounted cavalry had crawled so near the fort that it was impossible to depress the guns sufficiently to repel them. The Negro gunners were now without a single commissioned officer, and had suffered terribly from the enemy's sharp-shooters, who had gained possession of a row of wooden buildings immediately in front of the fort. At length, with the rebel yell of "*No quarter!*" the enemy assaulted the exhausted and decimated garrison with a savage impetuosity that brooked no resistance. The fort was carried. As rapidly as the men surrendered they were murdered, and the Negroes, believing that no mercy would be shown them, rushed at top speed down the bluff to the river. The enemy pursued, and shot them down as soon as overtaken. Many of the wounded, to escape brutal treatment, feigned death, but they were revived by cruel kicks and blows, compelled to rise to their knees, and then shot. Some sought refuge in the merciful river; but the enemy fired upon them until, bleeding and exhausted, they found ample sepulchre in the placid waters of the Mississippi. In one place under the bluff white and black soldiers had huddled together for safety, but the enemy discovered them long after the conflict had ended, and called them forth to a cruel death. First a white soldier would be called out and ordered to stand up and be shot down; then a black soldier would have to respond to the cruel summons, and meet death. The women and children of the garrison, white and black, young and old, mistress and servant, were shot down with indiscriminate inhumanity.

The slaughter went on until night closed over the revolting sight, and the stars shone upon murderer and victim with an impartial and peerless light.

Next morning, no reinforcements having arrived, the surviving Union soldiers, regardless of wounds, were set upon by the enemy and robbed; the wounded were conveyed to a frame building, with the promise that medical aid would be sent, but in a few minutes the doors were heavily barred and the building fired. Being dry, it was only a short time before the building and the wounded, helpless prisoners of war were consumed. Other wounded, who had crawled to their tents during the night, were nailed to the floor by their clothing, and in this condition were burned to death. Their piteous cries touched no heart, brought no succor, but only received the curses of the enemy. A Confederate lieutenant had taken a Negro child to his saddle, intending to save it; but General Chalmers, seeing this "womanish conduct," ordered the lieutenant to put the child upon the ground and shoot it. The lieutenant refused to kill an innocent child. The order was given again with brutal oaths and the child was murdered.

Is the evidence of these facts demanded? It is complete. First-lieutenant Mack J. Leaming, under oath before the Committee on the Conduct and Expenditures of the War, testified:

"The Negroes ran down the hill towards the river, but the rebels kept shooting them as they were running; shot some again after they had fallen, robbed and plundered them. After everything was all gone, after we had given up the fort entirely, the guns thrown away and the firing on our part stopped, they still kept up their murderous fire, more especially on the Colored troops, I thought, although the white troops suffered a great deal. I know the Colored troops had a great deal the worst of it. I saw several shot after they were wounded; as they were crawling around, the secesh would step out and blow their brains out.

"About this time they shot me. It must have been four or half-past four o'clock. I saw there was no chance at all, and threw down my sabre. A man took deliberate aim at me, but a short distance from me, certainly not more than fifteen paces, and shot me."

"Q. With a musket or pistol?"

"A. I think it was a carbine; it may have been a musket, but my impression is that it was a carbine. Soon after I was shot I was robbed. A secesh soldier came along, and wanted to know if I had any greenbacks. I gave him my pocket-book. I had about a hundred dollars, I think, more or less, and a gold watch and chain. They took everything in the way of valuables that I had. I saw them robbing others. That seemed to be the general way they served the wounded, so far as regards those who fell in my vicinity. Some of the Colored troops jumped into the river, but were shot as fast as they were seen. One poor fellow was shot as he reached the bank of the river. They ran down and hauled him out. He got on his hands and knees, and was crawling along, when a secesh soldier put his revolver to his head and blew his brains out. It was about the same thing all along, until dark that night.

"I was very weak, but I finally found a rebel who belonged to a society that I am a member of (the Masons), and he got two of our Colored soldiers to assist me up the hill, and he brought me some water. At that time it was about dusk. He carried me up just to the edge of the fort, and laid me down. There seemed to be quite a number of dead collected there. They were throwing them into the outside trench, and I heard them talking about burying them there. I heard one of them say, 'There is a man who is not quite dead yet.' They buried a number there; I do not know how many.

"I was carried that night to a sort of little shanty that the rebels had occupied during the day with their sharp-shooters. I received no medical attention that night at all. The next morning early I heard the report of cannon down the river. It was the gunboat 28 coming up from Memphis; she was shelling the rebels along the shore as she came up. The rebels immediately ordered the burning of all the buildings, and ordered the two buildings where the wounded were to be fired. Some one called to the officer who gave the order, and said there were wounded in them. The building I was in began to catch fire. I prevailed upon one of our soldiers who had not been hurt much to draw me out, and I think others got the rest out. They drew us down a little way, in a sort of gully, and we lay there in the hot sun without water or anything.

"About this time a squad of rebels came around, it would seem for the purpose of murdering what Negroes they could find. They began to shoot the wounded Negroes all around there, interspersed with the whites. I was lying a little way from a wounded Negro, when a secesh soldier came up to him, and said, 'What in hell are you doing here?' The Colored soldier said he wanted to get on the gunboat. The secesh soldier said, 'You want to fight us again, do you? Damn you, I'll teach you,' and drew up his gun and shot him dead. Another Negro was standing up erect a little way from me—he did not seem to be hurt much. The rebel loaded his gun again immediately. The Negro begged of him not to shoot him, but he drew up his gun and took deliberate aim at his head. The gun snapped, but he fixed it again, and then killed him. I saw this. I heard them shooting all around there—I suppose killing them."

Major Williams, a private in Company B, Sixth United States Heavy Artillery, testified as follows:

"Q. Was there anything said about giving quarter?"

"A. Major Bradford brought in a black flag, which meant no quarter. I heard some of the rebel officers say, 'You damned rascals, if you had not fought us so hard, but had stopped when we sent in a flag of truce, we would not have done anything to you.' I heard one of the officers say, 'Kill all the niggers;' another one said, 'No; Forrest says take them and carry them with him to wait upon him and cook for him, and put them in jail and send them to their masters.' Still they kept on shooting. They shot at me after that, but did not hit me; a rebel officer shot at me. He took aim at my side; at the crack of his pistol I fell. He went on, and said, 'There's another dead nigger.'"

"*Q.* Was there any shot in the hospital that day?"

"*A.* Not that I know of. I think they all came away and made a raft, and floated across the mouth of the creek and got into a flat-bottom."

"*Q.* Did you see any buildings burned?"

"*A.* I stayed in the woods all day Wednesday. I was there Thursday and looked at the buildings. I saw a great deal left that they did not have a chance to burn up. I saw a white man burned up who was nailed up against the house."

"*Q.* A private or an officer?"

"*A.* An officer; I think it was a lieutenant in the Tennessee cavalry."

"*Q.* How was he nailed?"

"*A.* Through his hands and feet, right against the house."

"*Q.* Was his body burned?"

"*A.* Yes, sir; burned all over—I looked at him good."

"*Q.* When did you see that?"

"*A.* On the Thursday after the battle."

"*Q.* Where was the man?"

"*A.* Right in front of the fort."

Ransom Anderson, private in Company B, Sixth United States Heavy Artillery, testified as follows:

"*Q.* Describe what you saw done there."

"*A.* Most all the men that were killed on our side were killed after the fight was over. They called them out and shot them down. Then they put some in the houses and shut them up, and then burned the houses."

"*Q.* Did you see them burn?"

"*A.* Yes, sir."

"*Q.* Were any of them alive?"

"*A.* Yes, sir; they were wounded, and could not walk. They put them in the houses, and then burned the houses down."

"*Q.* Do you know they were in there?"

"*A.* Yes, sir; I went and looked in there."

"*Q.* Do you know they were in there when the house was burned?"

"*A.* Yes, sir; I heard them hallooing there when the houses were burning."

"*Q.* Are you sure they were wounded men, and not dead men, when they were put in there?"

"*A.* Yes, sir; they told them they were going to have the doctor see them, and then put them in there and shut them up, and burned them."

"*Q.* Who set the house on fire?"

"*A.* I saw a rebel soldier take some grass and lay it by the door, and set it on fire. The door was pine plank, and it caught easy."

"*Q.* Was the door fastened up?"

"*A.* Yes, sir; it was barred with one of those wide bolts."

John F. Ray, private in Company B, Thirteenth Tennessee Cavalry, testified:

"*Q.* Will you state what you saw there?"

"*A.* After I surrendered they shot down a great many white fellows right close to me—ten or twelve, I suppose—and a great many Negroes too."

"*Q.* How long did they keep shooting our men after they surrendered?"

"*A.* I heard guns away after dark shooting all that evening somewhere; they kept up a regular fire for a long time, and then I heard the guns once in a while."

"*Q.* Did you see any one shot the next day?"

"*A.* I did not; I was in a house, and could not get up at all."

"*Q.* Do you know what become of the quartermaster of your regiment, Lieutenant Ackerstrom?"

"*A.* He was shot by the side of me."

"*Q.* Was he killed?"

"*A.* I thought so at the time; he fell on his face. He was shot in the forehead, and I thought he was killed. I heard afterwards that he was not."

"*Q.* Did you notice anything that took place while the flag of truce was in?"

"*A.* I saw the rebels slipping up and getting in the ditch along our breastworks."

"*Q.* How near did they come up?"

"*A.* They were right at us, right across from the breastworks. I asked them what they were slipping up there for. They made answer that they knew their business."

"*Q.* Are you sure this was done while the flag of truce was in?"

"*A.* Yes, sir. There was no firing; we could see all around; we could see them moving up all around in large force."

"*Q.* Was anything said about it except what you said to the rebels?"

"*A.* I heard all our boys talking about it. I heard some of our officers remark, as they saw it coming, that the white flag was a bad thing; that they were slipping on us. I believe it was Lieutenant

Ackerstrom that I heard say it was against the rules of war for them to come up in that way."

"*Q.* To whom did he say that?"

"*A.* To those fellows coming up; they had officers with them."

"*Q.* Was Lieutenant Ackerstrom shot before or after he had surrendered?"

"*A.* About two minutes after the flag of truce went back, during the action."

"*Q.* Do you think of anything else to state? If so, go on and state it."

"*A.* I saw a rebel lieutenant take a little Negro[1] boy up on the horse behind him, and then I heard General Chalmers—I think it must have been—tell him to 'take that Negro down and shoot him,' or 'take him and shoot him,' and he passed him down and shot him."

"*Q.* How large was the boy?"

"*A.* He was more than eight years old. I heard the lieutenant tell the other that the Negro was not in the service; that he was nothing but a child; that he was pressed and brought in there. The other one said, 'Damn the difference; take him down and shoot him, or I will shoot him.' I think it must have been General Chalmers. He was a smallish man; he had on a long gray coat with a star on his coat."[2]

In addition to the outrages committed at Fort Pillow, many wounded were cast into the ditches and buried alive. The evidence is ample, and the enemy may testify to his own inhumanity. Writing from Okalona, Mississippi, to the *Atlanta Appeal*, under date of June 14, 1864, a rebel said:

"You have heard that our soldiers buried Negroes alive

---

[1] General Chalmers has denied with vehemence that he did any cruel act at Fort Pillow, but the record is against him. Soldiers under brave, intelligent, and humane officers could never be guilty of such cruel and unchristian conduct as these rebels at Pillow. General Chalmers is responsible. As an illustration of the gentle and forgiving spirit of the Negro, it should be recorded here that many supported the candidacy of General Chalmers for Congress, and voted for him at the recent election in Mississippi.—G. W. W.

[2] *Vide* Report of Committee on Conduct of War, etc., "Rebellion Record," vol. viii., Doc., pp. 1–80.

at Fort Pillow. That is true. At the first fire, after Forrest's men scaled the walls, many of the Negroes threw down their arms and fell as if they were dead. They perished in the pretence, and could only be restored at the point of the bayonet. To resuscitate some of them, more terrified than the rest, they were rolled into the trenches made as receptacles for the fallen. Vitality was not restored until breathing was obstructed, and then the resurrection began. On these facts is based the pretext for the crimes committed by Sturgis, Grierson, and their followers. You must remember, too, that in the extremity of their terror, or for other reasons, the Yankees and Negroes in Fort Pillow neglected to haul down their flag. In truth, relying upon their gunboats, the officers expected to annihilate our forces after we had entered the fortifications. They did not intend to surrender.

"A terrible retribution, in any event, has befallen the ignorant, deluded Africans."

In a long and curiously interesting correspondence with General C. C. Washburn, General Forrest practically admitted and sought to justify the atrocities at Fort Pillow. He asserted that Negroes were *not* prisoners of war, but *property;* that the desperate fighting of the Negro troops invited and provoked cruel treatment, but did not deny the barbarous treatment inflicted upon Negro soldiers after they had surrendered. And thus General N. B. Forrest struck his name from the roll of brave professional soldiers, and wrote it in dishonor on the black list of men who have disgraced the profession of arms and insulted and outraged humanity.

After the civilized world had had time to breathe again, General Forrest saw where he stood, and sought by unfair means to extort testimony favorable to himself from a Union officer who had been taken prisoner at Fort Pillow.

Papers were drawn up by General Forrest, and sent to Captain John T. Young, a Union prisoner, to sign. After reading the papers Captain Young found that to sign them would be to exonerate General Forrest from the charge of brutality, of which he stood guilty before the civilized world. A report was circulated in the Confederate hospital, where he was sick, that he was recognized as a deserter from the rebel army, and that he was to be tried by court-martial and shot. Finally, General Forrest sent Judge P. T. Scooggs to induce the sick captain to sign some kind of a paper. This was done, ultimately, with the understanding and agreement that it was only to be used at Confederate headquarters, and would not be gazetted. This was in May, 1864. In September, soon after Captain Young had been returned to the Union lines, he wrote a letter to General C. C. Washburn, commanding the District of West Tennessee, explaining how he came to sign the document for General Forrest, and repudiating its contents.

Even General Forrest's chief, Lieutenant-general S. D. Lee, attempted no apology for the Fort Pillow massacre, but, on the contrary, exulted in the conduct of General Forrest's men.

"I respectfully refer you," wrote General Lee to General Washburn, "to history for numerous cases of indiscriminate slaughter, even under less aggravated circumstances.

"It is generally conceded by all military precedents that where the issue has been fairly presented, and the ability displayed, fearful results are expected to follow a refusal to surrender."

General Washburn replied:

"The record in the case is plainly made up, and I leave it. You justify and approve it, and appeal to history for precedents.

"As I have said, history furnishes no parallel. True, there are instances where, after a long and protracted resistance, resulting in heavy loss to the assailing party, the garrison has been put to the sword, but

I know of no such instance that did not bring dishonor upon the commander that ordered or suffered it.

"There is no Englishman that would not gladly forget Badajos, nor a Frenchman that exults when Jaffa or the Caves of Dahra and Shelas are spoken of. The massacre of Glencoe, which the world has read of with horror for nearly two hundred years, pales into insignificance before the truthful recital of Fort Pillow.

"The desperate defence of the Alamo was the excuse for the slaughter of its brave survivors after it surrendered, yet that act was received with just execration, and we are told by the historian that it led more than anything else to the independence of Texas.

"At the battle of San Jacinto the Texans rushed into action with the war-cry 'Remember the Alamo!' and carried all before them.

"You will seek in vain for consultation in history, pursue the inquiry as far as you may.

"Your desire to shift the responsibility of the Fort Pillow massacre, or to find excuses for it, is not strange. But the responsibility still remains where it belongs, and there it will remain."[1]

On the 13th of May, 1865, at Meridian, Mississippi, General Forrest gave the following account, or confession, of the Fort Pillow massacre to Bryan McAlister:

"At Fort Pillow I sent in a flag of truce, and demanded an unconditional surrender, or I would not answer for my men. This they refused. I sent them another note, giving them one hour to determine. This they refused. I could see on the river boats loaded with troops. They sent back asking for an hour more. I gave them twenty minutes. I sat on my horse during the whole time.

"The fort was filled with niggers and deserters from our army: men who lived side by side with my men. I waited five minutes after the time, and then blew my bugle for the charge. In twenty minutes my men were over the works, and the firing had ceased. The citizens and Yankees had broken in the heads of whiskey and lager-beer barrels, and were all drunk. They kept up firing all the time as they went down the hill. Hundreds of them rushed to the river and tried to swim to the gunboats, and my men shot them down. The Mississippi was red with their blood for three hundred yards. During all this time their flag was still flying, and I rushed over the works and cut the hal-

---

[1] For the correspondence between General Lee and General Washburn, *vide* "Rebellion Record," vol. x., pp. 721-730.

yards and let it down and stopped the fight. Many of the Yankees were in tents in front, and they were in their way, as they concealed my men, and some of them set them on fire. If any were burned to death it was in those tents."[1]

The Joint Committee on the Conduct and Expenditures of the War despatched the Hon. B. F. Wade, on the part of the Senate, and the Hon. D. W. Gooch, on the part of the House, as a sub-committee to investigate the Fort Pillow butchery. In their report, among many statements corroborated by the strongest evidence, they said:

"Then followed a scene of cruelty and murder without parallel in civilized warfare, which needed but the tomahawk and scalping-knife to exceed the worst atrocities ever committed by savages. The rebels commenced an indiscriminate slaughter, sparing neither age nor sex, white nor black, soldier nor civilian. The officers and men seemed to vie with each other in the devilish work; men, women, and even children, wherever found, were deliberately shot down, beaten, and hacked with sabres; some of the children, not more than ten years old, were forced to stand up and face their murderers while being shot; the sick and the wounded were butchered without mercy, the rebels even entering the hospital building and dragging them out to be shot, or killing them as they lay there unable to offer the least resistance. All over the hill-side the work of murder was going on; numbers of our men were collected together in lines or groups and deliberately shot; some were shot while in the river, while others on the bank were shot and their bodies kicked into the water, many of them still living, but unable to make any exertions to save themselves from drowning. Some of the rebels stood on the top of the hill or a short distance down its side, and called to our soldiers to come up to them, and as they approached, shot them down in cold blood; if their guns and pistols missed fire, forcing them to stand there until they were again prepared to fire. All around were heard cries of 'No quarter!' 'No quarter!' 'Kill the damned niggers! Shoot them down!' All who asked for mercy were answered by the most cruel taunts and sneers. Some were spared for a time, only to be murdered under circumstances of greater cruelty. No cruelty which the most fiendish malignity could devise was omitted by these murderers. One white soldier, who was wounded in one leg so as to be unable to walk, was made to stand up while his

---

[1] "Rebellion Record," vol. viii., poetry, pp. 55, 56.

tormentors shot him; others who were wounded and unable to stand were held up and again shot. One Negro who had been ordered by a rebel officer to hold his horse was killed by him when he remounted; another, a mere child, whom an officer had taken up behind him on his horse, was seen by Chalmers, who at once ordered the officer to put him down and shoot him, which was done. The huts and tents in which many of the wounded had sought shelter were set on fire, both that night and the next morning, while the wounded were still in them —those only escaping who were able to get themselves out, or who could prevail on others less injured than themselves to help them out; and even some of those thus seeking to escape the flames were met by those ruffians and brutally shot down, or had their brains beaten out. One man was deliberately fastened down to the floor of a tent, face upward, by means of nails driven through his clothing and into the boards under him, so that he could not possibly escape, and then the tent set on fire; another was nailed to the side of a building outside of the fort, and then the building was set on fire and burned. The charred remains of five or six bodies were afterwards found, all but one so much disfigured and consumed by the flames that they could not be identified, and the identification of that one is not absolutely certain, although there can hardly be a doubt that it was the body of Lieutenant John C. Ackerstrom, quartermaster of the Thirteenth Tennessee Cavalry, and a native Tennesseean; several witnesses who saw the remains, and who were personally acquainted with him while living, have testified that it is their firm belief that it was his body that was thus treated.

"'These deeds of murder and cruelty ceased when night came on, only to be renewed the next morning, when the demons carefully sought among the dead lying about in all directions for any wounded yet alive, and those they found were deliberately shot. Scores of the dead and wounded were found there the day after the massacre by the men from some of our gunboats who were permitted to go on shore and collect the wounded and bury the dead. The rebels themselves had made a pretence of burying a great many of their victims, but they had merely thrown them, without the least regard to care or decency, into the trenches and ditches about the fort, or the little hollows and ravines on the hill-side, covering them but partially with earth. Portions of the heads and faces, hands and feet, were found protruding through the earth in every direction. The testimony also establishes the fact that the rebels buried some of the living with the dead, a few of whom succeeded afterwards in digging themselves out, or were dug out by others, one of whom your Committee found in Mound City Hospital, and there examined. And even when your Committee visited the spot, two weeks afterwards, although parties of men had been sent on shore from time to time to bury the bodies unburied and re-bury the others, and were even then engaged in the same work, we found the evidences of this murder and cruelty still most painfully apparent. We saw bodies still unburied (at some distance from the fort) of some sick men who had been met fleeing from the hospital, and beaten down and brutally murdered, and their bodies left where they had fallen. We could still see the faces, hands, and feet of men, white and black, protruding out of the ground, whose graves had not been reached by those engaged in reinterring the victims of the massacre; and although a great deal of rain had fallen within the preceding two weeks, the ground, more especially on the side and at the foot of the bluff, where most of the murders had been committed, was still discolored by the blood of our brave but unfortunate men, and the logs and trees showed but too plainly the evidences of the atrocities perpetrated there.

"Many other instances of equally atrocious cruelty might be enumerated, but your Committee feel compelled to refrain from giving here more of the heart-sickening details, and refer to the statements contained in the voluminous testimony herewith submitted. Those statements were obtained by them from eye-witnesses and sufferers; many of them, as they were examined by your Committee, were lying upon beds of pain and suffering, some so feeble that their lips could with difficulty frame the words by which they endeavored to convey some idea of the cruelties which had been inflicted on them, and which they had seen inflicted on others.

"How many of our troops thus fell victims to the malignity and barbarity of Forrest and his followers cannot yet be definitely ascertained. Two officers belonging to the garrison were absent at the time of the capture and massacre. Of the remaining officers but two are known to be living, and they are wounded, and now in the hospital at Mound City. One of them, Captain Porter, may even now be dead, as the surgeons, when your Committee were there, expressed no hope of his recovery. Of the men, from three hundred to four hundred are known to have been killed at Fort Pillow, of whom at least three hundred were murdered in cold blood after the post was in possession of the rebels, and our men had thrown down their arms and ceased to offer resistance. Of the survivors, except the wounded in the hospital at Mound City, and the few who succeeded in making their escape unhurt, nothing definite is known, and it is to be feared that many have been murdered after being taken away from the Fort.

"In reference to the fate of Major Bradford, who was in command of the Fort when it was captured, and who had up to that time received no injury, there seems to be no doubt. The general understanding everywhere seemed to be that he had been brutally murdered the day after he was taken prisoner."[1]

On the morning of the engagement at Fort Pillow there were two hundred and sixty-two Negro soldiers in the garrison. The War Department record shows that three officers were killed, one wounded, and five missing: total nine; that there were eight enlisted men killed and two hundred and twenty-one missing: total two hundred and twenty-nine; grand total of two hundred and thirty-eight! These figures are significant. This is only the loss of the Negro troops. The entire force in the garrison was five hundred and fifty-seven, and at least three-fourths of it was annihilated. In his official report of the assault upon Fort Pillow General Forrest says: "My loss in the engagement was twenty killed and sixty wounded, that of the enemy unknown; *two hundred and twenty-eight were buried on the evening of the battle*, and quite a number were buried the next day by a detail from the gunboat fleet. . . .

"We captured one hundred and sixty-four Federals, seventy-three Negro troops, and about forty Negro women and children."[2]

History records, and the record will remain as long as the English language endures, that at Fort Pillow General Forrest and General Chalmers violated the honor of a flag of truce, the laws of civilized warfare—outraged every sentiment of humanity, and dishonored the uniform of Lee and Jackson, the Christian soldiers of the Confederacy. As long as brave deeds blaze in the firmament of national glory, as long as patriotism is revered and valor honored, so long will the gallant defence of Fort Pillow by the Negro Spartans be held in sacred remembrance by the loyal friends of a ransomed and reunited nation.

---

[1] "Rebellion Record," vol. viii., Doc., pp. 3, 4.
[2] Ibid., vol. viii., Doc., pp. 598–600.

CHAPTER XIII.

IN THE ARMY OF THE CUMBERLAND (1864.)

ALTHOUGH the recruitment of Negro soldiers began in the early autumn of 1863, at Nashville, Tennessee, there was little disposition to bring them into conflict with the enemy in the Department of the Cumberland. The great battles, with but few exceptions, had been fought while the effort to arm Negroes in this Department was in a tentative form. The entire effective force of this army was in the field, and most of the troops were from the Border States, with strong prejudices against the Negro. The officers had little or no time to discuss the fighting qualities of Negro soldiers, and were quite willing to be relieved of the question altogether. Major-general Geo. H. Thomas was inspecting the camp of the Fourteenth United States Colored Troops, when he suddenly turned to the colonel of the regiment and asked, "Will they fight?" "Yes," responded Colonel Thomas J. Morgan. " Yes, I think they will—behind breastworks," General Thomas added.

Meanwhile the Negro volunteers were silently and diligently at work upon the drill-ground and in the trenches. Fatigue duty had a very unhappy effect upon these troops. They had enlisted to fight, not to be hewers of wood. They were proud of their uniform, and desired above all things to be led against their ancient and inveterate foes. It was natural, therefore, that they should feel disappointed, and in some instances doubt the Government that had broken faith with them.

On the 15th of August, 1864, General Joseph Wheeler attacked the Union forces in garrison at Dalton, Georgia. General James B. Steedman was in command of the District of the Etowah, with headquarters at Chattanooga. Although he had been a leading Democrat before the war, he had entered the army as a patriot, and was singularly free from prejudice. Other general officers had been appealed to in vain for permission to bring the Negro troops in the Department into conflict with the enemy. But General Steedman promised, as soon as appealed to, that if there were any hard fighting to do, the Negro troops should participate. As soon, therefore, as he heard Wheeler's guns, he despatched a relief column to the beleaguered garrison, containing the Fourteenth United States Infantry (Negroes), Colonel T. J. Morgan. The Negro regiment held the left during the engagement, and behaved nobly. General Steedman was naturally anxious to know how these ex-slaves would stand fire. His orders to Captain Davis, one of his aides, were to look after the Negro regiment and report how it was fighting. Under the brave and competent officers of the Fourteenth its line of battle was perfect, and the firing regular and effective. Captain Davis looked on with amazement at these Negroes so recently from bondage fighting like veterans. Finally he rode back to General Steedman, and reported that "The regiment is holding dress parade over there under fire!" The Fifty-first Indiana Infantry, Colonel A. D. Streight, which was not in love with the idea of the incorporation of Negro troops in the army, had fought on the right of this Negro regiment and had witnessed its gallantry. When the battle was over, and the Fourteenth Regiment marched into Dalton, the Fifty-first gave three rousing cheers for the "Fourteenth Colored," and ever after, when asked "What regiment?" these brave and generous white soldiers would answer, "The Fifty-first Colored!" This was the first action in which Negro troops of the Army of the Cumberland had participated, and their splendid bearing had won the admiration of the white soldiers. They had secured the confidence of the army at a single bound, and thenceforth the equality of comradeship was recognized, and greatly contributed to the military unity of the Army of the Cumberland. The prejudice that had chilled these children of the sunny South was gone, and they now felt that it was a high privilege to fight for the Stars and Stripes. Those stars and stripes had once been the symbol of their degradation under the lash, but now those stars, gleaming with a peerless lustre, lighted their future with the hope of free citizenship in a free republic—to preserve which they were enlisted to fight. Just before the engagement at Dalton, an officer observed to the men of his company that some of them would doubtless be killed, but suggested to them the inspiring idea that they were fighting for liberty. A private spoke up, "I am ready to die for liberty!" He fell on that field with a ball through his heart, a willing offering to the cause of *Liberty*.

The following account of the fight appeared in the Chattanooga *Gazette* of August 16th:

"Late last night we learned from official sources the particulars of the rebel raid on the railroad at Dalton, the fight, and final repulse of the rebels.

"The raiders numbered about five thousand mounted infantry and cavalry, with six brass howitzers, commanded by Major-general Wheeler.

"The garrison at Dalton numbered only about four hundred men of the Second Missouri Volunteers, under Colonel Laiboldt.

"On Sunday morning the rebels approached the town in line of battle. Arriving at a convenient distance from the place, Wheeler sent in a formal demand for the surrender, couched in the following words:

"'*To the Officer Commanding U. S. Forces:*

"'To prevent the unnecessary effusion of blood, I have the honor to demand the immediate and unconditional surrender of the forces under your command at this garrison.

(Signed) "'Jos. WHEELER, Maj.-gen.,
"'Commanding Confederate Forces.'

"To which Colonel Laiboldt responded in the following laconic terms:

"'I have been placed here to defend the Post, but not to surrender.
(Signed) "'B. LAIBOLDT,
"'Colonel commanding.'

"Seeing he was outnumbered ten to one, Colonel Laiboldt with his command at once sought protection in his earthworks and in a large brick building.

"The invaders swarmed into the town, but were gallantly kept at bay from capturing the heroic garrison, who from behind their works mowed down the rebels.

"Yesterday morning at six o'clock the gallant and well-tried leader, General Steedman, arrived with reinforcements. Skirmishing at once commenced. The garrison sallied out from behind their earthworks. At this stage the Fourteenth United States Colored Infantry, who were commanded by Colonel Morgan, were ordered to charge. With a yell and a rush that were irresistible, they charged the chivalry, who turned tail and fled in the utmost confusion. Words are inadequate to describe the gallantry and impetuosity of the Colored troops on this occasion.

"The entire Union loss is between thirty and forty, the rebel loss one hundred and fifty."

Having earned a reputation for steady and gallant fighting, the Fourteenth was despatched in pursuit of the routed and decimated columns of General Wheeler through East and Middle Tennessee. On the march and in camp they exhibited the highest soldierly qualities, and displayed enthusiasm that their white comrades could not comprehend.

On the 27th of September, 1864, this regiment joined General Rousseau's command at Pulaski, Tennessee, where it participated in an action against the enemy under General Forrest. Rousseau had been driven all day, and his cavalry was about exhausted; but when Forrest met the steady and effective fire of the two Negro regiments which Colonel T. J. Morgan had brought from Nashville, he recoiled. These were the Fourteenth, Colonel Morgan's regiment, and the Sixteenth, Colonel William B. Gaw. Colonel Morgan gives the following account of this engagement:

"Colored troops and Forrest's cavalry now confronted each other, and a brisk fire was being kept up between them. Several of our men had been wounded. The enemy advanced; the fire grew hotter. At length the enemy, in full force, with banners flying, was plainly seen from our position on the ridge, advancing directly upon us. I passed along the line, and pointing to the rebel lines, said, 'Boys, it looks very much like fight. Keep cool, do your duty.' I was answered all along the line from the men most cheerfully, 'Colonel, dey can't whip us;' 'Dey neber dribe de ole Fourteenth out ob dis;' 'Dey neber will git de ole Fourteenth away widout a mighty lot ob dead men,' etc., etc. The enemy came on until within good range of the skirmish line, from which he received a severe steady fire. The line remained unshaken. The enemy halted, then withdrew, and night came on."

Two days before the engagement at Pulaski, Wheeler had summoned the Union garrison at Johnsonville, Tennessee, but the Thirteenth Infantry (colored), Colonel John A. Hottenstein, drove the enemy, inflicting upon him severe punishment. Johnsonville was a military *entrepôt*, situate at the end of the North-western Railroad, extending to Nashville, and upon the bank of the Tennessee

River. The enemy desired to occupy this position and possess himself of the stores, and made an impetuous attack.

When General Sherman led his army against Atlanta, Georgia, and began his march to the sea, General Hood with a considerable army decided to move against General Thomas, and destroy him by a turning movement. General Grant believed, as early as the first week in October, 1864, that if Sherman began his march to the sea, Hood, instead of following him, would turn his veteran columns northward. Sherman thought Hood would follow him to the sea. Grant desired Sherman to turn suddenly and annihilate Hood, and then march to the seaboard; but if he could not do this, to cut the Confederate army in twain and destroy it in detail. The following despatch shows how clear-headed he was:

"City Point, Virginia, *October* 11, 1864—11 A.M.

"Your despatch of October 10th received. Does it not look as if Hood was going to attempt the invasion of Middle Tennessee, using the Mobile and Ohio, and Memphis and Charleston roads to supply his base on the Tennessee River, about Florence or Decatur? If he does this he ought to be met and prevented from getting north of the Tennessee River. If you were to cut loose, I do not believe you would meet Hood's army, but would be bushwhacked by all the old men and little boys, and such railroad guards as are still left at home. Hood would probably strike for Nashville, thinking that by going north he could inflict greater damage upon us than we could upon the rebels by going south. If there is any way of getting at Hood's army I would prefer that; but I must trust to your own judgment. I find I shall not be able to send a force from here to act with you on Savannah. Your movements, therefore, will be independent of mine; at least, until the fall of Richmond takes place. I am afraid Thomas, with such lines of road as he has to protect, could not prevent Hood from going north. With Wilson turned loose, with all your cavalry, you will find the rebels put much more on the defensive than heretofore.

"U. S. GRANT, Lieutenant-general.

"Major-general W. T. SHERMAN."

Sherman sent the following despatch to his chief the same day:

"Kingston, Georgia, *October* 11th—11 A.M.

"Hood moved his army from Palmetto Station across by Dallas and Cedartown, and is now on the Coosa River, south of Rome. He threw one corps on my road at Acworth, and I was forced to follow. I hold Atlanta with the Twentieth Corps, and have strong detachments along my line. This reduces my active force to a comparatively small army. We cannot remain here on the defensive. With the twenty-five thousand men and the bold cavalry he has, he can constantly break my roads. I would infinitely prefer to make a wreck of the road, and of the country from Chattanooga to Atlanta, including the latter city, send back all my wounded and worthless, and, with my effective army, move through Georgia, smashing things, to the sea. Hood may turn into Tennessee and Kentucky, but I believe he will be forced to follow me. Instead of my being on the defensive, I would be on the offensive; instead of guessing at what he means to do, he would have to guess at my plans. The difference in war is full twenty-five per cent. I can make Savannah, Charleston, or the mouth of the Chattahoochee.

"Answer quick, as I know we will not have the telegraph long.

"W. T. SHERMAN, Major-general.

"Lieutenant-general GRANT."

Near midnight Grant sent Sherman permission to march to the sea in the following brief but explicit despatch:

"City Point, Virginia, *October* 11, 1864—11.30 P.M.

"Your despatch of to-day received. If you are satisfied the trip to the sea-coast can be made, holding the line of the Tennessee River firmly, you may make it, destroying all the railroad south of Dalton or Chattanooga, as you think best. U. S. GRANT,

"Lieutenant-general.

"Major-general W. T. SHERMAN."

While Sherman was preparing to cut loose from Atlanta, Georgia, Hood sent a considerable force against the garrison at Decatur, Alabama. This place was held by General R. S. Granger, and the assault was the first of a series of movements having the reduction of Nashville in view. Grant had rightly anticipated the movements of

Hood's army. Hood delivered battle at Decatur on the 26th[1] of October, 1864, and supposing the place could be easily carried, he turned with his main force towards Courtland. He forced a passage of the Tennessee River at Florence, where he halted to hear of the capture of Decatur. He was doomed to disappointment. Major-general James B. Steedman, who had learned to trust in the valor of Negro troops, hearing of the investment of Decatur, despatched the Fourteenth Regiment of Negro Infantry, Colonel Morgan, from Stevenson to relieve Granger. At 12 M. on the 28th General Granger ordered eight companies of the Fourteenth, under Colonel Morgan, to take a battery of the enemy that had been very troublesome. It was a splendid compliment to the gallantry of this Negro regiment that it was ordered to this hazardous task, while thousands of white troops were within the earthworks. The storming column was formed at a distance of seven hundred and eighty yards from the enemy's line, having moved under cover of the river bank until Granger's rifle-pits were passed. Flankers were thrown out, files were distributed for spiking the guns when taken; Colonel Morgan addressed the men upon the importance of taking the battery if only ten men survived; the colors were unfurled, and the order, "Forward, double-quick, march!" given, and the men moved forward to their work with enthusiasm. As soon as the assaulting column disclosed itself upon the crest of a hill in front of the battery the enemy delivered a severe fire. The column swept on, maintaining a perfect line, determined to carry the works with the bayonet. It was an unique spectacle as the white troops gazed in breathless awe at this Negro regiment charging a Confederate battery at a right shoulder shift

---

[1] "Rebellion Record," vol. xi., Doc., p. 344.

arms, without firing a shot! In less than fifteen minutes the assaulting column had charged over the enemy's works, taken the guns, and spiked them, making prisoners, and planting their colors over their undisputed trophies. This gallant feat thrilled the hearts of the white troops who had been passive lookers-on, and they made the country ring with hearty cheers.

This daring but successful movement attracted the attention of the enemy, who was in large force towards Courtland. Several regiments were despatched to retake the captured guns. Captain H. Romeyn, of the Fourteenth, had discovered from the opposite bank of the river that the enemy was preparing to flank Colonel Morgan's force, and finding also that the colonel was about to pursue the enemy, he rode at high speed and great peril to prevent the daring pursuit. Although Colonel Morgan was unable to remove the captured guns from the field, he spiked and dismantled them, and with colors floating, retired to Decatur and marched into the Union earthworks. The white troops who had witnessed the gallantry of this Negro regiment cheered it during the return march, and as a part of the garrison at Decatur, it was afterwards treated with distinguished consideration.

Four officers and sixty men were killed, wounded, and missing in the assault; but this was the price of a good reputation for the Negro volunteer in the Department of the Cumberland.[1] In General Orders No. 50, dated November 23, 1864, Colonel Morgan said:

"The colonel commanding desires to express to the officers and men of the Fourteenth United States Colored Infantry his entire satisfaction with their conduct during

---

[1] "Rebellion Record," vol. xi., p. 362; also "The American Conflict," vol. ii., p. 679.

the 27th, 28th, 29th, and 30th days of October, in the defence of Decatur, Alabama. On the march, on the skirmish line, in the charge, they proved themselves soldiers. Their conduct has gained for the regiment an enviable reputation in the Western army."

Hood had succeeded in getting his army into position in front of Nashville. It consisted of three corps under Lieutenant-generals S. D. Lee and A. P. Stewart, and Major-general B. F. Cheatham. These corps were composed of three divisions each. The infantry force exceeded 40,000, the cavalry was 12,000, and, with the artillery, Hood's army was about 55,000 men of all arms. On the other hand, Thomas was in command of the small force which Sherman had left behind when he started on his march to the seaboard, consisting of the Fourth Corps, General Stanley, 12,000 men; the Twenty-third Corps, General Schofield, 10,000 men; and a cavalry force of 8,000 men under Generals Hatch, Croxton, and Capron—in all 30,000 men.

If Hood should pursue Sherman, Thomas was instructed to follow persistently, but prudently; but in case he should turn into Tennessee, he was to fall upon him and annihilate him. Thomas was given plenary powers, and was expected to engage Hood as soon as he could concentrate his troops; but he did not intend to risk too much in the open field. On the 12th of November, 1864, Sherman moved out from Cartersville, Georgia, and Hood turned to feel for Thomas's flank. Without abandoning important garrisons, Thomas began to contract his lines, extending over a vast territory, evidently intending to impose upon Hood the necessity of striking at him over the strong works at Nashville. Hood declined this perilous initiative, as will be seen; he preferred to strike the fragments of Thomas's recoiling columns as they were falling back to

Nashville. He finally overtook Schofield at Franklin, Tennessee, and charged him with such impetuosity that his works were carried and his centre pierced. But the gallantry of Opdycke's brigade closed the breach and regained the lost works.

Schofield retired across the Harpeth and joined Thomas at Nashville.

By the 2d of December, 1864, Hood's entire army had reached Thomas's front, and was reorganized. Earthworks were constructed, siege-guns mounted, and every preparation made to remain under cover and invite Thomas to the onset.

It is true that Hood's army was not very large, but it was composed of well-seasoned veterans: men who were now on their native soil, and were ready to fight to the death for their homes. Moreover, Hood had told his army at Franklin that if he could break the Union lines there was nothing to obstruct his march to the Ohio River. It was certain, therefore, that it would require the most desperate fighting to drive the enemy from Nashville and expel him from Tennessee.

General Grant had grown somewhat impatient at Thomas's apparent inaction, and was amazed that he did not strike out at Hood and crush him at once. But Thomas, a brave and cautious soldier, did not propose to deliver battle until he was safely ready. Meantime he was contracting his lines and reorganizing his cavalry.

There were eight regiments of Negro troops in the Department of the Cumberland, and they were now ordered to Nashville, where their courage was to be tried against the veterans of Hood's army. On the 29th of November, 1864, Colonel T. J. Morgan assumed command of the Fourteenth, Lieutenant-colonel H. C. Corbin; the Sixteenth, Colonel William B. Gaw; and the Forty-fourth, Colonel L. Johnson—all Negro regiments of infantry. He reached Nashville from Chattanooga *via* Cowan on December 1st; but Colonel Lewis Johnson, in command of the Forty-fourth United States Negro Infantry, with A and D companies of the Fourteenth Regiment, under Captain C. W. Baker, was attacked by the enemy at a bridge over Mill Creek. At about 11 A.M. on the 2d of December, 1864, the assault was made upon the train containing Colonel Johnson's command. The artillery fire disabled the engine, and the troops were compelled to abandon it under a destructive fire from the enemy. The men displayed great coolness, and when in line were marched to Block-house No. 2, but it was found to be occupied by a detachment of twenty-five men belonging to the One Hundred and Fifteenth Ohio Infantry. Colonel Johnson deployed his men around the block-house, threw out a strong skirmish line, and against a very tempest of shells from three batteries and the rattle of musketry, he pushed his way up a hill to the eastward. He was unable to carry the enemy's position on the crest of the hill, where he was skilfully serving a battery with strong infantry support. He did not, however, retire, but clung gallantly to the side of the hill; his men took shelter behind trees and stumps, and fought with marked courage and coolness.

The artillery slackened towards sunset, and ceased its fire at nightfall. The enemy kept up a severe musketry fire all night, but Colonel Johnson's ammunition was nearly exhausted, and under cover of the friendly darkness he drew his command back to the block-house, which was now in ruins. His command did not reply to the enemy's fire, and the remaining four rounds of ammunition were reserved for a final effort. At 3.30 A.M. on the morning of the 3d of December, having placed his wounded in charge of Surgeon J. T. Strong and Chaplain Lycurgus Railsback, of the Forty-fourth Infantry, he determined to fight his way to Nashville. He skirmished slightly with the enemy, and reached Nashville about daylight.

Colonel Johnson only had three hundred and thirty-two muskets in this engagement, including the twenty-five in the block-house, and his loss in killed, wounded, and missing was one hundred and fifteen—more than one-third of his entire command. These Negro troops had contended with a force vastly superior in numbers, bearing all arms, and had successfully repelled desperate assaults, and after sixteen hours of hard fighting opened a way to Nashville.

All the available Negro troops in the Department of the Cumberland massed at Nashville were organized into a corps. All doubt as to the efficiency and gallantry of troops of this character had disappeared from the minds of general officers, and they were hailed by the white veterans of Lookout Mountain and Chickamauga as their peers. These troops had confidence in themselves as well, and abounded in zeal and military enthusiasm. They were now confronted by Hood's veteran army, and perilous work awaited them.

The winter just setting in was of unusual severity, but martial pride raised the black soldiers above their sufferings. They lived cheerfully in their light shelter tents, they drilled and paraded on the sleet and snow, they participated in several bold reconnoissances, they executed repeated movements on the enemy's right flank, constructed breastworks, and participated with intelligent zeal in all the duties of the Army of the Cumberland.

The week of rain, ice, and cold was over, and the weather-bound armies were ready for the impending conflict. It was determined that the "Negro Division" should open the battle of Nashville. On the night of the 14th of December, 1864, Colonel T. J. Morgan, commanding the division of Negro troops, was summoned to the headquarters of General Steedman. The plan of the battle was explained to Colonel Morgan, and he was ordered to open the action at daylight. Colonel Morgan was a gentleman of education and marked courage, but he was a civilian, and his command had rarely exceeded a regiment. To be placed suddenly in command of a division was indeed a compliment to his abilities as a soldier, but it was a trying position for a modest officer. Colonel Morgan endeavored to get General Steedman to inform him *how* the engagement should be opened, but the stern old soldier replied, "To-morrow morning, colonel, just as soon as you can see how to put your troops in motion, I wish you to begin the fight." Colonel Morgan rose, saluted, and bade the general good-night.

Accompanied by his adjutant, Colonel Morgan repaired to the picket line and made a tracing of the enemy's rifle-pits, outlined his plan of attack, and issued the necessary orders that night.

On the morning of the 15th of December a bank of dense fog settled down between the hostile armies, concealing their dispositions and delaying the assault. At length the curtain of fog was rolled up, and Morgan's Black Division marched out on the Murfreesboro pike, where the following disposition was made: the Fourteenth United States Colored Troops, under command of Lieutenant-colonel H. C. Corbin, was deployed as skirmishers; the Seventeenth and Forty-fourth United States Colored Troops were formed in line of battle, under command of Colonel William R. Shafter; one section of the Twentieth Indiana Battery, Captain M. A. Osborne, supported by a battalion of the Eighteenth United States Colored Troops, Major Lewis D. Joy. Colonel Charles

R. Thompson was in command of a brigade composed of the Twelfth, Thirteenth, and One Hundredth United States Colored Troops. The left wing of the army, by which the assault was to be made, was commanded by Major-general James B. Steedman. General Thomas's plan of battle contemplated a vigorous attack upon the enemy's right flank, well knowing that he would contract and weaken his left flank; then Wilson's cavalry and General Smith's corps were to attack the enemy's left flank, envelop it, and destroy Hood's army. Accordingly, at eight o'clock, Captain Osborne's battery opened upon the enemy; the skirmish line moved forward, driving the Confederate pickets, and at length Colonel Morgan's Negro troops assaulted the enemy's rifle-pits and cleared them. The vigor and spirit with which these troops assaulted the rebels left no doubt in the enemy's mind that this was a general attack. At the same time Colonel Charles R. Thompson's brigade moved across Brown's Creek, between the Nolensville and Murfreesboro turnpikes, and carried the left of his front line of works resting on the Nolensville turnpike.

After gallant and effective fighting Colonel Morgan's Negro troops were withdrawn and impelled against an earthwork east of the "Raine house." The Negro troops raised a yell and carried the works with the bayonet, getting possession of the Raine house and other brick buildings adjacent, which were loop-holed and turned to good account. All day these troops behaved with great courage. They executed every movement, obeyed every order, and with their white comrades shared the perils and glory of the first day's battle in front of Nashville. Thomas had succeeded in enveloping Hood's left wing, and the day's work was prophetic of final and complete victory.

At six o'clock on the morning of the 16th Steedman

led his Negro troops against the enemy's works in his front, but he had retired during the night. He moved his command out over the Nashville pike, encountering the enemy's cavalry, which he gallantly beat off. His troops formed a junction with those of the Fourth Corps, General T. J. Wood, his right resting on the railroad, and his left extending near the pike and covering the left wing of the entire army. During the forenoon he had several severe conflicts with the enemy in which his troops were victorious.

At about one o'clock Thomas ordered Steedman and Wood to assault the enemy in his strongly fortified position on Overton Hill. The troops moved forward gallantly until within striking distance, when they attempted to expel the enemy from his cover. Although brilliantly executed, the charge was received with undaunted courage, and the assailants driven back by a storm of shot, shell, and musketry, whereby the storming column sustained severe loss. The troops had delivered such a severe blow at Overton Hill that the enemy, while he did not recoil, contracted his line; and while Steedman, nothing daunted, was reforming his troops to renew the assault, a division of the Fourth Corps, from the right of the Franklin pike, executed a turning movement on the weakened flank of the enemy, and Hood's entire line gave way.

The rout of the enemy was complete. The Negro troops joined in the pursuit with zeal, always anxious to get within striking distance. But Hood's veteran army was now beaten and demoralized, and it fled, pursued by the Army of the Cumberland, over rough roads, through a devastated and inhospitable country, over swollen and freezing streams and snow-drifted paths in the mountains of Tennessee. Hood's army was annihilated, and Negro troops materially aided in the work; Sherman had no effective foe in his rear, and his path was open to the seaboard. On the other hand, Lee could not spare enough troops from the Army of Northern Virginia to annoy Sherman, but Grant was now enabled vigorously to assault Lee, to defeat him in the field, or capture him in the mountains of Virginia. The importance of the battle of Nashville cannot be over-estimated. It touched and modified all the plans of the commanders of both armies; it hastened the close of the civil war, and in this great achievement a division of Negro troops bore a conspicuous and creditable part. It will be seen that these troops purchased their reputation for martial valor at an awful price. The following table exhibits the losses they sustained:

BATTLE OF NASHVILLE.

Command.	Company.	Killed.		Wounded.		Missing.		Aggregate.	Remarks.
		Officers.	Enlisted Men.	Officers.	Enlisted Men.	Officers.	Enlisted Men.		
First Brigade.									
Fourteenth U. S. Col'd Troops.	F.&S.	..	4	..	41	..	20	65	Commanded by T. J. Morgan.
Sixteenth " " "	A	..	..	..	..	..	..	..	
Seventeenth " " "	B	2	14	4	64	..	..	84	
Eighteenth " " "	C	..	1	..	5	..	3	9	
Forty-fourth " " "	D	..	..	..	4	..	..	4	
Total—First Brigade.....	.....	2	19	4	114	..	23	162	
Second Brigade.									
Twelfth U. S. Colored Troops.	F.&S.	..	10	5	99	..	..	114	Commanded by C. R. Thompson.
Thirteenth " " "	A	4	51	4	161	..	1	221	
One Hundredth U. S. Col'd "	B	..	12	5	116	..	..	133	
Total—Second Brigade....	.....	4	73	14	376	..	1	468	

In his report of the battle General Steedman says:

"The larger portion of these losses, amounting in the aggregate to fully twenty-five per cent. of the men under my command who were taken into action, it will be observed, fell upon the Colored Troops. The severe loss of this part of my troops was in the brilliant charge on the enemy's works on Overton Hill on Friday afternoon. I was unable to discover that *color* made any difference in the fighting of my troops. All, white and black, nobly did their duty as soldiers, and evinced cheerfulness and resolution such as I have never seen excelled in any campaign of the war in which I have borne a part." [1]

---

[1] "Rebellion Record," vol. xi., Doc., p. 89.

CHAPTER XIV.

THE ARMY OF THE JAMES (1865).

During the winter of 1864–65 twenty-five regiments of Negro troops were concentrated on the James River, confronting the Confederate capital. With but few exceptions, those troops had seen severe service in the field. Many of them had been in spirited conflicts with the enemy in Florida, South Carolina, and Virginia, while quite all of them had attained proficiency in drill and field manœuvres.

The presence of so large a force of Negro troops in front of Richmond had a most salutary effect upon the Confederate authorities, both civil and military. The reputation won by Negro troops was respected in both armies, and the prejudice against their employment among conservative Northern representatives in Congress had almost wholly disappeared. Moreover, there was now a disposition in Congress to make amends for the bad treatment and neglect which Negro troops had suffered. Accordingly, on the 31st of January, 1865, a constitutional amendment prohibiting slavery passed the House by a vote of 119 to 56. The news of this noble action had a splendid effect upon the Negro troops in the field; they began to enjoy the rewards of their valor as soldiers.

Already, on the 15th of January, Negro troops had participated in the assault upon and capture of Fort Fisher, North Carolina.

On the last day of January General Robert E. Lee was appointed commander-in-chief of the Confederate army. Among the many new features which he immediately sought to incorporate in his war policy was the military employment of Negroes by the Confederate Government. This recommendation to the Confederate Congress was the result of General Lee's experience. He had witnessed the excellent fighting of Negro troops in the Union army, and entertained no prejudice against the military employment of Negroes to save the imperilled cause of the slaveholders' rebellion.

On the 28th of January the Lower House of the Confederate Congress had resolved to employ Negroes as soldiers, but on the 7th of February the Senate refused to concur in the action of the House. On the 18th of February General Lee urged his plan of the military employment of Negroes, and on the 20th the Confederate House passed a bill authorizing the employment of two hundred thousand Negroes in the armed service of the Government, but the Senate promptly rejected the measure. The Negro, who had been manifestly and confessedly the cause of the war, was now the hope of both Union and Confederate governments. Fair hands that had been stained with the blood of bondmen, but which were now impotent in disaster, were outstretched to Ethiopia. But "Ethiopia's hands long stretching mightily had plead with God," and the cause of the despised Negro had become the cause of humanity and civilization the world over.

But the movement finally received the force of law, as shown in the following, which is the last part of the last Special Order issued from the Adjutant and Inspector General's Office at Richmond:

"*Special Orders No.* 78.

"Adjutant and Inspector General's Office,
"Richmond, *April* 1, 1865.

* * * * * * * *

"XXIX. Lieutenant John L. Cowardin, Adjutant Nineteenth Battalion Virginia Artillery, is hereby relieved from his present command

and will proceed without delay to Halifax County, Virginia, for the purpose of recruiting Negro troops, under the Act of Congress approved March 13th, and General Orders No. 14, Adjutant and Inspector General's Office, current series."

On the 23d of March the first company of Negro State troops was mustered into the Confederate service, and by a strange coincidence President Lincoln left Washington city to review his Negro soldiers on the James River on the same day. The review was one of the most magnificent military spectacles of the civil war. The weather was fair and the atmosphere pleasant for the moving masses of troops. Twenty-five thousand Negro soldiers, in bright, new uniforms, well drilled, well armed, and well officered, passed in review before the President, General Grant, and the general officers of the Army of the James and the Army of the Potomac. The troops were reviewed between General William Birney's headquarters and Fort Harrison, in full view of the enemy at Fort Gilmer. The troops marched with company front, with banners flying and bands playing. Nearly every slave State had its representatives in the ranks of this veteran Negro army, while Massachusetts, New York, Connecticut, Pennsylvania, Indiana, Ohio, and Illinois, of the Northern States, had regiments in the line. President Lincoln was deeply moved at the sight of these Negro troops, against whose employment he had early and earnestly protested. Hundreds of white officers and thousands of white soldiers witnessed the review with keen interest, and were loud in their praise of the splendid soldierly bearing of their Negro comrades in arms. The entire review was highly satisfactory, and made a deep impression upon the minds of the civil and military chiefs who witnessed it.

On the 28th of March a council of war was held at General Grant's headquarters at City Point. President Lincoln, Generals Sherman, Sheridan, and Ord were present, and the result of the council was that the next day the Army of the Potomac was put in motion. As usual, the South-side Railroad was the objective point. To this force was added a portion of the Army of the James, a part of the Twenty-fourth Corps (Gibbon's), and one division of the Twenty-fifth Corps (Weitzel). The Twenty-fifth army corps was entirely composed of Negro troops, and its commander was anxious to lead them in person in the campaign now to begin. On the night of March 27th these troops were moved across the James and Appomattox rivers, under cover of the darkness, to the "White House," where they rested until nightfall of the 29th. As soon as darkness concealed their movements the Negro troops were hurried forward to assist in turning the enemy's left flank. On the previous day the Fifth Corps (Warren's) had been thrown across Hatcher's Run, and Griffin, followed by Crawford and Ayres, had encountered the enemy on Quaker Road. On Friday morning Sheridan's flying cavalry column joined Birney's Negro troops in motion.[1] Warren ordered Griffin to unite the divisions of Crawford and Ayres, and, by a movement to the left, to push forward to the White Oak Road. Although Miles's division was to support this movement, the enemy, by impetuous gallantry, hurled the Fifth Corps back on the Boydtown road. Having routed Warren's infantry, the enemy turned upon his cavalry and put it to flight. But just in the moment of exultation Sheridan appeared at the head of his splendid cavalry and saved the Fifth Corps from utter rout.

During the remainder of Friday a series of brilliant

---

[1] But while the entire division was included in the movement but one brigade engaged the enemy.—G. W. W.

manœuvres were executed creditable to military science, but not productive of valuable results. When all seemed lost, General J. L. Chamberlain's first brigade of Griffin's division of the Fifth Corps was impelled across Gravelly Run, and by the vigor of the assault swept the enemy from the field, capturing many flags and prisoners. The Fifth Corps bivouacked on the White Oak road Friday night, and the Second Corps joined it early Saturday morning, April 1st. At daylight the Fifth Corps moved down the Boydtown road until it joined Sheridan's cavalry, when the entire force moved towards Five Forks. It had been raining, and although now the morning was fair, the roads were heavy and the marching slow. Birney's Negro troops were in the moving column, eager for the onset. The cavalry dashed at the enemy, and the infantry moved steadily to the conflict. Sheridan soon swung around and enveloped the enemy's extreme left, while the infantry, in wheeling to the left, had struck the enemy's works in flank. From ten o'clock Saturday night a severe cannonade was opened along the entire lines from the Appomattox to Hatcher's Run. This was designed to assist Sheridan's turning movement and hold the enemy away from him. No artillery fire during the entire civil war exceeded this in quality and volume, in accuracy, and the extent of territory over which it raged. It was most effective. It is difficult to describe either the bombardment or the feeling it produced. The night was dark, the air damp, and the heavens sullen and threatening. Both armies lay close together, with their dead and wounded numerous and near, but neither knew what would be the next move. Suddenly the entire artillery, siege-guns, and mortars of the Army of the Potomac opened upon the unsuspecting enemy, and the earth reeled for miles, and houses were denuded of glass of every description, while the heavens were lighted up for sixteen miles, and the two crouching armies were uncovered to each other, like wild beasts waiting for the fatal leap. The enemy along his well-constructed line of earthworks, where he had wintered in substantial log quarters, was driven into his trenches by the storm of shell and shot, while substantial buildings and gun-carriages were shattered and demolished. Many rebels subsequently made prisoners declared that they were thrown from their bunks by the shock, while the Confederate army felt that the bombardment was literally a day of judgment to their cause. It was indeed an awe-inspiring spectacle, the sublimest and most awful scene of war.

It was a strange sensation for the ten thousand Negro troops to lie prone upon the earth a few hundred yards from the enemy, who, thinking this portion of the line weak, assaulted it with the energy of despair about four o'clock Saturday morning. But the Negro troops were nothing moved by the impetuosity of the onset or by the "rebel howl" so terrible in its shrillness. The rebels were warmly received, but sixteen hundred of them were made prisoners, while many were slain, wounded, or driven back. But it was a grander scene when, just as the sun was rising and discovering the carnage of the field, Birney's Negro troops uncovered the enemy's works, swept through and dealt deadly blows upon the foe as he fell back before the fury of Ayres's and Griffin's assault farther to the left. Within a few hours the enemy's right was doubled up against his centre.

The Negro troops, with their white comrades, swung around towards Petersburg, and swept every fragment of battle before them. General Sheridan, the senior officer upon the battle-field, cried out to all officers who attempted to communicate with him, "Smash them! smash them!

We have a record to make before the sun goes down. I want the South-side Railroad!" The daring impetuosity of his leadership had a profound influence upon the troops, and they accomplished his desire. Birney's Negro troops and Seymour's command cut their way through the enemy's lines and reached the South-side Railroad, Grant's objective point for many months. The work of destruction was wrought with skill and determination, and before the sun went down Sheridan's troops had made a record. Pickett's veteran rebel corps was caught by Birney's troops in their turning movement and torn into shreds, and then the pierced and broken rebel wing was hurled along inside the enemy's earthworks towards Petersburg. The orderly retreat of early morning became a rout. A. P. Hill endeavored to rally his shattered and decimated columns, but the effort was as impotent as Napoleon's at Waterloo to rally the Old Guard. The broken parts of a once magnificent army swept by the intrepid Hill as the merest drift-wood of battle. The tide was too strong, and the red waves of battle swept on towards Petersburg, where they were temporarily checked. The enemy endeavored to make a stand several times, but he was immediately caught by the fierce tide of battle and driven back. The path of this remarkable conflict was strewed with the enemy's dead, dying, and wounded, his dismantled artillery, disabled wagons, and disheartened stragglers.

The news of Sheridan's victory was proclaimed to the army in the immediate vicinity of Petersburg, and the pulse of patriotism beat high. The battle of Five Forks had been fought and won; and Sheridan was no longer a successful cavalry leader only, but a soldier capable of broad plans and brilliant execution.

The cannonade doubtless prevented Lee from falling upon Sheridan in the night, hurling him aside, and making good his escape. During the night Grant rectified his lines and perfected his plans for a final assault upon the enemy's lines about Petersburg. The general engagement was to extend from the Appomattox to Hatcher's Run, with Parke on the right, Ord on the left, and Wright in the centre. At 4 A.M. Sunday morning the cannonade slackened, and finally ceased.

Battery B, First United States Artillery, fired the signal for Birney's Negro troops to move forward to the assault. In the gray dawn of the morning these troops marched out of a grove on the side of a hill, then down the hill into an open field. Before them on a high hill sat a large fort covering the approach to the city. The enemy was waiting with bated breath and shotted guns, and as the column dashed up the hill with a yell the fort gleamed with fire. The enemy's shell and musketry tore Birney's ranks, but his gallant men only sprang forward with renewed vigor, and carried everything before them.

Coming closer to Petersburg, Ord's command, with Birney and Gibbon, was met by stubborn resistance from two of the enemy's forts—Alexander and Gregg. Fort Alexander was carried by desperate fighting, but Fort Gregg held out with almost matchless valor. It was here that the One Hundredth New York Regiment of infantry and the Twenty-second United States Regiment of Negro infantry generously contended for the flags and guns in the enemy's possession. The Negro regiment charged the fort, and when under the guns threw off caps and coats, rushed over the works, and seized the guns, hauling them away from the gallant gunners who had not yet acknowledged their defeat. The One Hundredth New York had entered the fort about the same time, and the black and white soldiers contended for a division of the trophies which they had so gallantly won. This fort was taken at a loss of about five hundred; while of the garrison of two hundred and fifty only thirty survived the action.

In other portions of the line the fighting was severe but triumphant. Wilcox's division of Parke's right had made a successful feint on Fort Steedman, and Hartranft's division had carried everything before it, capturing twelve guns and eight hundred prisoners. Wright's Sixth Corps charged through three lines of abatis, making thousands of prisoners, and cutting the Confederate line in two.

The 2d of April, 1865, was a beautiful day, but the bloody events in and about Petersburg made it a day of slaughter and destruction. By noonday the outer lines of Confederate defences had been carried by the besieging army, and Grant was preparing for a grand assault upon the city. Generals Lee, A. P. Hill, and William Mahone were in the doomed city consulting upon a plan of retreat before it should be too late. Grant's army was thundering at the very gates. The noise of battle grew nearer. "How is this, general?" asked Lee of Hill; "your men are giving way." At Manassas, Harper's Ferry, and Antietam he had saved the day for the Confederate army, and at critical moments, in his picturesque red battle-shirt, had struck with the right hand of Mars. So soon as Lee spoke to him he mounted his horse and rode off, accompanied by a single orderly, to reconnoitre. In a wooded ravine he suddenly came upon a few Union soldiers. They fired their pieces, and Major-general A. P. Hill fell dead. He was a splendid soldier; but the old charm was gone, and the once magnificent corps he had led on many victorious fields was now scattered and flying for life.

General Lee issued orders for the evacuation of Petersburg and Richmond, and began preparations to withdraw his army to the mountains about Lynchburg. The first news of the fate of the Confederacy was conveyed to Jefferson Davis as he sat in his accustomed place of worship. He read the note from Lee with a dazed look, and with blanched countenance and unsteady step went down the aisle and passed out of the church. The Confederate newspapers had concealed the real state of affairs, and had purposely misled the people as to the dangers that threatened their cause. So, when the news of Lee's disaster reached the Confederate capital, it fell like a thunder-bolt out of a cloudless sky. Amid the confusion and consternation, the disorder and disaster, the panic and pillage, the rapine and flames, the Negro population stood still to see the salvation of the Lord.

Sunday night Grant put his army in readiness and rectified his lines; but before the dawn of Monday morning the shattered remnant of Lee's famous Army of Northern Virginia had evacuated Petersburg. At early dawn Birney's Negro troops were led against Petersburg, but there was no enemy to dispute their entrance. The Negro population gave the black soldiers in blue a most cordial welcome. They were greeted with tears and cheers, with prayers and praise, with songs and phrases of high-sounding adulation. Many of the people rushed to the side of the moving column, embraced the conquerors, and covered their hands with kisses. The bands of the Negro regiments played "John Brown's Body," and thrilled the Negro populace with the sentiment, "We'll hang Jeff Davis on a sour apple-tree!" The whites were silent and sullen; it was not their day, although it was manifestly the funeral of their cause; the year of jubilee had come to the long-benighted bondman, however. Neither the pride of the Negro soldier nor the joy of the Negro citizen assumed offensive form; the quiet dignity of the former and the Christian humility of the latter were conspicuous on every hand.

Two divisions of Negro troops and a portion of the Twenty-fourth Corps were on the James River side of the rebel capital watching Ewell. About two o'clock Monday morning, April 3d, Captain Bruce, of General Devens's staff, discovered a bright light in the direction of Richmond, and heard loud explosions. Three men were sent forward to reconnoitre, and within a few minutes a Negro brought the news that Richmond had been evacuated. As soon as day broke General Weitzel passed through the enemy's deserted works, consisting of several lines of redoubts and bastioned forts. The ground was thoroughly sowed with torpedoes, and the troops were moved slowly. At length a cry was raised in the main street of the doomed capital, "The Yankees are coming!" and confusion reigned among the citizens. Fifty Negro cavalrymen dashed up to the Capitol, and Lieutenant Johnson De Peyster hauled the Union flag to its place upon that edifice. A regiment of Negro cavalry headed the Union column into the city, and another regiment of Negro cavalry was posted on the north side of the square about the Capitol to preserve order and to guard the property of their late masters! This beautiful city had been looted and burned by its own citizens; but as soon as the United States flag floated over the chaos order was restored, and every attempt made to save property as well as life. The Negro population behaved well, and the black soldiers bore themselves more like guests than conquerors.

It does not come within the scope of this work to describe the movements of the Army of the Potomac in this final and triumphant campaign, except so far as the Negro troops bore a part. The temptation is strong to describe the precipitous retreat of Lee's army towards Burkesville Junction; how his half-famished army struggled over heavy roads and swollen streams to reach Amelia Court-house, to which point Lee had ordered a quarter of a million of rations; how the civil authorities at Richmond had ordered the train that contained the rations back to Richmond without unloading, thus sacrificing the army for the safety of the politicians; how Lee, hungry and faint, was unable to move his army, and how Sheridan's cavalry passed between Amelia Court-house and Burkesville; how at Sailor's Creek, Sheridan, Crook, Custer, and Devens struck Ewell and Pickett's corps flank and rear, capturing five generals, seven thousand prisoners, hundreds of wagons, many guns and flags. But all this belongs to a general history of the campaign.

The Negro troops in Ord's Army of the James had moved by the South-side Railroad, and were hurrying forward to prevent the passage of Lee's army over the Appomattox at Farmville. In all the conflicts in which these troops participated they bore themselves as brave soldiers, and were equal to every emergency; and finally, when Grant had thrown a girdle of steel about Lee's invested army at Appomattox Court-house, Birney's black troops were nearest the enemy, with glinting bayonet and loaded musket. The Eighth Pennsylvania Cavalry had charged the enemy at Clover Hill, and had been repulsed; General Doubleday threw his brigade of Negro troops into line of battle to receive the enemy if he should assault the Union lines. He advanced the colors of the Forty-first Regiment, and, in a charge like a dress-parade, it cleared the enemy from its front. It was in this brilliant charge that the brave and accomplished soldier, Captain John W. Falconer, received a mortal wound.

When an aide-de-camp rode down the line of battle crying, "Cease firing! General Lee has made an unconditional surrender," the Negro troops, who had been driving the enemy into a ravine, discharged their pieces in the air, and gave a shout of joy that made the ground shake.

In the evening several Confederate bands serenaded the Union troops, and in return several bands, composed entirely of Negroes, complimented the Confederates with appropriate music.

After the Confederate army had been paroled the Negro troops cheerfully and cordially divided their rations with the late enemy, and welcomed them at their campfires on the march back to Petersburg. The sweet gospel of forgiveness was expressed in the Negro soldiers' intercourse with ex-rebel soldiers, who freely mingled with the black conquerors. It was a spectacle of magnanimity never before witnessed among troops that had hated and actually murdered one another.

CHAPTER XV.

AS PRISONERS OF WAR.

The capture and treatment of Negro soldiers by the enemy is a subject that demands dispassionate and judicial scrutiny. No just judge of historical events would seek to tear a single chaplet from the brow of any brave soldier, it matters not what uniform he wore or what flag he fought under. Valor is valor the world over. But whatever may be said of the gallantry of Confederate soldiers or the chivalry of the South, it remains true that the treatment bestowed upon Union prisoners of war in general, and upon Negroes in particular, has no parallel in the annals of modern civilized warfare.

Slavery destroyed the Southern conscience, blunted the sensibilities and affections, and depreciated human life. The Confederate army exhibited a fierceness in battle and a cold cruelty to their prisoners that startled the civilized world. Confederate military prisons became places of torture wherein every species of cruelty was perpetrated. Among the many hells erected for the reception and retention of Union prisoners Andersonville was, perhaps, the most notorious. It was situated on the South-western Railroad, about sixty-two miles south of Macon, Georgia. On the side of a hill where the timber was thick a space was cleared for the prison, in the form of a parallelogram, 1540 feet long and 750 feet wide. The ground was of red clay, and sloped gently to the south. Logs measuring twenty-four feet in length were firmly embedded in the ground, and closely joined together all the way up, with the upper end sharpened. Beyond and outside of this was a lower stockade for greater security. Within the main prison-wall, and thirty feet from it, a railing three feet high, upon posts ten feet apart, ran around the entire prison. This was known as the "dead-line." On the top of the main wall were thirty-five sentry-boxes, while at the angles of the prison stood artillery commanding the entire space. For recapturing escaped prisoners a large pack of blood-hounds was kept constantly on hand. There was not a tree or shrub left in the entire prison, and thus the sun had full power. In the summer the thermometer registered 110° Fahrenheit, while its mean for the heated term was 88° in the shade. The only water near this prison was a little stream five feet wide and six inches deep, that had its origin in a deadly, unhealthy swamp; and this stream passed through the prison grounds, flowing from east to west.

On the 15th of February, 1864, the first detachment of Union prisoners of war, numbering eight hundred and sixty, was received. Within four months there were twelve thousand prisoners in Andersonville, and before the end of August there were 31,693—leaving about thirty-six feet for each man! The prison was in use about thirteen months, and its reports show that during that period 44,882 prisoners were received.

The prisoners were allowed as rations each day two ounces of bacon or boiled beef, one sweet potato, and one piece of bread two and one-half inches square and thick, made of corn and ground pease.

There was no shelter from rain or sun. Some men dug holes in the ground, where they remained during the day, and at night wandered forth under the open sky, while others made little houses of sticks and red clay. When it rained this vast army of forlorn captives wandered about in mud a foot deep. "Into the brook there flowed the filth and excrements of more than thirty thousand men. The banks of the stream were covered with ordure, and appeared to be alive with working maggots. Through this reeking mass wandered about, elbowing and pushing one another, the shoeless, hatless, famished captives, many of them with scarcely a tatter to cover them. ... Attracted by the smell of this mass of living carrion, flocks of vultures—the 'turkey-buzzards' of the South—soared in the air over this den of human putridity, or, gorged with human flesh, sat nodding on the dead pines of the adjacent forest."

The death-rate soon reached the alarming figures of $8\frac{1}{2}$ per hour, and of the 44,882 incarcerated 12,462 died; while a large proportion of those who lived to get out of this atrocious lazar-house died soon after in Union hospitals or at home. Those who died in the prison were piled in heaps outside of the stockade; they were hauled away by the wagon-load, cast into a common ditch without coffins and covered with quick-lime. If the dead had rings on their fingers, the axe was often used to secure these jewels.

There were three hundred men shot near the dead-line, while hundreds were torn by the half-starved blood-hounds in attempting to escape. Many were put in stocks and chains for alleged breaches of the laws of the prison, and others were murdered by the hands of the keeper, Wirz, who was subsequently tried by the United States authorities and hanged.

Not only physical suffering, but mental ruin, often resulted from this diabolical prison system, and men wandered about the loathsome pen raving maniacs. Some fought their battles over again, and hysterically laughed at the imaginary foes they vanquished; some wandered forth in delirium to meet kindred, and were murdered on the "dead-line;" others stood shaking their shrivelled fists at the sky pronouncing wild imprecations; while still others drifted in listless apathy from one end of the den to the other, clinching a bone or dramatically drawing their tattered garments about their emaciated forms.

But who were the victims of this organized cruelty of which the Inspector-general of the Confederate army, Colonel Chandler, said, "It is a place the horrors of which it is difficult to describe—it is a disgrace to civilization?" White officers and enlisted men from the North. Many of them had the blood of revolutionary patriots in their veins; some were from Harvard and Yale, Williams and Brown; some were justly distinguished in literature and science; many were the sons of rich men, millionaires, without food or raiment. If such men endured such hardships as prisoners of war, what was in reserve for the poor Negro?

Although the Confederate authorities had first inaugurated the policy of arming Negroes as soldiers, the moment the United States Government announced its intention to do likewise the Rebel Government proscribed the Negro as a prisoner of war. In fact, the message of Jefferson Davis on the treatment of Negroes as prisoners of war was prior to any action on this matter by either President Lincoln or Congress. The first Emancipation Proclamation of President Lincoln, issued on the 22d of September, 1862, a few days after the battle of Antietam, was rather a measure of military policy than of humanity. It was regarded by the Confederate authorities as contemplating the employment of emancipated slaves in the armed service of the United States. Before this, on the 22d of August, 1862, General B. F. Butler, then in command of the Union forces at New Orleans, had appealed to the free Negro citizens of Louisiana to rally in defence of their common country; and this fact, followed so soon by Mr. Lincoln's proclamation, imbittered and alarmed the enemy. The independent action of General Butler was regarded as indicating the policy of the Government.

On the 23d of December, 1862, Jefferson Davis, President of the Confederate States, issued the following proclamation, aimed at General Butler in particular, and all Negro soldiers and their officers in general:

"*First.* That all commissioned officers in the command of said Benjamin F. Butler be declared not entitled to be considered as soldiers engaged in honorable warfare, but as robbers and criminals, deserving death; and that they and each of them be, whenever captured, reserved for execution.

"*Second.* That the private soldiers and non-commissioned officers in the army of said Butler be considered as only the instruments used for the commission of crimes perpetrated by his orders, and not as free agents; that they, therefore, be treated, when captured, as prisoners of war, with kindness and humanity, and be sent home on the usual parole that they will in no manner aid or serve the United States in any capacity during the continuance of this war, unless duly exchanged.

"*Third.* That all Negro slaves captured in arms be at once delivered over to the executive authorities of the respective States to which they belong, to be dealt with according to the laws of said States.

"*Fourth.* That the like orders be executed in all cases with respect to all commissioned officers of the United States, when found serving in company with said slaves in insurrection against the authorities of the different States of this Confederacy.

"[Signed and sealed at Richmond, December 23, 1862.]

"JEFFERSON DAVIS."

This message was laid before the Confederate Congress, and on the 12th of January, 1863, the following action was had:

"*Resolved, by the Congress of the Confederate States of America,* in response to the message of the President, transmitted to Congress at the commencement of the present session, That, in the opinion of Congress, the commissioned officers of the enemy ought *not* to be delivered to the authorities of the respective States, as suggested in the said message, but all captives taken by the Confederate forces ought to be dealt with and disposed of by the Confederate Government.

"Sec. 2. That, in the judgment of Congress, the proclamation of the President of the United States, dated respectively September 22, 1862, and January 1, 1863, and the other measures of the Government of the United States and of its authorities, commanders, and forces, designed or tending to emancipate slaves in the Confederate States, or to abduct such slaves, or to incite them to insurrection, or to employ Negroes in war against the Confederate States, or to overthrow the institution of African slavery, and bring on a servile war in these States, would, if successful, produce atrocious consequences, and they are inconsistent with the spirit of those usages which, in modern warfare, prevail among civilized nations; they may, therefore, be properly and lawfully repressed by retaliation.

"Sec. 3. That in every case wherein, during the present war, any violation of the laws of war, among civilized nations, shall be, or has been, done and perpetrated by those acting under the authority of the Government of the United States, on the persons or property of citizens of the Confederate States, or of those under the protection or in the land or naval service of the Confederate States, or of any State of the Confederacy, the President of the Confederate States is hereby authorized to cause full and ample retaliation to be made for every such violation, in such manner and to such extent as he may think proper.

"Sec. 4. That every white person, being a commissioned officer, or acting as such, who, during the present war, shall command Negroes or mulattoes in arms against the Confederate States, or who shall arm, train, organize, or prepare Negroes or mulattoes for military service against the Confederate States, or who shall voluntarily aid Negroes or mulattoes in any military enterprise, attack, or conflict in such service, shall be deemed as inciting servile insurrection, and shall, if captured, be put to death, or be otherwise punished at the discretion of the Court.

"Sec. 5. Every person, being a commissioned officer, or acting as such in the service of the enemy, who shall, during the present war, excite, attempt to excite, or cause to be excited, a servile insurrection, or shall incite, or cause to be incited, a slave or rebel, shall, if captured, be put to death, or be otherwise punished at the discretion of the Court.

"Sec. 6. Every person charged with an offence punishable under the preceding resolutions shall, during the present war, be tried before the military court attached to the army or corps by the troops of which he shall have been captured, or by such other military court as the President may direct, and in such manner and under such regulations as the President shall prescribe; and, after conviction, the President may commute the punishment in such manner and on such terms as he may deem proper.

"SEC. 7. All Negroes and mulattoes who shall be engaged in war, or be taken in arms against the Confederate States, or shall give aid or comfort to the enemies of the Confederate States, shall, when captured in the Confederate States, be delivered to the authorities of the State or States in which they shall be captured, to be dealt with according to the present or future laws of such State or States."

This document is cited in full that the official record may be before the reader. Several points in it deserve special consideration. The Confederate Congress was unwilling, on the recommendation of Mr. Davis, to allow the prisoners which their army might take to pass into the control of the several Confederate States. While devoted to "State Rights," for once the sovereign Confederate Government raised its majestic voice and demanded possession of Union prisoners. The several States could be trusted in everything but the delicate matter of dealing with Union prisoners of war. Congress did not hesitate to take issue with President Davis. The civil and criminal law of the States in ante-bellum days had always been regarded as adequate to deal with Abolitionists, Negroes, and other criminals; but when those laws were to be applied to Union prisoners of war their efficiency was called in question, and the Confederacy now conferred upon the States authority to make new laws upon the subject. The high prerogative of murdering Union prisoners having not been delegated to the States, was reserved to the Confederate Congress.

Just where, when, and in what manner the United States ever violated " the laws or usages of war among civilized nations" is not clear. Certainly there is no record of any such violation. But of this the Confederate Government determined to be the sole judge of what constituted a violation of "the laws or usages of war;" and from its judgment there was no appeal.

Brave white officers, the laurelled leaders of gallant Negro soldiers, were marked for a felon's death. The military employment of slaves by the United States Government was justified by historical precedents ancient and modern, Christian and pagan; and last, if least, it had before it the example of the Confederate Government already alluded to. Consequently the murdering of officers who belonged to organizations composed of Negroes was "a most flagrant violation of the laws or usages of war among civilized nations." It had become manifest that either "the institution of African slavery" or the free institutions of the American Union must perish, and therefore the United States Government was justified in using the Negro as a military instrument in preserving the autonomy of the States, and in securing the freedom of the slaves.

The proclamation of Mr. Davis and the subsequent legislative action of the Confederate Congress aroused the attention and stirred the indignation of the friends of humanity everywhere. On the 14th of April, 1863, the *New York Tribune* said, editorially, "At all events, the policy of the Government to employ Black Troops in active service is definitely established, and it becomes—as indeed it has been for months—a very serious question what steps are to be taken for their protection. The Proclamation of Jefferson Davis remains unrevoked. By it he threatened death or slavery to every Negro taken in arms, and to their white officers the same fate. What is the response of our Government? Hitherto, silence. The number of

Negroes in its service has already increased; in South Carolina they have already been mustered into regiments by a sweeping conscription, and now in the West apparently the same policy is adopted and rigorously enforced."

In reply to the pertinent and humane sentiments of Horace Greeley and other leaders of public sentiment at the North, the *Richmond Examiner*, speaking for the Confederate Government, said, "It is not merely the pretension of a regular Government affecting to deal with 'Rebels,' but it is a deadly stab which they are aiming at our institutions themselves, because they know that, if we were insane enough to yield this point, to treat Black men as the equals of White, and insurgent slaves as equivalent to our brave soldiers, the very foundation of Slavery would be fatally wounded."

A few bold and conscientious Southern newspapers urged that the Confederate Government had no authority to proscribe Union soldiers on account of color, and clearly pointed out the dangers that such a course as the Government had marked out would invite. The Confederate Government adhered to its views, and its army in the field carried out its policy with zeal and cruelty.

The Confederate army at Port Hudson would not permit a flag of truce to bury the brave black soldiers who fell in the memorable engagement in May, 1863. In the spring and summer of 1863 a number of Negro soldiers were made prisoners in their conflicts with the enemy, and were subjected to barbarous treatment. When an exchange of prisoners took place in front of Charleston, although the rebels held many Negro prisoners, they gave up none but white soldiers. When this fact was brought to the attention of commissioners for the exchange of prisoners on behalf of the Confederate Government, they explained that it was against the law of their Government to exchange Negro prisoners. This statement aroused the North, and President Lincoln issued the following order:

"Executive Mansion, Washington, *July* 30, 1863.

"It is the duty of every government to give protection to its citizens of whatever class, color, or condition, and especially to those who are duly organized as soldiers in the public service. The law of nations, and the usages and customs of war, as carried on by civilized powers, permit no distinction as to color in the treatment of prisoners of war as public enemies. To sell or enslave any captured person, on account of his color, and for no offence against the laws of war, is a relapse into barbarism, and a crime against the civilization of the age.

"The Government of the United States will give the same protection to all its soldiers; and if the enemy shall sell or enslave any one because of his color, the offence shall be punished by retaliation upon the enemy's prisoners in our possession.

"It is therefore ordered that, for every soldier of the United States killed in violation of the laws of war, a Rebel soldier shall be executed; and for every one enslaved by the enemy or sold into Slavery, a Rebel soldier shall be placed at hard labor on public works, and continued at such labor until the other shall be released and receive the treatment due to a prisoner of war. ABRAHAM LINCOLN.

"By order of the Secretary of War.

"E. D. TOWNSEND,

"Assistant Adjutant-general."

On the 12th of August, 1863, the *Charleston Mercury*, an able and conservative journal, called attention to the severe treatment of Negro prisoners of war. The humane sentiments expressed appealed strongly to the general officers of the Confederate army. General Beauregard felt that the criticism applied to him. It was certainly a case of conscience, for he had sent the following despatch the year before which lowered him from the honorable position of a general and branded him forever as a murderer:

"Charleston, South Carolina, *October* 13, 1862.

"*Hon. Wm. P. Miles, Richmond, Virginia:*

"Has the bill for the execution of Abolition prisoners after January next been passed? Do it, and England will be stirred into action! It is high time to proclaim the black flag after that period. Let the execution be with the garrote.

    (Signed)   "G. T. BEAUREGARD."

Previous to this, on the 3d of August, 1862, General Beauregard wrote to General Wm. E. Martin from Bladen, Alabama, as follows:

"We will yet have to come to proclaiming this war 'a war to the knife,' when no quarter will be asked or granted. I believe it is the only thing which can prevent recruiting at the North. As to ourselves, I think that very few will not admit that death is preferable to dishonor and ruin."[1]

His chief of staff sent the following letter to the *Mercury:*

    "Headquarters Department of S. C., Ga., and Fla.,
     "Charleston, South Carolina, *August* 12, 1863.

"*Colonel R. B. Rhett, Jr., Editor of 'Mercury:'*

"In the *Mercury* of this date you appear to have written under a misapprehension of the facts connected with the present *status* of the Negroes captured in arms on Morris and James islands, which permit me to state as follows:

"The Proclamation of the President, dated December 24, 1862, directed that all Negro slaves captured in arms should be at once delivered over to the executive authorities of the respective States to which they belong, to be dealt with according to the laws of said States.

"An informal application was made by the State authorities for the Negroes captured in this vicinity, but as none of them, it appeared, had been slaves of citizens of South Carolina, they were not turned over to civil authority, for at the moment there was no official information at these headquarters of the Act of Congress by which 'all Negroes and mulattoes who shall be engaged in war, or be taken in arms against the Confederate States, or shall give aid or comfort to the enemies of the Confederate States,' were directed to be turned over to the authorities of 'State or States in which they shall be captured, to be dealt with according to the present or future laws of such State or States.'

"On the 21st of July, however, the commanding general telegraphed to the Secretary of War for instructions as to the disposition to be made of the Negroes captured on Morris and James islands, and on

---

[1] "Rebellion Record," vol. viii., P., p. 36.

the 22d received a reply that they must be turned over to the State authorities, by virtue of the joint resolutions of Congress in question.

"Accordingly, on the 29th of July, as soon as a copy of the resolution or act was received, his Excellency Governor Bonham was informed that the Negroes captured were held subject to his orders, to be dealt with according to the laws of South Carolina.

"On the same day (29th of July) Governor Bonham requested that they should be retained in military custody until he could make arrangements to dispose of them; and in that custody they still remain, awaiting the orders of the State authorities.

"Respectfully, your obedient servant,
"THOMAS JORDAN, Chief of Staff."

The enemy was inflexible in his purpose to deny Negro soldiers the immunities of prisoners of war. Some whom the fortunes of civil war threw into the hands of the enemy were murdered after they had surrendered; others were placed at work on fortifications, where they were exposed to the fire of the Union army; many were crowded into common jails, and made to toil in the streets like felons, or were sold at public auction. In many instances where Negro soldiers had surrendered their arms on the battle-field they were shot down in cold blood. On the 17th of December, 1863, the *Richmond Enquirer* said: "The Yankees are not going to send their Negro troops in the field; they know as well as we do that no reliance can be placed upon them; but as depot-guards, prison-guards, etc., they will relieve their white troops. This is the use that will be made of them. Should they be sent to the field, and be put in battle, none will be taken prisoners: our troops understand what to do in such cases."

Such advice from the organ of the Confederate administration at Richmond had its influence upon the rebel army. The following correspondence between Generals Peck and Pickett needs no explanation or comment:

"Headquarters of the Army and District of North Carolina,
"Newbern, North Carolina, *February* 11, 1864.
"*Major-general Pickett, Department of Virginia and North Carolina, Confederate Army, Petersburg:*

"GENERAL,—I have the honor to enclose a slip cut from the *Richmond Examiner*, February 8, 1864. It is styled 'The Advance on Newbern,' and appears to have been extracted from the *Petersburg Register*, a paper published in the city where your headquarters are located.

"Your attention is particularly invited to that paragraph which states 'that Colonel Shaw was shot dead by a Negro soldier from the other side of the river, which he was spanning with a pontoon-bridge,' and that 'the Negro was watched, followed, taken, and hanged after the action at Thomasville:'

"'THE ADVANCE ON NEWBERN.—The *Petersburg Register* gives the following additional facts of the advance on Newbern: Our army, according to the report of passengers arriving from Weldon, has fallen back to a point sixteen miles west of Newbern. The reason assigned for this retrograde movement was that Newbern could not be taken by us without a loss on our part which could find no equivalent in its capture, as the place was stronger than we had anticipated. Yet, in spite of this, we are sure that the expedition will result in good to our cause. Our forces are in a situation to get large supplies from a country still abundant, to prevent raids on points westward, and keep Tories in check, and hang them when caught.

"'From a private who was one of the guard that brought the batch of prisoners through we learn that Colonel Shaw was shot dead by a Negro soldier from the other side of the river, which he was spanning with a pontoon-bridge. The Negro was watched, followed, taken, and hanged after the action at Thomasville. It is stated that when our troops entered Thomasville a number of the enemy took shelter in the houses and fired upon them. The Yankees were ordered to surrender, but refused, whereupon our men set fire to the houses, and their occupants got, bodily, a taste in this world of the flames eternal.'

"The Government of the United States has wisely seen fit to enlist many thousand colored citizens to aid in putting down the rebellion, and has placed them on the same footing in all respects as her white troops.

* * * * * * *

"Believing that this atrocity has been perpetrated without your knowledge, and that you will take prompt steps to disavow this violation of the usages of war, and to bring the offenders to justice, I shall refrain from executing a rebel soldier until I learn your action in the premises.

"I am, very respectfully, your obedient servant,

"JOHN J. PECK, Major-general."

Reply of General Pickett.

"Headquarters of the Department of North Carolina,
"Petersburg, Virginia, *February* 16, 1864.

"*Major-general John J. Peck, U.S.A., Commanding at Newbern:*

"GENERAL,—Your communication of the 11th of February is received. I have the honor to state in reply that the paragraph from a newspaper enclosed therein is not only without foundation in fact, but so ridiculous that I should scarcely have supposed it worthy of consideration; but I would respectfully inform you that had I caught *any* Negro, who had killed either officer, soldier, or citizen of the Confederate States, I should have caused him to be immediately executed.

"To your threat expressed in the following extract from your communication, namely, 'Believing that this atrocity has been perpetrated without your knowledge, and that you will take prompt steps to disavow this violation of the usages of war, and to bring the offenders to justice, I shall refrain from executing a rebel soldier until I learn of your action in the premises,' I have merely to say that I have in my hands, and subject to my orders, captured in the recent operations in this department, some four hundred and fifty officers and men of the United States army, and for every man you hang I will hang ten of the United States army.

"I am, General, very respectfully, your obedient servant,
"J. E. PICKETT,
"Major-general Commanding."[1]

On the 14th of June, 1864, a correspondent, writing from Mississippi to the *Atlanta Appeal*, speaking of Forrest's fighting in Tennessee, said:

"Very few Negroes, it seems, have been captured. Perhaps not more than forty or fifty have appeared at headquarters. Most of them fled as soon as it was known that Forrest was on the battle-field. Those that were taken escaped (?). The soldiers say that they lost them."

In plainer terms, the soldiers murdered the Negro prisoners, and Forrest knew it and approved of the butchery. As at Fort Pillow, so here and elsewhere during the Rebellion, Forrest murdered his Negro prisoners of

---

[1] "Rebellion Record," vol. viii., Doc., pp. 418, 419.

war. His government never disapproved of his conduct, because he was simply carrying out its policy in the main.

In many instances Negro captives would be marched all day, escorted by the enemy's cavalry, and towards evening some rebel soldier would exclaim, "Halt there! These niggers are tryin' to git away!" and immediately begin an indiscriminate slaughter of their Negro prisoners. The verbal report would be that they attempted to escape and were shot by the guards. But no investigation would be instituted, and so the Confederate soldier came to understand that it was his privilege and his duty to murder Negro prisoners of war. The search has been made in vain for a single military or political protest against these enormous crimes. On the contrary, there is ample proof that the murder of Negro prisoners was authorized by the Confederate Congress, since that body regarded them as engaged in insurrection, the crime whereof was punishable with death.

The following despatch shows that the War Department knew that the Confederate Government would not treat Negro soldiers as prisoners of war, and that it was the duty of the United States Government to protect them:

"War Department, *November* 17, 1863.
"*Major-general Butler, Fort Monroe:*
"'The whole subject of exchange of prisoners is under direction of Major-general Hitchcock, to whom, as Commissioner of Exchange, that branch of the service has been committed. He will be glad to have any aid or suggestions you may be pleased to furnish, but there should be no interference without his assent. It is known that the rebels will exchange man for man and officer for officer, except blacks, and officers in command of black troops. These they absolutely refuse to exchange. This is the point on which the whole matter hangs. Exchanging man for man and officer for officer, with the exception the rebels make, is a substantial abandonment of the Colored Troops and

their officers to their fate, and would be a shameful dishonor to the Government bound to protect them. When they agree to exchange all alike there will be no difficulty.

"EDWIN M. STANTON, Secretary of War."

The men who disgraced their uniform by murdering Union prisoners of war may not be willing to remember, but will be unable to forget, their crime against the profession of arms. Every sentiment of patriotism, every instinct of humanity, every principle of justice, every element of Christian ethics, revolts at these dark deeds. The Southern conscience of to-day may seek, like Cain, to hide from the bar of public sentiment, but, like the first murder, neither the Confederate Congress nor its hired assassin, the Confederate army, can ever escape the fierce light of impartial history. A cause that could authorize and seek to justify such horrors is forever and irrevocably "the lost cause." No descendant will be proud of its memory, no friend of humanity will mourn at its sepulchre. Christian civilization the world over will rejoice that such a cause has perished from among the governments of mankind; while the Negro, with unexampled charity, if not able to forget, freely forgives the murderers of his kinsmen under the pretext of law.

CHAPTER XVI.

THE CLOUD OF WITNESSES.

TESTIMONY to the martial valor of the Negro soldier comes from the lips of friend and foe alike. He disappointed his enemies and surprised his friends. He was not only impetuous in the onset, but cool and stubborn in repelling an assault. He exhibited the highest qualities of soldiership at Port Hudson in repeatedly assaulting the enemy in strong works with great physical obstructions to contend with. It was true he had the inspiration and poetry of numbers to incite him to deeds of valor; but at Milliken's Bend he was a raw recruit, and yet he did his fighting with the bayonet, often dying with his antagonist's steel in his body. Often he transfixed the enemy, and showed himself possessed of great personal courage when every semblance of order and organization had melted in the heat of battle. At Olustee and Honey Hill, at Poison Springs and Chaffin's Farm, he proved that he was endowed with that military intelligence of unit that makes the concrete strength of an army. The Negro was a soldier in every sense of the word.

Secretary of War Edwin M. Stanton said of Negro troops at Petersburg: "The hardest fighting was done by the black troops. The forts they stormed were the worst of all. After the affair was over, General Smith went to thank them, and tell them he was proud of their courage and dash. He says they cannot be exceeded as soldiers, and that hereafter he will send them in a difficult place as readily as the best white troops." [1]

In a letter to Senator Henry Wilson, dated May 30, 1864, Lorenzo Thomas, Adjutant-general of the Army, said: "Experience proves that they manage heavy guns very well. Their fighting qualities have also been fully tested a number of times, and I am yet to hear of the first case where they did not fully stand up to their work. I passed over the ground where the First Louisiana made the gallant charge at Port Hudson, by far the stronger part of the rebel works. The wonder is that so many have made their escape. At Milliken's Bend, where I had three incomplete regiments, one without arms until the day previous to the attack, greatly superior numbers of the rebels charged furiously up to the very breastworks. The Negroes met the enemy on the ramparts, and both sides freely used the bayonet—a most rare occurrence in warfare, as one or the other party gives away before coming in contact with steel. The rebels were defeated with heavy loss. The bridge at Moscow, on the line of railroad from Memphis to Corinth, was defended by one small regiment of blacks. A cavalry attack of three times their number was made, the blacks defeating them in three charges made by the rebels.

"They fought them hours, till our cavalry came up, when the defeat was made complete, many of the dead being left on the field.

"A cavalry force of three hundred and fifty attacked three hundred rebel cavalry near the Big Black with signal success, a number of prisoners being taken and marched to Vicksburg. Forrest attacked Paducah with seven thousand five hundred men. The garrison was between five

---

[1] *New York Herald*, June 18, 1864.

hundred and six hundred, nearly four hundred being colored troops recently raised. What troops could have done better? So, too, they fought well at Fort Pillow, till overpowered by greatly superior numbers."

Major-general James G. Blunt, writing of the battle of Honey Springs, Arkansas, said of Negro troops: "The Negroes (First Colored Regiment) were too much for the enemy, and let me here say that I never saw such fighting as was done by that Negro regiment. They fought like veterans, with a coolness and valor that is unsurpassed. They preserved their line perfect throughout the whole engagement, and although in the hottest of the fight, they never once faltered. Too much praise cannot be awarded them for their gallantry. The question that Negroes will fight is settled; besides, they make better soldiers in every respect than any troops I have ever had under my command." [1]

Major-general S. A. Hurlbut, on the 24th of April, 1864, said of Negro troops in his command: "I have two or three regiments at Memphis that I am willing to put anywhere that I would put any soldiers which I have ever seen, with the same amount of experience."

General George C. Strong, who so gallantly led the troops that charged Fort Wagner, said of the brave Negro troops: "The Fifty-fourth did well and nobly, only the fall of Colonel Shaw prevented them from entering the fort. They moved up as gallantly as any troops could, and with their enthusiasm they deserve a better fate."

Major-general Alfred H. Terry, on the 16th of July, 1863, said to the adjutant of the Fifty-fourth Regiment, "Tell your colonel that I am exceedingly pleased with

---

[1] *New York Tribune*, August 19, 1863.

the conduct of your regiment. They have done all they could do."

Major-general W. F. Smith, speaking of the bravery of Negro troops at Petersburg, said: "There were thirteen guns pouring a constant fire of shot and shell upon those troops, enfilading the line, cutting it lengthwise and crosswise, 'yet they stood unmoved for *six hours*. Not a man flinched.' [These are the words of the General.] 'It was as severe a test as I ever saw. But they stood it, and when my arrangements were completed for charging the works, they moved with the steadiness of veterans to the attack. I expected that they would fall back or be cut to pieces, but when I saw them move over the field, gain the works, and capture the guns, I was astounded. They lost between five hundred and six hundred in doing it. There is material in the Negroes to make the best troops in the world, if they are properly trained.'"[1]

Brevet-major-general Thomas J. Morgan, speaking of the courage of Negro troops in the battle of Nashville, and its effect upon Major-general George H. Thomas, said: "Those who fell nearest the enemy's works were colored. General Thomas spoke very feelingly of the sight which met his eye as he rode over the field, and he confessed that the Negro had fully vindicated his bravery, and wiped from his mind the last vestige of prejudice and doubt."

Colonel John A. Foster, of the One Hundred and Seventy-fifth New York, speaking of the conduct of the Negro brigade at Port Hudson, said: "We witnessed them in line of battle under a very heavy fire of musketry and siege and field pieces. There was a deep gully or bayou before them which they could not cross nor ford in the

---

[1] *New York Tribune*, July 26, 1864.

presence of the enemy, and hence an assault was wholly impracticable. Yet they made five several attempts to swim and cross it, preparatory to an assault on the enemy's works, and in this, too, in fair view of the enemy, and at short musket-range. Added to this, the nature of the enemy's works was such that it allowed an enfilading fire. Success was impossible, yet they behaved as cool as if veterans, and when ordered to retire, marched off as if on parade. I feel satisfied that if the position of the bayou had been known, and the assault made a quarter of a mile to the left of where it was, the place would have been taken by this Negro brigade on that day.

"On that day I witnessed the attack made by the divisions of Generals Grover and Paine, and can truly say I saw no steadier fighting by those daring men than did the Negroes in this their first fight."

Hundreds of other witnesses would cheerfully give their testimony to the valor of the Negro soldier, but no more need be summoned. There is no testimony offered in rebuttal; there is but one opinion—"*The Colored Troops fought nobly.*"

From first to last there were 178,975 Negro soldiers in the United States Volunteer army, and of this number 36,847 were killed, wounded, and missing. They participated in four hundred and forty-nine battles, and served in nearly every military department of the United States Army. Besides this large military force there were at least one hundred and fifty thousand Negro laborers in the Quartermaster and Engineering departments. When Ohio was threatened by invasion a large number of Negro citizens of Cincinnati were impressed to construct military roads and fortifications. This band of patriotic laborers, seven hundred and six in number, has been designated "*The Black Brigade of Cincinnati.*" It was not even a regiment, and that it never performed military service there is evidence in its record, compiled in 1864. The services of this fatigue party lasted just eighteen days, with compensation at the rate of one dollar and one dollar and a half per day. The compiler of the record of these men says, in the second paragraph, that this "was the first organization of the colored people of the North actually employed for military purposes;" while Judge Wm. M. Dickson, who had charge of them, says: "During the first week they labored, as did the whole fatigue force, without compensation. During the second week they received a dollar a day per man, and during the third week a dollar and a half, as did also all the fatigue force, black and white" (page 20). And on the next page the judge says: "Many of the members of the brigade have *since* entered the *military* service." It is plain, therefore, that these men were not a "brigade;" that they were never called upon to perform military service, but were simply employed on fatigue duty for a term less than three weeks.

Not alone these brave black men of Cincinnati, but their kinsmen all along the seaboard defences of the Union army, were part of the muscle and sinew of the republic, and what they did in their humble capacity as laborers should never be forgotten or underestimated.

The result of this long and sanguinary fratricidal conflict was the attainment of two noble ends—American Nationality and National Freedom. The metamorphoses of the United States Government had been slow: Continentalism, Federalism, then the struggle between State and National Sovereignty. The character of the Government had always been equivocal. The armed attempt to disturb the autonomy of the United States Government was regarded by the enemies of Democracy, here and abroad, as the beginning of the end of the republic. Abraham Lincoln was elected, by all the solemn forms of law, President of these United States; the Southern States, coerced by ambitious politicians, appealed from the decision of the ballot to the Supreme Court of Civil War. Following the plaintiff into that awful tribunal, the United States Government, as defendant, won the right of national existence as well as the authority to enforce its laws in States as in the Territories.

Coupled with and inseparable from the doctrine of State Sovereignty was the dogma of Negro slavery. The overturning of State Rights carried with it, logically and inevitably, the local, sectional, and patriarchal institution of slavery. They were united in life, they were not divided in death, and they found a common grave under the feet of a victorious army. American nationality is sealed forever, and the one flag of a great nation will float as the sovereign symbol of a free and united people; while the Constitution of these United States knows no sect nor section, no party nor partisan, no black nor white, only American citizens.

The United States Government added no star to its flag, nor did it wage war for conquest, but in defending its life against the insidious and dangerous doctrine of disunion it struck down human slavery, the bane of American civilization. Nor was it an accident that the Negro soldier became a profound and determinative factor in the problem of war. In the Universe of God there are no accidents. From the fall of a sparrow to the sweep of a planet, all is in accord with His will whose laws are divine! The Southern Pharaoh, as the Egyptian Pharaoh, pursued his slaves into the red sea of civil war, where the Nemesis of retribution overtook him. The handwriting was upon the walls of the institution of slavery from the first hour of the civil strife; only the eyes of the South were blind to the fate that awaited the enemies of humanity. The Negro slave, at first despised and rejected, at least became the stake of the game of war to be won or lost. But the most impressive fact in this strange history is that the Negro himself helped win the victory. There was no time during the war when he was not, in one way or another, helpful to the cause of the Union. During the first year of the conflict, when the hostile armies were mastering technicalities and learning the art of practical warfare, the Negro was besieging Heaven with his potent prayers for the Union. He could not be inactive, passive, indifferent; and although illiterate, he read the signs of the times aright. He believed from the first that the war was all about him, and for his redemption. It was the answer to the uncounted prayers of generations of pious slaves; and although many died without the sight, the promise was unto the faithful.

It was a grand achievement in the history of the Democracy of the world that the United States Government was taken from the shifting sands of the delusion of State Rights and built upon the adamantine foundation of National Unity. But the brightest star, the one that shall shine with undimmed lustre while Republican institutions endure among men, is that which symbolizes the disinthralment of 4,500,000 bondmen. To wash out the foul stain of human slavery by the blood of patriots, to elevate the slave to the dignity of a soldier, and to invite him into the arena of civil war, where every element of manhood, every sentiment of patriotism, every attribute of valor could have full play, was an achievement hardly ever vouchsafed to a government before. And where upon the face of the whole earth has a race of slaves gone in a single bound from abject, servile subjection to the imperial heights of military accomplishments? History contains no parallel.

In passing in review the military services of the Negro soldier some lessons may be learned. Hamlets and villages, towns and cities, counties and States, have erected monuments and cenotaphs to commemorate the valor of their citizens. The ineffable, mute eloquence of these soldier-monuments is invaluable to the cause of National Unity, while the story of the civil war is forever an object lesson. The songs of a nation are the heart-beats of patriotism; but the surest way to teach national history is in monumental marble and brass. The deathless deeds of the white soldier's valor are not only embalmed in song and story, but are carved in marble and bronze. But nowhere in all this free land is there a monument to brave Negro soldiers, 36,847 of whom gave up their lives in the struggle for national existence. Even the appearance of the Negro soldier in the hundreds of histories of the war has always been incidental. These brave men have had no champion, no one to chronicle their record, teeming with interest and instinct with patriotism.

A government of a proud, patriotic, prosperous, and free people would make a magnificent investment by erecting at the capital of the nation a monument dedicated to its brave black soldiers. The large and beautiful Government Park, immediately in front of Howard University, would be an admirable place for a monument to the Negro soldiers who fell in their country's cause. A commanding monument made of Southern granite, surmounted by a private soldier in great-coat, equipments, fixed bayonet, gun at parade rest, looking south towards the Capitol, would be most impressive. At the four corners the three arms of the field-service and the navy would be represented. *First figure*, a Negro artilleryman in full-dress uniform, with folded arms, standing by a field-piece. *Second figure,* a cavalryman in full-dress uniform, with spurs and gloves, and sabre unhooked at his left side. *Third figure,* an infantryman in full-dress uniform, accoutrements, and musket at in place rest. *Fourth figure,* a Negro sailor in uniform standing by an anchor or mortar.

On the *first* side of the monument:

A GRATEFUL NATION CONSECRATES THIS MONUMENT TO THE 36,847 NEGRO SOLDIERS WHO DIED IN THE SERVICE OF THEIR COUNTRY.
"THE COLORED TROOPS FOUGHT NOBLY."

On the *second* side of the monument:

THEY EARNED THE RIGHT TO BE FREE BY DEEDS OF DESPERATE VALOR; AND IN THE 449 ENGAGEMENTS IN WHICH THEY PARTICIPATED THEY PROVED THEMSELVES WORTHY TO BE INTRUSTED WITH A NATION'S FLAG AND HONOR.

On the *third* side of the monument:

DURING THE CIVIL WAR IN AMERICA, FROM 1861 TO 1865, THERE WERE 178,975 NEGRO SOLDIERS ENROLLED IN THE UNITED STATES VOLUNTEER ARMY. OF THIS NUMBER 99,337 WERE ENLISTED BY AUTHORITY OF THE GOVERNMENT, AND 79,638 WERE ENLISTED BY THE SEVERAL STATES AND TERRITORIES.

On the *fourth* side of the monument:

PORT HUDSON,	MILLIKEN'S BEND,
FORT WAGNER,	OLUSTEE,
HONEY HILL,	FAIR OAKS,
NEW MARKET HEIGHTS,	PETERSBURG,
POISON SPRINGS,	NASHVILLE,
DEEP BOTTOM,	FORT FISHER,
FORT PILLOW,	FORT BLAKELY,
CHAFFIN'S FARM,	HATCHER'S RUN.

These inscriptions are merely suggestive; the United States Congress would charge the appropriate committee with this as with other matters of detail. And the matter of naming the park in which such a monument should stand belongs to the Congress, and is very important. Among all the white officers who were identified with Negro troops, Colonel Robert Gould Shaw was the most conspicuous, and of most commanding character. He came of a noble race of men, and his broad views of humanity were an inheritance; he was pure as he was just, beautiful as he was good, patriotic as he was brave. He was a born leader of men, and, had he lived, would have attained high rank. He had studied at Harvard College with diligence, and was an heir to fortune, and yet he heard his country's call for defenders in the midst of luxury and ease, and responded. When other officers not only despised the Negro, but had no faith in his manhood or courage, Colonel Shaw chose to lead the first Massachusetts Colored troops to the battle-field. And so he resigned his commission in one of the best veteran white regiments of Massachusetts and became the colonel of the Fifty-fourth Massachusetts (Negro) Regiment. His influence over his regiment, his gentle kindness, and yet his firmness as a disciplinarian, his rectitude in camp and his courage in battle, are remembered by all whose good fortune it was to come within the sphere of his military activity.

Alas! that he should have fallen so early in the cause he so eagerly served! But who can record that death without emotion! There come a choking sensation, the fugitive tear, the swelling heart, the soul's deep sigh, as memory turns to the parapets of Wagner where patriotism offered up one of its most valiant votaries. The story of the fall of Colonel Shaw at the head of his gallant regiment is known by heart throughout the land, and in the humble huts of the unlettered blacks of the South his name is a household word. His stainless memory is the amulet that will forever preserve, untouched by calumny or the corroding mutations of time, the valor of the American Negro soldier.

To name for Colonel Robert Gould Shaw a park wherein a national monument to the Negro should stand would be eminently proper. It would quicken the pulse of national patriotism, it would elevate the feelings of the Negro, it would inform the Present, instruct the Future, and bind the friends of freedom to the generous heart of the nation. He was representative of the sentiment of anti-slavery New England, and was also the embodiment of all that was noble and upright in national character. He harbored no narrow, provincial sentiments, for his mind was broad as his ideas of the National Government were far-reaching. He was a splendid type of the most unselfish and exalted American patriot, and in recognizing his consummate services and in hallowing his precious memory the nation, for whose preservation he yielded up his life, would honor itself. The old Commonwealth of Massachusetts would beg of the Government the privilege of placing a statue of Colonel Shaw at the entrance of the proposed park.

Many Spartans fell at Thermopylæ, but in the battle-picture of that heroic defence the student of history sees alone the commanding form of Leonidas. Many brave men fell at the storming of Battery Wagner, yet nevertheless but one figure will be conspicuous in the eye of history for all time, Colonel Robert Gould Shaw, crying, "*Forward! my brave boys!*"

Looking back over the centuries, there would be little else to record of the poor, patient Negro save his sufferings and degradation were it not for the luminous flashes of his martial glory, which cast a light upon the background of an otherwise sombre picture. But a monument such as is here proposed would surely and safely elevate the Negro to a proud place in the history of the nation. There are hundreds of thousands of ignorant people in the streets of Paris, but the great French nation can never lack patriotic defenders so long as its multitudinous monuments teach the unerring and inspiring lessons of its history. No people can be dangerously ignorant if their government build monuments.

The masses of Negroes in the United States are ignorant; but from their loins will spring only a race of patriots so long as a monument records the magnificent military achievements of the Negro soldier. Under such an object lesson, held by the sacred spell, touched by such an immutable influence, centuries might pass, treasures corrode, cities disappear, tribes perish, and even empires whose boast was their duration might crumble, but a republic that remembers to defend its defenders in tracing their noble conduct in monumental marble and brass can never decay. Heaven and earth may pass away, but God's word endures forever. Truth only is immortal.

THE ROLL OF HONOR.

The roll of honor is luminous with the names of Negro soldiers who, by deeds of personal valor, won the applause of the commanding generals and the Congress of the United States. Such a roll must necessarily be inadequate, for many as deserving as those whose names are here inscribed have been overlooked, but with very few exceptions the entire force of colored troops in the War of the Rebellion is worthy of special mention.

For gallantry while acting as color-sergeant of the Thirty-ninth United States Colored Troops at the battle of Petersburg, July 30, 1864, Decatur Dorsey was awarded a medal by Congress. Sergeant-major Thomas Hawkins, Sixth United States Colored Troops, for rescuing a regimental flag in the battle of Deep Bottom, Virginia, July, 1864, was awarded a medal by Congress.

CONGRESS MEDAL.

In an address to the Army of the James, Headquarters Department of Virginia and North Carolina, before Richmond, October 11, 1864, General Butler made the following special and significant mention of the valor of colored troops through the campaign which the army had just passed:

"*Of the colored soldiers* of the Third Divisions of the Eighteenth and Tenth corps, and the officers who led them, the general commanding desires to make special mention.

"In the charge on the enemy's works by the colored division of the Eighteenth Corps at Spring Hill, New Market, better men were never better led, better officers never led better men. With hardly an exception, officers of colored troops have justified the care with which they have been selected. A few more such gallant charges, and to command colored troops will be the post of honor in the American armies. The colored soldiers, by coolness, steadiness, and determined courage and dash, have silenced every cavil of the doubters of their soldierly capacity, and drawn tokens of admiration from their enemies —have brought their late masters, even, to the consideration of the question whether they will not employ as soldiers the hitherto despised race. Be it so this war is ended when a musket is in the hands of every able-bodied Negro who wishes to use one.

* * * * * *

"*Third Division.*

"Brigadier-general Charles J. Paine has received the thanks of Major-general D. B. Birney for the conduct of his division while temporarily acting with the Tenth Corps in the action of the 29th of September, near New Market.

"Colonel S. A. Duncan, Fourth United States Colored Troops, commanding Third Brigade, in addition to other gallant services in the field heretofore, fell wounded near the enemy's works. He is recommended to the President for a brevet rank as brigadier-general.

"Colonel A. G. Draper, Thirty-sixth United States Colored Troops, commanding Second Brigade, carried his brigade in column of assault with fixed bayonets over the enemy's works through a double line of abatis, after severe resistance. For incessant attention to duty and gallantry in action, Colonel Draper is also recommended to brevet rank as brigadier-general.

"Lieutenant-colonel G. W. Shurtleff, Fifth United States Colored Troops, gallantly led his regiment in the assault of the 29th, although at the commencement of the charge was shot through the wrist and again wounded until he received a third, and probably mortal, wound close to the enemy's works. He has nobly earned his promotion and his commission as colonel of his regiment, to date from the 29th of September, subject to the approval of the President.

"First-lieutenant Edwin C. Gaskill, Thirty-sixth United States Colored Troops, for distinguished gallantry in leading his men, when shot through the arm, within twenty yards of the enemy's works. He is promoted to a captain.

"First-lieutenant Richard F. Andrews, Thirty-sixth United States Colored Troops, has honorable mention. Having been two months sick and relieved from duty, he volunteered and charged with his command through the swamp, where he received a wound. He is promoted to the rank of captain.

"First-lieutenant James B. Backup, Thirty-sixth United States Colored Troops, excused from duty for lameness, from which he could walk but a short distance, volunteered and charged with his command through the swamp, and received a wound through the breast. He is promoted to a captain

"Private James Gardner, Company I, Thirty-sixth United States Colored Troops, rushed in advance of his brigade, shot at a rebel officer who was on the parapet cheering his men, and then ran him through with his bayonet. He will have a sergeant's warrant and a medal for gallant daring.

"Captain Philip Weinmann, Sixth United States Colored Troops, commanding division of sharp-shooters, and in charge of the skirmish line, is promoted to major for excellent conduct in making his line of assault on the 29th of September.

"Milton M. Holland, Sergeant-major Fifth United States Colored Troops, commanding Company C; James H. Bronson, first-sergeant, commanding Company D; Robert Pinn, first-sergeant, commanding Company I, wounded; Powhatan Beaty, first-sergeant, commanding Company G, Fifth United States Colored Troops — all these gallant colored soldiers were left in command, all their company officers being killed or wounded, and led them gallantly and meritoriously through the day. For these services they have most honorable mention, and the commanding general will cause a special medal to be struck in honor of these gallant colored soldiers.

"Captain Peter Schlick, Thirty-eighth United States Colored Troops, was the first of his regiment to enter the rebel works in the assault of the 29th, and is promoted to major

"Lieutenant Samuel B. Bancroft, Thirty-eighth United States Colored Troops, has honorable mention for daring and endurance. Being shot through the hip at the swamp, he crawled forward on his hands and knees, waving his sword, and cheering his men to follow.

"First-sergeant Edward Ratcliff, Company C, Thirty-eighth United States Colored Troops, thrown into command of his company by the death of the officer commanding, was the first enlisted man in the enemy's works, leading his company with great gallantry, for which he has a medal.

"Private Wm. H. Barnes, Company C, Thirty-eighth United States Colored Troops, among the very first to enter the rebel works, although himself previously wounded, has a medal for his gallantry.

"Sergeant Jas. H. Harris, Company B, Thirty-eighth United States Colored Troops, has a medal for gallant conduct in the assault on the 29th inst.

"First-lieutenant J. Murray Hoag, Fourth United States Colored Troops, although on the sick list, and suffering from the effects of fever, insisted on leading his company, until he fell, wounded in two places, at the enemy's inner line of abatis. He is promoted to captain.

"Alfred B. Hilton, Color-sergeant Fourth United States Colored Troops, the bearer of the national colors, when the color-sergeant with the regimental standard fell beside him, seized the standard, and struggled forward with both colors, until disabled by a severe wound at the enemy's inner line of abatis, and when on the ground he showed that his thoughts were for the colors and not for himself. He has a special medal for gallantry, and will have his warrant as first-sergeant.

"Christian A. Fleetwood, Sergeant-major Fourth United States Colored Troops, when two color-bearers had been shot down, seized the national colors and bore them nobly through the fight. He has a special medal for gallant conduct.

"Charles Veal, Color-bearer Company D, Fourth United States Colored Troops, after two bearers of the regimental color had been shot down, seized it close to the enemy's works and bore it through the remainder of the action. He has a medal for gallantry, and will have the warrant of color-sergeant.

"Lieutenant N. H. Edgerton, Adjutant Sixth United States Colored Troops, when the color-bearer was shot down, seized the colors and carried them forward, even after his own hand was pierced by a bullet which severed the flag-staff. He is promoted to the rank of captain.

"Corporal Miles James, Thirty-sixth United States Colored Troops, after having his arm so badly mutilated that immediate amputation was necessary, loaded and discharged his piece with one hand, and urged his men forward—this within thirty yards of the enemy's works. He has a medal and a sergeant's warrant.

"First-sergeant William Davis, Company E, Thirty-sixth United States Colored Troops, has honorable mention and a medal for gallantry.

"Sergeant Samuel Gilchrist, Company K, Thirty-sixth United States Colored Troops, showed great bravery and gallantry in commanding his company after his officers were killed. He has a medal for gallantry.

"Alexander Kelley, First-sergeant Company F, Sixth United States Colored Troops, gallantly seized the colors, which had fallen near the enemy's inner abatis, raised them, and rallied the men, at a time of confusion and a place of the greatest possible danger. He has a medal for his gallantry.

"Sergeant Ellsbry, First-sergeant Company G, Sixth United States Colored Troops, has a medal for bravery and remarkable coolness during the engagement of September 29, 1864.

"Major J. B. Cook, Twenty-second United States Colored Troops, commanding his regiment as a skirmish line, behaved most gallantly himself, and managed his men with marked ability in the assault on the enemy's lines near New Market. In the attempt of the enemy to take Fort Harrison he unfortunately fell wounded through his utter neglect of personal safety. He is promoted to lieutenant-colonel.

"Captain Robert Dollard, Second United States Colored Cavalry, acting as field-officer, and in charge of the skirmish line in the assault on New Market, September 29th, inspired his command by his great personal bravery, coolness, and ability, until he fell severely wounded near the enemy's main line. He is promoted to major.

"First-lieutenant Henry Peterson, Second United States Cavalry, is promoted to a captaincy for gallantry and ability in conducting his company at New Market on the 29th of September, and for meritorious conduct in the field and camp.

"Sergeant George Honesty, Company I, Second Colored Cavalry; First-sergeant Isaac Harris, Company F, Sergeant Gilbert Harris, Company F; Sergeant Reuben Parker, Company F; First-sergeant Randolph Driver, Company I, have honorable mention for conspicuous bravery on the skirmish line in the assault on the enemy's works September 29th. Each has a medal.

"The regiments of this division having behaved with great gallantry in several actions, earning thereby the right to official notice, it is ordered that there be inscribed upon the colors of the First and Tenth United States Colored Troops the name 'Wilson's Wharf,' that being the place where they defeated the cavalry of Fitzhugh Lee

"That the Second United States Colored Cavalry have the word

'Suffolk' on their colors for their conduct in the battle of March 9th near that place.

"That the First, Fourth, Fifth, Sixth, and Twenty-second United States Colored Troops have the word 'Petersburg' inscribed on their banners for their gallantry in capturing the line of works and the enemy's guns on the 15th of June, 1864, at that place.

"That the First, Fourth, Fifth, Sixth, Twenty-second, Thirty-sixth, Thirty-seventh, Thirty-eighth United States Colored Troops, and the Second United States Colored Cavalry, have the words 'New Market Heights' inscribed upon their colors for their gallantry in carrying the enemy's works at that point on the 29th of September.

"The quartermaster is directed to furnish a new stand of colors to each of these regiments, with the inscription ordered.

* * * * * *

"*Third Division, Tenth Army Corps.*

"First-lieutenant Waldo B. Ryder, Seventh United States Colored Troops; First-lieutenant Joseph E. Lockwood, Seventh United States Colored Troops; First-lieutenant Sumner E. Warren, Seventh United States Colored Troops, are promoted to be captains for meritorious conduct during their connection with the regiment.

"Second-lieutenant Alpheus K. Long, Seventh United States Colored Troops; Second-lieutenant Charles H. C. Brown, Seventh United States Colored Troops; Second-lieutenant Russel Hall, Seventh United States Colored Troops, are promoted to first-lieutenants for meritorious services during their connection with the regiment.

"Lieutenant-colonel Samuel C. Armstrong, Ninth United States Colored Troops, is promoted, for gallant and meritorious services at Deep Bottom and Fussell's Mill on the 14th of August, 1864, as Colonel of the Eighth United States Colored Troops, *vice* Colonel Loren Burrett, who has failed to be mustered on account of physical disability.

"First-lieutenant Thomas Young, Eighth United States Colored Troops, is promoted to be captain for meritorious services.

"Second-lieutenant William H. Brooks, Eighth United States Colored Troops, is promoted to first-lieutenant.

"First-lieutenant Haskell M. Phelps is promoted to be captain in the Ninth United States Colored Troops for meritorious services during his connection with the regiment.

"Second-lieutenant Edward E. Fairchild, Ninth United States Colored Troops, is promoted to first-lieutenant for meritorious services during his connection with the regiment.

"Second-lieutenants Edward Coe and John Bishop, Twenty-ninth

Connecticut Colored Volunteers, are appointed first-lieutenants for uniform attention to duty.

"Major George E. Wagner, Eighth United States Colored Troops, is specially mentioned for gallantry, and is appointed lieutenant-colonel, *vice* Lieutenant-colonel Armstrong, Ninth United States Colored Troops.

"Captain Oscar E. Pratt, Seventh United States Colored Troops, has honorable mention for meritorious conduct, and is appointed major in the Eighth United States Colored Troops, *vice* Major Wagner promoted.

"Captains Julius A. Weiss, Thomas McCarty, First-lieutenants George R. Sherman, David S. Mack, Second-lieutenants Sylvester Ehler, J. Ferguson, R. M. Spinney, of the Seventh United States Colored Troops, are all entitled to the highest praise and commendation for their gallantry and good conduct in the assault on Fort Gilmer, for which they are not now promoted, being either killed or in the hands of the enemy.

"The commanding general is quite conscious that in his endeavors to put on record the gallant deeds of the officers and soldiers of the Army of the James, he has almost, of necessity, because of the imperfection of reports, omitted many deserving of mention; yet, as these gallant men will on other occasions equally distinguish themselves, they can then take their due place in their country's history.

"By command of Major-general Butler.

"EDWARD W. SMITH,
"Assistant Adjutant-general."

The following enlisted men of the Fifty-fourth Massachusetts Infantry received the Gillmore medal for gallantry in the assault on Fort Wagner, July 18, 1863: Sergeant Robert J. Simmons, Company B; Sergeant William H. Carney, Company C; Corporal Henry F. Peal, Company F; and Private George Wilson, Company A.

The following order was issued in recognition of the conspicuous gallantry of colored soldiers in the Department of the South:

"Headquarters Department of the South,
"Hilton Head, South Carolina, *April* 12, 1865.

"On March 7, 1865, a party of Colored soldiers and scouts, thirty in number, commanded by Sergeant-major Henry James, Third United States Colored Troops, left Jacksonville, Florida, and penetrated into the interior through Marion County. They rescued ninety-one Negroes from slavery, captured four white prisoners, two wagons, and twenty-four horses and mules; destroyed a sugar-mill and a distillery, which were used by the rebel government, together with their stocks of sugar and liquor, and burned the bridge over the Oclawaha River. When returning they were attacked by a band of over fifty cavalry, whom they defeated and drove off with a loss of more than thirty to the rebels. After a long and rapid march they arrived at St. Augustine on March 12th, having lost but two killed and four wounded.

"This expedition, planned and executed by Colored men under the command of a Colored non-commissioned officer, reflects credit upon the brave participants and their leader.

"The major-general commanding thanks these courageous soldiers and scouts, and holds up their conduct to their comrades in arms as an example worthy of emulation.

"By command of Major-general Q. A. Gillmore.
        "W. L. M. BURGER.
     "Assistant Adjutant-general."

      "War Department, Adjutant-general's Office,
        "Washington, *December* 22, 1864.
"*General Orders No.* 303.

"The following General Order, No. 81, from the Headquarters Military Division of West Mississippi, is approved by the President of the United States:
     "Headquarters Military Division of West Mississippi,
      "New Orleans, Louisiana, *December* 9, 1864.
"*General Orders No.* 81.

"Subject to the approval of the President of the United States, Major J. B. Cook, Third United States Colored Cavalry, is hereby promoted to the lieutenant-colonelcy of that regiment, to date from the 27th of November, 1864, in consideration of the gallantry displayed by him on that day, when, with his men dismounted, and having nothing but railroad ties for a path, he charged over the Big Black Bridge, near Canton, Mississippi, in face of a heavy fire, drove off the rebel force stationed on the opposite shore behind a strong stockade, and destroyed the bridge, by which the main line of the rebel general Hood's communications with his depots in South Mississippi and Alabama was effectually cut off. The major-general commanding the Districts of West Tennessee and Vicksburg styles this affair as '*One of the most daring and heroic acts of the war.*'

"By order of Major-general E. R. S. Canby.
        "C. F. CHRISTENSEN,
     "Lieut.-col., Ass't Adjt.-general."

"By order of the Secretary of War.
     "E. D. TOWNSEND, Assistant Adjutant-general."

"Headquarters Twenty-fifth Army Corps, Army of the James,
"In the Field, Virginia, *February* 20, 1865.

"*Orders:*

"In view of the circumstances under which this corps was raised and filled, the peculiar claims of its individual members upon the justice and fair dealing of the prejudiced, and the regularity of the conduct of the troops, which deserve those equal rights that have been hitherto denied the majority, the commanding general has been induced to adopt the Square as the distinctive badge of the Twenty-fifth Corps. Wherever danger has been found and glory to be won, the heroes who have fought for immortality have been distinguished by some emblem, to which every victory added a new lustre. They looked upon their badge with pride, for to it they had given its fame; in the homes of smiling peace it recalled the days of courage, endurance, and the hour of deadly strife, and it solaced the moments of death, for it was a symbol of a life of heroism and self-denial. The poets will sing of the 'Templar's Cross,' 'The Crescent' of the Turk, 'The Chalice' of the hunted Christian, and the 'White Plume' of Murat, that crested the wave of valor sweeping resistlessly to victory. Soldiers, to you is a chance in this spring campaign of making this badge immortal. Let history record that on the banks of the James River thirty thousand freemen not only gained their own liberty, but shattered the prejudice of the world, and gave to the land of their birth peace, union, and glory.

"GODFREY WEITZEL,
"Major-general Commanding."

To this list of valiant Negro soldiers may be added the name of Captain Robert Smalls, the captor of the steamer *Planter.*

This task is done with as much completeness as the condition of the War Records, many of which are in the hands of the printer, will allow at this time; and this poetical tribute, with the entire work, is offered with grateful patriotic sentiments by the author to his comrades wherever they may be throughout a free country which their valor helped to save:

THE NEGRO VOLUNTEER.

> They struggled and fought, with courage fraught,
>   With love for the cause of the Nation;
> They knew in the strife for the Union's life
>   They must buy Emancipation.

INDEX.

ADAMS, JOHN QUINCY, on the war powers of the Government, 147.
Administration, wavering policy of the, in 1862, 105.
African slave-trade, the, a Southern convention favors reopening of, 59; bewildering effect of, on Northern Democrats, 59.
Alabama, secession of, 63.
American Army, number of Negroes in the, during Revolutionary War, 35 (*note*).
Andersonville Prison, description of, 304; treatment of prisoners confined in, 305; death-rate in, 306; action of confinement in, on prisoners, 306.
Andrew, John A., Governor, of Massachusetts, criticises action of General Butler concerning hostile Negroes, 69; secures authority to raise Negro troops, 103; orders their recruitment, 104; enthusiasm of the Negro citizens over, 104.
Arming of Negroes, Northern statesmen urge the, 86.
Army Appropriation Bill, sections of, covering pay, etc., of Negro soldiers, 152; decision of Attorney-general Bates respecting, 153.

Army of King Pepi, Negroes in the, 3, 4.
Army of the Cumberland, Negro soldiers in the, 273.
Army of the James, Negro soldiers in the, 291.
Army of the Potomac, Negro soldiers in the, 231.

BANKS, GENERAL N. P., organizes Corps d'Armée of Negro troops, 113; enthusiastic response to, 113.
Barns, H., of Michigan, urges the military employment of Negroes, 131; writes to Secretary of War concerning, 131; authorized to raise a regiment of Negro volunteers, 133; organizes the One Hundred and Second United States Colored Troops, 133.
"Battle of the Hundred Pines," Negroes in the, 186.
Battle of Olustee, gallantry of Negro troops in the, 204–208.
Battle of Poison Springs, Negro troops in the, 228.
Beauregard, General G. T., letter of, on the treatment of Negro prisoners of war, 313, 314.
"Black Brigade of Cincinnati," the, 324; Judge Wm. M. Dickson on, 325.

Border States, feeling against the Negro in the, 177.

Brazil, Negroes employed in the police and military forces of, 40.

Brown, Captain John, takes United States arsenal at Harper's Ferry, 59; throws town into excitement, 59; hanging of, 60; execution of Hazlitt and Stevens, compatriots of, 60.

Buell, General D. C., declaration of, on the harboring of fugitive slaves, 76.

Butler, Major-general B. F., inaugurates a new policy concerning slaves, 68; letter of, to Governor Hicks, of Maryland, in this connection, 69; his action criticised by Governor Andrew, of Massachusetts, 69; declares fugitive slaves contraband of war, 70; escaped slaves employed by, 70; action of, approved by the Secretary of War, 71; comment in political and military circles concerning order of, respecting fugitive slaves, 71; rates Negroes with mules, wagons, etc., 72; orders the discharge of a Negro soldier, 77; correspondence between, and General J. W. Phelps, 97; issues appeal to Negroes of New Orleans to enlist, 98; response to appeal of, 99; describes the part taken by Negro troops at New Market Heights, 254.

CAILLOUX, CAPTAIN ANDRÉ, 218; bravery of, during Port Hudson assault, 219; *New York Times* comments on, 220.

Cass, Lewis, Secretary of State, resignation of, 63.

Charleston Convention, seceding delegates of, nominate Breckinridge and Lane for President and Vice-President, 61.

Chetlain, A. L., Brigadier-general, assigned as chief of the recruitment of Negro troops in Tennessee, 124; recommendation of, by General Grant, 125; establishes his headquarters at Memphis, 126; his sphere of influence extended to Kentucky, 126; order of, to candidates applying for commissions in Negro regiments, 126; regiments organized and inspected by, 127; awarded a brevet major-generalship, 128.

Clergy of the North urge upon the President the emancipation of the slaves and the arming of the Negroes, 89.

Clinton, Sir Henry, proclamation of, in 1779, to discourage the employment of Negroes, 28.

Cobb, Howell, Secretary of Treasury, resignation of, 62.

Colored officers in United States Volunteer Army, 141; initiative taken in Massachusetts in commissioning, 141; commanding independent battery at Leavenworth, Kansas, 142.

Computation of number of Negroes in the American army of the Revolutionary War, 35.

Confederate Congress, an act of the, to increase the efficiency of the army, 84; act of, denying the Negro the immunity of a prisoner of war, 180; considers the employment of Negroes in the army, 292.

Congress, act of, in 1779, for raising Negro troops, 23; passes law in 1861 for the confiscation of property used for insurrectionary purposes, 73; act of, emancipating the slaves of rebels, 87.

Connecticut, governor of, organizes Negro troops, 135; casualty of these troops on the field, 135.

Constitutional Union Convention, meeting of, in 1860, 60; nominates Bell and Everett for President and Vice-President, 61.

Cumberland, Negro soldiers in the Army of the, 273; they secure the confidence of the white soldiers by their bravery, 275; account of the fight at Dalton, Ga., 275; Colonel Morgan's account of engagement by, at Pulaski, Tenn., 277; in the defence of Decatur, Ala., 280; casualty of, in this defence, 281; commended in General Orders, 281; ordered to Nashville to confront Hood's army, 283; skirmishes during the march, 284; hailed by the white veterans as their peers, 285; they open the battle of Nashville, 286; assistance given by, in routing Hood's army, 288; tabulated statement of casualty of, 289; General Steedman's comment upon the gallantry of, 289.

DAVIS, JEFFERSON, election of, as President of the Southern Confederacy, 64.

Deep Bottom, Va., Negro troops in action at, 250; commended by Major-general D. B. Birney, 251.

Democratic Party, the, degeneration of, prior to the Rebellion, 58; Southern wing of, asserts the right to buy, sell, and transport slaves, 61; Douglas wing of, adheres to the doctrine of State sovereignty, 62.

Department of the South, Negro troops in the, 181; leading a forlorn hope in, 209; commendation of, for gallantry by the War Department, 339, 340.

Dix, General John A., proclamation by, to people of Virginia, 74; issues orders to the troops regarding persons held to domestic servitude, 74.

Draft Riots, the, in New York, 174; inoffensive Negroes the objects of the rioters' wrath, 174; savagery of the mob, 174; diabolical work of human fiends during, 175; the quality of men who forced the, 176.

Drilling of Negroes by "nomarchs, chancellors," etc., 3, 4.

Dumas, General Alexander Davy, military career of, in France, 36; valor of, at the Battle of Brixen, 37; death of, 37.

Dunmore, Earl of, issues proclamation to Virginia slaves, 16; effect of proclamation on civil and military officials, 16; Virginia Convention issues an answer to, 18; waning influence of, 21.

EGYPTIAN ARMY, strength of, estimated by Herodotus, 2; by Diodorus, 2; divisions of the, 2.

Egyptian Empire, beginning of military epoch of the, 1.

Egyptians, position of soldiers among the, 1 (*note*).

Emilio, Captain Luis F., in the assault upon Fort Wagner, 196; bravery of, 196; receives the thanks of General Stevenson for his assistance, 198.

England, employment of Negro troops in the army of, 38; exclusive Negro regiments in the British West Indies, 39.

"Enrolment Act," Negroes included under, 136; provisions of, 137, 138; opinion of Judge Advocate Holt on passages in, concerning the employment of Negroes, 138, 139.

Establishment at Washington of a bureau for the conduct of matters referring to Negro troops, 113.

Estimate of slave population at the beginning of the Revolution, 19.

Estimated number of Negroes recruited by the Bureau for the Organization of Colored Troops, 136.

Exclusion of the Negro slave from printing-offices, etc., 67.

Execution of Hazlitt and Stevens, compatriots of John Brown, 60.

FEDERALISTS and planters, excitement of, at Lord Dunmore's proclamation to Virginia Negroes, 18.

Fifty-fourth Massachusetts Regiment, the, 191; under General Terry on James Island, 192; "two-o'clock-in-the-morning" courage of, 192; exhaustive march of, to participate in the assault upon Fort Wagner, 193; arrival of, at General Strong's headquarters, 195; addressed by Colonel Shaw and General Strong, 195; participation of, in the assault upon Fort Wagner, 196; interesting letter concerning bravery of, during the assault, 196; casualty of, during action, 199; medals awarded to soldiers of, 199; in the battle of Olustee, 204; in the battle of Honey Hill, 211.

First North Carolina Regiment, the, in the battle of Olustee, 207.

First South Carolina Regiment, the, at St. Helena Island, 181; in the expedition along the coasts of Georgia and East Florida, 181; bravery of, in this expedition, 182; in an expedition from Beaufort, S. C., to Deboy River, Ga., 182; report of, by General Saxton, 182; in an expedition to secure Negro recruits in Georgia and Florida, 182; indefatigable courage of, 185; action of, on the St. Mary's River, 186; success of, in the Georgia and Florida expedition, 187; company of, under Captain Trowbridge, on the Florida coast, 187; comment by the *New York Times* on the expedition, 188; in an expedition up the St. John's River, 189; graphic account by a war correspondent of the expedition, 189, 191.

Florida, secession of, 63.

Floyd, John B., Secretary of War, resignation of, 63.

Fort Harrison, capture of, 252; brilliant and daring work by Negro troops at, 252; gallant defence of, 253; the Negro troops commended in General Orders for courage at, 253.

Fort Pillow, massacre at, 257; brutal slaughter of the garrison of, 260; official testimony given before a Congressional committee concerning the massacre at, 261–265; rebel testimony on the burying alive of Negroes at, 265; General Forrest's attempt to justify his action at, 266; extracts from correspondence between Generals Lee and Washburn concerning, 267; report of sub-committee from the Senate and House to investigate, 269–272; War

Department record of casualty at, 272.

Fort Powhatan, battle of, 233; gallant defence of, by the Negro soldiers in, 233; casualty of the Negro troops at, 234; the *New York Times* comments on, 234.

Fort Wagner, assault upon, 193; participation of the Fifty-fourth Massachusetts in, 196; list of casualties during, 199.

France, Negroes not proscribed from entering army of, 36; mulattoes not addressed as Negroes in, 36; no obstruction to ambition of the Negroes in, 36.

Fremont, General John C., proclamation of, declaring Negroes free men, 73; moral influence of proclamation throughout the South, 73; his action not approved by the President, 74; removal of, 74.

GEORGIA and Florida expedition, Negro soldiers in the, 181; their bravery in the, 182; success of the, 187.

Government, United States, Northern Negroes pledge themselves to support the, 87; their offers unnoticed by the, 87; John Quincy Adams on the war powers of the, 147; policy of the, respecting the arming of Negroes, 160, 161.

Grant, General U. S., orders issued by, respecting slaves at Fort Donelson, 75; letter of General Halleck to, on the arming of Negroes, 106; hastens the organizing of Negro troops in his Department, 108.

Greeley, Horace, editorial of, to the President relative to the question of slavery, 79; urges the enforcement of the "Confiscation Act," 80; views of, respecting the Negro troops in garrison, 165.

HALLECK, GENERAL, W. H., orders issued by, forbidding slaves within his lines or camps, 75; letter of, to General Grant outlining the policy of the Government in arming Negroes, 106; reply of General Grant to, 108.

Hamlin, Hannibal, election of, as Vice-President, 62.

Hayti, Negro soldiers in, 40.

Higginson, Colonel T. W., quoted concerning the bounty and pay of the Negro troops, 155, 156; letters from, to the *New York Tribune* and *New York Times* on the subject, 157-160; first colonel to lead a Negro regiment, 181; commands the First South Carolina Volunteers in the Beaufort, S. C., expedition, 182; commands the same regiment in the St. John's River expedition, 189.

Honey Hill, battle of, 209; Negro troops in, 210; desperate fighting of the Fifty-fourth Massachusetts in, 211; Confederate account of the, 212.

Hooker, General Joseph, authorizes citizens of Maryland to search for fugitive slaves in his camp, 76; result of such authority, 77.

Hunter, Major-general David, declares the States of Georgia, Florida, and South Carolina under martial law, 79; proclaims the slaves of these States "forever free," 79; abrogation of the order of, by the President, 79; issues orders for the recruitment of a Negro regiment, 90; organizes the "First South Carolina Regiment," 90; opposed for this action, 90; resolution introduced in Congress respecting his Negro regiment, 91; letter of, to Secretary of War in answer to the resolution, 92–94; his communication ordered read in the House, 94; gives freedom papers to slaves who enlisted, 95; not supported by the Administration in his noble effort, 95 (*note*).

IDIOSYNCRACIES of the Negro, 167–169.
Indiana, Governor of, authorized to raise a Negro regiment, 136; it serves in the Army of the James, 136.
Indies, British West, exclusive Negro regiments in the, 39.
Inscriptions of Una, Negroes mentioned in the, 1.

JACKSON, GENERAL ANDREW, issues appeal to free Negroes to join his army, 55; addresses the Negro troops in front of New Orleans, 56; promises Negro volunteers equal pay, etc., of white soldiers, 151.
James, Army of the, Negro troops in, 291; they participate in the battle of Five Forks, 294; courage of, in the fight, 296; in the assault before Petersburg, 298; reception of, on entering Petersburg, 300; they head the Union column on entering Richmond, 301; magnanimity of, after Lee's surrender, 303.
James Island, Negroes under General A. H. Terry on, 192
Joux, dungeon of, imprisonment of Toussaint L'Ouverture at, 53.

KANSAS, initiative taken by, in raising Negro troops, 101; organizes the first regiment of Northern Negroes, 101.
Kench, Thomas, presents plan in 1778 for raising Negro troops, 25; letter of, to the Council in Boston concerning the freedom of Negroes, 26.
King Pepi, Negroes in the army of, 3, 4.

LEGAL status of the Negro soldier, the, 145.
Legislature, New York, enacts a law, in 1814, for the incorporation of two Negro regiments, 57.
Lincoln, Abraham, election of, as President, 62; feeling in the South and North regarding, 62; formal declaration of the election of, by the Electoral College, 64; inauguration of, as President, 65; opposition of, to the employment of Negroes as soldiers, 88; the *New York Herald* on decision of, 88; issues an emancipation proclamation, 105; declares the slaves *forever free*, 106; extracts of letters from, referring to the enemies of the Negro, 176, 177; treats on the Negro question in his message to Congress in 1863, 178; reviews the Negro troops in the Army of the James, 293.
Louisiana Native Guards, First and Third regiments of, 215; in the assault upon Port Hudson, 215; undaunted valor of, 217; conduct of the, cited, 219; remarks of General Halleck on heroism of, 221.
Louisiana Native Guards, Second Regiment of, 221; under Colonel Daniels in the battle of East Pascagoula, 222; success of, 223; re-

port of, to General T. W. Sherman, 223.

Louisiana, secession of, 64.

L'Ouverture, Toussaint, birth of, 41; espouses the cause of Spain, 42; commissioned a brigadier-general, 42; his first battle, 42; as a student of military books, 43; defeats the French at Dondon, 43; origin of the affix to his name, 43; administrative ability of, 44; hailed as *Le noir Napoleon* in military circles, 44; appointed commander-in-chief of the army of Santo Domingo, 44; speech of, at his inauguration, 45; issues a general amnesty at Cayes in 1800, 45; his noble sentiments in the constitution of, 46; Napoleon plots the destruction of, 47; repulses the French at Santo Domingo, 48–51; Napoleon's strategy to apprehend, 52; imprisonment of, in the dungeon of Joux, 53; death of, 54.

McCLELLAN, GENERAL GEORGE B., proclamation of, against forcible abolition of slavery, 77; correspondence of, with William H. Seward, Secretary of State, regarding, 78.

Martial valor of the Negro soldier, 320; Secretary of War quoted on, 320; testimony of prominent military men on, 321–323.

Massachusetts, roll of Negro representatives of, in the army, 33.

Mexico, Negroes not discriminated nor proscribed in, 55.

Military rendition of slaves, 66.

Milliken's Bend, battle of, 224; Negro troops in the, 224; casualty at the, 225; account of the, by Captain Matthew Miller, 226.

Mississippi, secession of, 63.

Mississippi Valley, Negro troops in the, 214.

Monument, a proposed, to brave Negro soldiers, 328, 329, 332.

Morgan, Lieutenant-colonel Thomas J., appointment of, to recruit Negroes in the Department of the Cumberland, 130; fitness of, for the command, 130; extracts of letters from, on the position of colored troops in the army, 162, 163; forces the Secretary of War to change the policy of employing Negroes as laborers, 164.

"Mulatto War," the, in Hayti, beginning of, 42.

NATIONAL Democratic party, meeting of, in 1860, 60; fruitless labor of, on slavery question, 60.

Negro, the, in the military history of Egypt, 1–6; sudden disappearance of, in Egyptian history, 7; depiction of, on ancient tombs, 7, 8; military employment of the, three thousand years before the Christian era, 8; reappearance of, in history, 10; as a solution of the labor problem in North America, 10; non-combativeness of, during the slave traffic, 11; part taken by, in the beginning of the struggle for independence in America, 11, 12.; conspicuous in the first battle of the Revolutionary War, 12; his employment as a soldier considered in 1775, 13; prohibited from being employed in the army, 14; General Gates forbids the enlistment of the, 14; his military status discussed by the Continental Congress, 14; arming of, discussed at a council of war in 1775, 15;

Royalists awake to the policy of the Continental authorities concerning the, 16; General Thomas quoted concerning prejudice against the, 17; solicited to adopt the Continental uniform, 21.

Negro chaplains commissioned during the war, 144.

Negro surgeons commissioned during the war, 143.

Negroes, official return of number of, under General Washington, 22; enactment by Congress in 1779 for the raising of troops of, 23; Act of General Assembly in 1778 giving freedom to, who enlist, 24; letter to Boston Council concerning freedom of, 26; New England colonies accept the arming of, as inevitable, 27; proclamation of Sir Henry Clinton to discourage employment of, in the Continental Army, 28; roll of Massachusetts, represented in the army, 33; number of, in American army of the Revolution, 35 (*note*); position of, in France, 36; employment of, in the British army, 38; position of, in Brazil and Hayti, 40; in the War of 1812, 55; incorporation of two regiments of, in New York, in 1814, 57; recruits in the United States army in 1815, 57; their employment in the Union army derided, 66; Northern statesmen urge the arming of, 86; provisions of the "Enrolment Act" appertaining to the, 137, 138; idiosyncracies of the, 167–169; martial valor of the, as soldiers, 320–323; proposed monument to commemorate bravery of, as soldiers, 328, 329, 332.

OBSTACLES confronting the employment of the Negro, 173.

Official return of the number of Negroes under General Washington, 22.

Ogé, Lieutenant-colonel, 41; bravery of, at Cape Haytien, 41; effect of the death of, on the Negroes, 42.

Olustee, battle of, Negro troops in the, 204, 208.

PERU, canonization of Negro priests in, 40.

Petersburg, reduction of, 234; participation of a Negro division in, 235; graphic account of the, 236; casualties sustained in, 239; Major-general Smith's report of, 240; the Negro division commended for bravery at, 242; loss sustained by the Negro division in front of, 243; the fitness of the "Black Division" to charge the fort at, considered, 244; mining of the fort at, 248; gallantry of the Negro soldiers in the action, 249; testimony of officers as to the bravery of the Negro soldiers at, 250.

Phelps, General J. W., favors the employing of Negroes, 96; communicates with General Butler concerning, 97; result of the correspondence, 98.

Philadelphia, recruitment of Negroes in, 119, 120.

Poison Springs, battle of, 228; Negro volunteers in, 228; casualty sustained in, 230.

Policy of the Government on the employment of Negroes, 160, 161.

Potomac, Army of the, 231; Negroes in, 231.

Public confidence *versus* the Negro, 170; the *New York Times* comments on, 171-173.

RAWLINSON, PROFESSOR, assertion of, regarding Negroes in Egyptian army, 4; criticism on, 4; quoted concerning Negroes in the army of Pepi, 5.

Reed, Lieutenant-colonel William N., 141.

Representatives, House of, enacts law prohibiting the return of fugitive slaves, 87.

Republican Party, the, before the Rebellion, 58; opposition of, to the extension of slavery into the Territories in 1860, 61.

Retrospect of the Civil War, 325-327.

Rider, Sidney S., criticised concerning the black regiment of Rhode Island, 31, 32 (*note*).

Ripley, General R. S., returns State colors lost at Fort Wagner, 201; letter of, to Governor of Massachusetts, 201.

Roll of Honor of Negro soldiers, the, 333-339.

SECRETARY OF WAR, order of, in 1862, to enlist Negroes, 100.

Shaw, Colonel Robert Gould, in the assault upon Fort Wagner, 195; addresses the Fifty-fourth Massachusetts Regiment, 195; death of, at Fort Wagner, 202; letter from the father of, protesting against the removal of his son's body, 203; poem on the death of, 203; the commanding character of, 330; his memory cherished by the blacks of the South, 331; proposed park to be named for him, 331; a type of the exalted American patriot, 331.

Sherman, General Thomas W., proclamation of, to the people of South Carolina, 74; assures the people of South Carolina that their "local institution" would remain undisturbed, 74.

Slavery question, the, before the Rebellion, 58; appealed to the Court of Civil War, 65; has no place in the early military policy of the Union Army, 68; wavering policy of the United States Government regarding, 68.

Slavery, position occupied by, in the United States, 147.

Slaves, prohibition of the manumission of, in Maryland in 1860, 61; Major-general Benjamin F. Butler inaugurates a new policy concerning, 68.

South, initiative taken by the, in 1861, in employing Negroes as soldiers, 81; opens recruiting office for free Negroes at Memphis, 81; establishes Bureau for Conscriptions, 85.

Sprague, Governor, of Rhode Island, appeals to the Negroes to enlist, 98.

Stearns, Major G. L., appointment of, to organize Negro troops, 120; refusal of General Couch to accept troops from, 121; letter to, from the Secretary of War, 122; opposition of, to the wholesale impressment of Negroes, 122; an abolitionist, not a slave-catcher, 123; telegrams between the War Department and, 123, 124; resignation of, 124; makes good the dishonored faith of the Government in the paying of Negroes, 155.

TENNESSEE, enactment of law by,

in 1861, for the relief of Negro volunteers, 82.

Texas, secession of, 64.

Thomas, General Lorenzo, announces the policy of the Administration in 1863 to the United States Army, 109, 111; charges the soldiers to receive and encourage Negroes, 110; enthusiasm at the North regarding this action of, 111; despatched to the Southwest to enlarge the scope of the enlistment of Negroes, 114; success of, 136.

Thomas, General, in 1775, concerning prejudice to the Negroes, 17.

Thompson, Jacob, Secretary of the Interior, resignation of, 63.

Times, New York, editorial of, on the employment of the Negro, 171-173.

"*Tirailleurs Algériens*," 38.

Tod, Governor, of Ohio, insists on equal pay and bounty for Negro troops, 133; encourages the recruitment of Negro troops in Ohio for Massachusetts, 133, 134; organizes two regiments and forwards them to the field, 135.

Tyler, Colonel, speech of, to West Virginia rebels, 72.

ULLMANN, BRIGADIER-GENERAL Daniel, urges upon President Lincoln the employment of Negroes, 102; authorized to organize Negro troops, 102; remarks of, concerning Negro troops, 102.

Una, Inscription of, 1 (*note*).

Union Army, number of Negroes in the, during the Civil War, 139, 140.

Union League Club of New York, the, devises means for raising Negro troops, 116; obtains the consent of the War Department to recruit a regiment of Negroes, 117; organizes the Twentieth Regiment of United States Colored Troops, 117; reception given by, to the Twentieth Regiment United States Colored Troops, 179; comment of a New York paper on, 179.

VOLUNTEER ARMY, United States, Negro officers in, 141; number of Negro soldiers in, 324; casualty of these troops in, 324.

WALL, CAPTAIN O. S. B., as recruiting-officer in Ohio, 142; proposition of Secretary Stanton to, 142; Colonel Foster refuses to examine, for a captaincy, 143; executive ability of, 143.

Wall, Sergeant John, mention of, 199.

War Department, the, establishes Negro recruiting-stations, 115; credits State and county with furnishing recruits, 115; creates boards to determine the claims of owners, 116; appointment of a commissioner by, to organize Negro troops, 120; order of, to General W. T. Sherman respecting the employment of Negroes, 150; interprets the pay of the Negro volunteer, 154.

War, treatment of Negro soldiers as prisoners of, 304; proclamation of Jefferson Davis on, 308; editorial extract of *New York Tribune* on, 311; action of the Confederate Army concerning, at Port Hudson, 312; President Lincoln issues order relative to, 313; letter of General Beauregard on, 314; cruelty of the Confederates to, 315; correspondence between Generals Peck and Pickett on, 316, 317; cowardly action of rebel soldiers to, 318; the Secretary of War orders the protection of, 318; arraignment of the Confederate Army and Congress for their, 319.

War of 1812, the, participation of Negroes in the land and naval forces of, 55.

Washington, General George, quoted concerning Lord Dunmore's proclamation, 19; authorizes the enlistment of "free Negroes," 19.

YATES, RICHARD, Governor of Illinois, authorized to raise Negro troops, 133; organizes the Twenty-ninth Regiment of United States Colored Troops, 133.

THE END.

About The Naval & Military Press Ltd

Military book enthusiasts have a place on the internet dedicated to themselves. Our site is the most extensive devoted to military history on the web. You can browse and shop through our vast range of titles by time period or by theme, or use our advanced search facilities to find areas of specific interest.

The Naval & Military Press Ltd was founded in 1991 and quickly established itself as a mecca for the military enthusiast. Over 25,000 customers worldwide enjoy receiving our regular booklist which contains many hundreds of first-class books.

With the advances in modern technology we are now pleased to show all of you with access to the internet our full catalogue.

Our own publications feature strongly on both our list and our website. The innovative approach we have to military bookselling and our commitment to publishing have made us Britain's leading independent military bookseller

There is not another Military Book seller like
naval-military-press.com

THREE MONTHS IN THE SOUTHERN STATES
April - June 1863
By Captain Arthur Fremantle, Coldstream Guards

A very interesting and detailed account of the officer's time with the Confederate forces of the South, Fremantle was a notable British witness to The Battle of Gettysburg, one of the bloodiest battles during the American Civil War. This is an important account that was a best seller when published in 1864, in both the North and South.

Most specifically mentioned in the book are Fremantle's travels through Texas, the deep south, and finally when he arrived in the company of the Army of Northern Virginia on June 27, and witnessed the Battle of Gettysburg firsthand, with of a cadre of foreign observers attached to the headquarters of Lt. Gen. James Longstreet. Contrary to popular belief, Fremantle was not an official representative of the United Kingdom; instead, he was something of a war tourist.

9781474539159

GRANT'S CAMPAIGNS of 1864 and 1865
The Wilderness and Cold Harbor (May 3 - June 3, 1864)
By Lieutenant C F Atkinson, 1st Batt. City of London (Royal Fusiliers)

This a detailed and scholarly account of Lee and Grant's first encounter. When the Grant's Overland Campaign ended, it left behind numbing losses: the dead, missing, and wounded totalled 55,000 for the Union and 33,000 for the Confederacy. Spotsylvania Court House (30,000 combined casualties) and the Wilderness (29,8000 combined casualties) were the third- and fourth-bloodiest battles of the American Civil War, trailing only Gettysburg and Chickamauga. The Confederate victory at the Battle of Cold Harbor would be one the war's most lopsided engagements.

9781783315635

BLACK PHALANX

A History of the Negro Soldiers of the United States in the wars of 1775-1812 & 1861-1865
By Joseph T. Wilson late Louisiana Native Guard Volunteers & 54th Massachusetts Regiment

The bulk of Wilson's compelling book concerns African Americans military service during the American Civil War, including the free Blacks who served in the Confederate army: "Descriptions of a number of the battles in which Negro troops took part in the late war of the Rebellion, are given to call attention to the unsurpassed carnage which occurred, and to give them proper place in the war's history rather than to present a critical account of the battles."

9781783315741

THE WAR OF SECESSION 1861-1862

Bull Run To Malvern Hill
By Major G.W. Redway

The American Civil War, known in Europe as the 'War of Secession', was marked by the ferocity and frequency of battles. Over four years, 237 named battles were fought, as were many more minor actions and skirmishes, which were often characterised by their bitter intensity and high casualties. As per the customs of the time, Prussian, French and British military observers were sent to the North American continent to observe the tactics of both armies, taking notes and reporting back to their homelands with observations and ideas about new tactics.

Covered in succinct chapters, Major Redway details subjects including: The Army System, The Command of the Seas, Organisation & Strategy, Tactics, Operations in 1866, Campaign in West Virginia, The Bull Run Campaign, Valley Campaign and Yorktown Peninsula.

9781783315482

THE BATTLE OF BUENA VISTA
With the Operations of the "Army of Occupation"
for One Month
By Captain James Henry Carleton U.S. Cavalry

This is the best account by a participant of the Battle of Buena Vista, the largest battle fought during the Mexican-American War of 1846-48, a war that was caused by the invasion of Mexico by the United States Army. It followed the 1845 American annexation of Texas, which Mexico still considered its territory. In the US this war was almost forgotten after the cataclysm of the American Civil War.

The author Captain James Henry Carleton was an officer in the US Army and a Union general during the American Civil War. Carleton and is best known as an Indian fighter in the South-western United States.. Partly on the strength of 'The Battle of Buena Vista' he received an appointment from Secretary of War Jefferson Davis in 1856 to make a study of European cavalry tactics.

9781474540780

A GUIDE TO THE WW1 BATTLEFIELDS OF EUROPE
Prepared by the American Battle Monuments Commission

A solid reference for those who wish to know about the American evolvement in the Great War, and also good for family members discovering where a doughboy great-grandfather fought – this classic is a good place to start.

This 1927 guide is organised by region and campaign: Aisne-Marne, St. Mihel, Meuse-Argonne, Champagne, and the areas north of Paris including Flanders, Ypres, the St. Quentin Canal Tunnel and Cantigny. It includes narrative, photographs and maps.

9781474540483

US INFANTRY TACTICS 1861
(SCHOOL OF THE BATTALION)

By Authority The Secretary of War May 1, 1861.

On 20 April 1861 the Civil War in the United States opened with the capture of Norfolk Navy Yard by the Confederate forces from the South, and the war raged for four more years, with, as usual, the greater number of casualties being among the infantry. Infantry battle tactics were determined at the time by the firearms with which they were issued, and the main infantry weapon was the Springfield rifle musket. This muzzle loaded weapon was slow to fire, and marginally accurate, even with the new Minie ball: this meant that the tactics on the field of battle were almost unchanged from those of the Napoleonic wars, fought fifty years previously. This book shows how such evolutions (they were little more than drills) at battalion level were adapted and used to enable commanders to deliver the weight of their firepower on to the enemy. All the prescribed manoeuvres could be practised on the drill square, so that once the men were in battle, all they had to do was obey orders, present their weapons and fire. Of course, all the drills in the world do not prevent panic, and records show that despite all the training, some men reloaded their weapons so many times without firing that the weapons were rendered useless. The book is extremely well illustrated with 67 plates of all the movements in plan form.

9781843426202

1862 FREDERICKSBURG
A Study In War
By Major G.W. Redway

Part of the acclaimed "Special Campaign" series of works intended for serious professional students of military history, each volume is interspersed with strategical and tactical comments and illustrated by numerous sketches.

Fredericksburg is remembered as one of the most one-sided battles of the American Civil War, with Union casualties more than twice as heavy as those suffered by the Confederates. A visitor to the battlefield described the battle to US President Abraham Lincoln as a "butchery".
9781783315444

A NEW SYSTEM OF SWORD EXERCISE

With a Manual of the Sword for Officers, Mounted and Dismounted

By Matthew O'Rourke Late Captain US Volunteers

Illustrated with delicately clear line drawings, and first published on the eve of the American Civil War (this revised edition 1872) this Edged Weapon Manual tells the aspiring swordsman - mounted or fighting on foot - all he needs to know to defeat, wound and/or kill his opponent by the sword. A must for the American Civil War, and Indian Wars Reenactor.
9781783312887

HISTORY OF MORGAN'S CAVALRY

by Basil Wilson Duke

Important account of General Morgan who served with the Confederate forces.

This is a classic work about John Hunt Morgan's legendary exploits, written by Morgan's brother-in-law and a brigadier in his own right. The narrative describes many soldiers of Morgan's command in their adventures in Kentucky, Ohio, Tennessee and elsewhere. A focused military narrative of Morgan's operations, this work is valuable for Basil Duke's eyewitness recollections recorded so soon after the war.
9781474540797

www.ingramcontent.com/pod-product-compliance
Lightning Source LLC
Chambersburg PA
CBHW021759220426
43662CB00006B/121